February 2017.

Andy:

Best - Wishes,

Happy Birthday and
Good luck on your

writing project.

Dave

HIDDEN HEROES

FINDING SUCCESS IN THE SHADOWS

Also by David Heenan

Leaving On Top

Bright Triumphs From Dark Hours

Flight Capital

Double Lives

Co-Leaders
WITH WARREN BENNIS

The New Corporate Frontier

Re-United States of America

Multinational Organization Development
WITH HOWARD PERLMUTTER

HIDDEN HEROES

FINDING SUCCESS IN THE SHADOWS

DAVID HEENAN

WATERMARK
PUBLISHING

ISBN 978-1-935690-83-2
Library of Congress Control Number: 2016953449

Design and production
Jen Tadaki Canzariti

Cover design
Andy Carpenter

Watermark Publishing
1000 Bishop St., Ste. 806
Honolulu, HI 96813
Toll-free 1-866-900-BOOK
sales@bookshawaii.net
www.bookshawaii.net

10 9 8 7 6 5 4 3 2 1

Printed in Korea

Contents

1   In Praise of Hidden Heroes   1

2   Hoop Dreams   14

3   Football-Lite   30

4   Supporting Acts   46

5   Perfect Gentlemen   62

6   Disposable Dons   76

7   Halls of Ivy   96

8   Underdogs of the Air   114

9   Meals on Wheels   130

10   Ghost Stories   146

11   Into Thin Air   164

12   Top Billing for Heroes   181

Notes   192
Index   234

To Issei Marcelo Heenan
My hero

Acknowledgments

MANY FRIENDS AND COLLEAGUES contributed to this book. The earliest version of my manuscript was critiqued by Brett Uprichard, who brought a journalist's eye to the process. Larry Pulley, Dave Bess, Randy Roth, Dick Tomey, Zap Zlatoper and Peter Drewliner provided both inspiration and important inputs. I also owe very special thanks to Bill Hamilton, Michael Schmicker and Kent Keith. I benefited tremendously from their wisdom and rigor.

Hats off to Vance Roley, Avi Soifer, Mufi Hannemann, Chris Kormis, Gary Yoshida, Rob Kay, Mayur Chaudhari, Y. C. Boon, Tadanobu Kashiwa, Hiroshi Yasuda, Dick Gushman, Clint Churchill, and Marc, Eric, Nozomi and Jennifer Heenan.

Many thanks to all those who helped me tell these stories: Tim Kelly, Doug Stewart, Bill Wagner, Dave Zeitlin, Terry Cullen, Mike Beamish, Mike McCurdy, Stuart Helgeon Jr. and Sr., Bob Dale, Paul Seilar, Alex Smith, Lt. Col. Mark West, Harry and Carol Ann Maurer, Mark Bernstein, Jim Nabors, Stanley Cadwallader, Peter Carlisle, Carole Kai, Doug Jones, Carol Sussman, Tracy Robison, Ronne Infeld, Harry Norton, Reuben Chong, Beth Kupper-Herr, Matthew Tuthill, John Morton, Erika Lacro, Richard and Deborah Van Treuren, Fred Morin, George Allen, Ross Wood, Mark Lutz, Don Kaiser, Mort Eckhouse, John Fahey, Iva Kinimaka, Jo McGarry, Julia Gallo-Torres, Poni Askew, Madeleine Morel, Sally Collings, Gary Guller, Mike McCurdy, Carl Jablonski, John and Sandra Nowlan, Catherine Toth Fox, Unyong Nakata, Dolly Omiya and Robert Hatanaka.

At Watermark Publishing, I've had the pleasure of working with a talented team of wonderful professionals: first and foremost, publisher George Engebretson, but also Dawn Sakamoto and Erin Shishido, who copyedited the manuscript and saved me from many potential gaffes. Any remaining errors are mine.

Once again, Martha Miller's competence, diligence and unfailing good cheer contributed greatly to the book's completion. She was assisted by Jenny Okano and Linda Perrin.

Finally, my wife, Nery, has been at my side throughout this project. As with my earlier books, she organized my interviews and read and commented on successive versions of the manuscript. To this loving and most constructive critic goes a very special mahalo.

David Heenan
Honolulu
September 2016

"A hero is someone who has given his or her life to something bigger than oneself."

—JOSEPH CAMPBELL

CHAPTER 1

IN PRAISE OF HIDDEN HEROES

"Fame is the least important quality
in being a hero. It's personal sacrifice
for the good of others that makes a hero."

—JOHNNY CASH

"T HE HISTORY OF THE WORLD is but the biography of great men," wrote Thomas Carlyle, the nineteenth-century historian. The myth of the Great Man remains deeply ingrained in the American psyche. We live in a star-struck society. We love our heroes, be they athletes, astronauts or chief executives. We are enamored of their talents and cherish their boldness—these rugged champions who meet challenges and overcome adversity. We cling to the distinctively top-doggy image and fairy tale appeal of the Great Man or Great Woman, the larger-than-life individual working alone, as the prototypical American hero.

Whether it's puffed up billionaires on Wall Street or alpha professionals on Main Street, idolatry abounds. It is a genuine part of our national character. So we continue to make celebrities of Bill Gates, Elon Musk, Richard Branson and other fascinating leaders, just as we make legends of rock stars, screen actors and professional athletes. It is a fallacy that dies hard. In our hearts, we know that the world is more complex than ever and that we must look beyond the superstar to understand what makes contemporary life work. That work is being done not by organizational gods, but by everyday and, for the most part, hidden heroes: firefighters, policemen, emergency service personnel, men and women in uniform—those who put their lives on the line for others.

This book is intended to sound a loud wake-up call to a nation often blinded by celebrity. Designed to provoke and inspire, it celebrates those selfless individuals who find success in the shadows—motivated by the opportunity to serve others and to make a difference irrespective of the risks.

In the summer of 2015, for example, we were inspired by the selfless courage exhibited by Airman First Class Spencer Stone, who, with two boyhood friends, helped foil a terrorist attack on a high-speed train from Amsterdam to Paris, and saved a wounded passenger. Shortly before the train crossed the Belgian border into France, Stone was abruptly awakened by gunfire only to engage a shirtless man standing in the aisle, cocking an AK-47.

"It felt like it took forever to get to him," the twenty-three-year-old airman said. In a desperate fight for the assault rifle, the terrorist lost the weapon but produced a handgun, cocked it and pointed it at close range at Stone. It clicked, but didn't go off. The attacker next grabbed a box cutter and stabbed Stone in the neck and thumb. Despite significant loss of blood, the medically trained airman then moved to help save the life of another passenger, who had earlier been shot by the assailant. Fifteen minutes later, paramedics boarded the train and took Stone to the hospital.

In the days after the incident, Stone recovered from his wounds. French President François Hollande said that Stone's quick action had given the world "a lesson in courage, in will, and thus in hope." For this, he and his two friends received the French Legion of Merit. Back home, President Barack Obama praised these three ordinary citizens for their bravery and gave them a hero's welcome at the White House. It's worth remembering, the president reminded us, that America is filled with everyday heroes who inspire hope at times like this of tragedy.

"We can't all be heroes," said humorist Will Rogers, who was known for his pithy wisdom. "Some of us have to stand on the curb and clap as they go by." In the French attack, we were reminded once again of countless others who, every day, prove their mettle on the world stage.

"Success," as John F. Kennedy once put it, "has many fathers." Rather than depreciate the inspirational value of those like Airman Stone who often fly under the radar, we need them as surely as much as we need water, food and air. Routinely called upon to do the work and forgo the credit, hidden heroes often have character when lionized leaders have only flash. Their selfless acts reflect the true American spirit. Therefore, in a world often turned dark and cold, we need to give these invisible but invaluable stalwarts the credit they so richly deserve.

Historically, Americans, in fact, have had a long-standing affection for these unsung heroes. For example, the United States Marine Corps, with its fiercely proud tradition of excellence in combat, its hallowed rituals and its unbending code of honor, personifies its time-tested valor, an ethos that dominates its culture. The Iwo Jima monument in the nation's capital captures the essence of the corps' dedication to the mission, not celebrity. It's a faceless team of men struggling to achieve a larger goal. Indeed, two of the men have their backs turned to the spectators, two are seen only from the side, and the fifth is hidden except for his arms and hands, which support the flag. There are no famous generals here, just five nameless riflemen signifying a turning point in modern history.

As a former Marine, I discovered long ago that the genius of our age is truly collaborative. In all but the simplest tasks, we need legions of talented men and women committed to serving others for a common purpose without consideration for status or standing. Indeed, the shrewd leaders of the future are those who recognize the significance of creating alliances with others whose fates are correlated with their own.

Hidden Heroes lays to rest the destructive mania of the chest-beating solo star. "The real power is in the swarm," David Brooks of *The New York Times* correctly points out. That swarm consists of an undervalued minority of hidden talent who don't aspire to become larger-than-life heroes. Dedicated men and women who focus on others, not themselves. Through the prism of their personal stories, you will see how gifted leaders and their talented subordinates can make their organizations stronger, more equitable...and ultimately more successful.

The time to act is now. The next global war will be fought not over terrorism or weapons of mass destruction, but over human capital. In today's talent-tight world, the winners will be those nations with deep reservoirs of bench strength—unselfish men and women devoted not to title, but to the tasks at hand. But for this to happen, all segments of society will have to pool their talents. Henry Ford perhaps put it best: "Coming together is a beginning; keeping together is progress; working together is success."

This, then, is a defining moment. We cannot afford to equivocate. The glib solution to a nation sometimes viewed as elitist and inequitable is to withdraw from it—a topic of countless articles, blogs and talk shows. If America is to regain the hearts and minds of *all* its people, it must re-establish the virtues of trust and selflessness.

In the following pages, we'll examine how organizations can leverage their hidden gems more effectively. The answers call for very different actions—actions highlighted on the opposite page and amplified in Chapter 12.

❖ ❖ ❖

To better understand this emerging challenge, I spent several years researching this book. Eventually, I settled on ten sets of hidden heroes, from history and contemporary life. Each of these subjects has or had a distinctive personality. They are as different as chalk and cheese. Their stories illuminate every field, from business and entertainment to education and sports. But there is one pattern that dominates: All those profiled possess an egoless commitment to the tasks at hand. They do the real work—literally, the heavy lifting—not just the few charismatic, often isolated, stars who are regally compensated.

The dedicated men and women described in these pages ply their skills in very different fields of endeavors. Crafty ghostwriters serve in the shadow as invisible wordsmiths, satisfied with magnifying someone else's ego. Courageous Sherpas put their crampons on every day to ensure the safety of foreign climbers. In the halls of ivy, devoted adjunct faculty labor away, teaching more than half of America's undergraduates. Similarly, our community colleges effectively open doors for the underserved: immigrants,

A CALL TO ACTION

1. Get Personal

2. Develop Good Chemistry

3. Take Risks

4. Dare to Dream

5. Don't Beat Yourself Up

6. Focus on the End Game

7. Build Alliances

8. Don't Sell Your Soul (or Ruin Your Body)

9. Don't Quit Your Day Job...Yet

10. Don't Dillydally

minorities and first-generation college students. In the world of big-time entertainment, backups, openers and supporting actors toil away in relative obscurity, propping up the careers of their respective stars. On the gridiron, scrappy sprint footballers epitomize the Greek ideal that sports can be an outstanding preparation for life. In sixty-three years of losing to the beloved Harlem Globetrotters, the unheralded Washington Generals put smiles on the faces of fans around the world. Others, although not always players on the world stage, demonstrate that you don't have to be captain of the team to find happiness on the team and that doing something important and doing it well can be its own reward.

"If a man aspires to the highest place," Cicero once wrote, "it is no dishonor to him to halt at second place." Indeed, the prevailing winds may well be blowing in subordinates' favor. We are witnessing a populist backlash imperious against No. 1s, particularly those chest-beaters and loudmouths who earn far more than they deliver. Clearly, the emperor's crown today isn't nearly as comfortable as it used to be. The toxic climate of the treadmill economy, coupled with the mass surveillance of social media, have made public lynching commonplace in all walks of life.

Being on top of the mountain nowadays is akin to being one of the kings in ancient Crete who had extraordinary power and access to every perk and pleasure—but only for a time. After his year of absolute power, the king was put to death. For contemporary bigwigs, it's become impossible to remain on the pedestal. Their charisma tends to wear off. "Many don't last as long as a refrigerated fruitcake," says *USA Today*'s Del Jones.

Even the most iconic personality is more likely to inspire cynicism than respect. Witness, for example, the demise of Bill Cosby, Lance Armstrong and former House Speaker Dennis Hastert. As top dogs have lost the aura of infallibility and celebrity has become less associated with genuine achievement, sacrifice through subordination is gaining steam. Hence, "we should study the practices of people who occupy the second-best tier of their respective fields," argues *TIME*'s Annie Murphy Paul.

In researching this book, I analyzed how hidden heroes contribute to the success of their organizations and to society in general. In the course of examining them, I was constantly reminded that serving in the shadows is a role, not an identity—and certainly not a destiny. There is no single personality type that consigns people to the shadows. But in the course of my research, I found that, however they differed, each person demonstrated several common traits.

For starters, successful subordinates are willing to suppress their egos, a sacrifice that seems all the more remarkable in an age that continues to celebrate the star. Vocalist Lisa Fischer, for example, has no problem checking her ego at the door. For four decades, she has backed up Luther Vandross, Tina Turner, Beyoncé, Dolly Parton and the Rolling Stones. "I just love supporting other artists," she says. "Part of the beauty of backup is that you're invisible. It's not about you. It's about being selfless, and that to me is the most joyous thing."

Although these unselfish cohorts have the ability to put "self" on the shelf, they are extraordinarily confident and self-reliant. That may seem a paradox. But these men and women understand that the majority of credit is going to accrue to the top dog. Nevertheless, other than title, they view themselves as equal to their superiors or their more highly acclaimed peers. Simply put, insecure people do not make high-performing lieutenants.

The University of Pennsylvania's sprint football players, for example, rarely experience the lofty dividends enjoyed by their "big boy" counterparts on the flagship varsity team. No bonfires, pep rallies, marching bands or raucous crowds with thousands of cheering fans. Yet they view themselves—and their often-underappreciated sport—as equal to, if not better than, Penn's heavyweight prima donnas.

Not surprising then, hidden heroes have thick skin. To many luxury-liner loyalists, the most important member of the crew is not the captain, the cruise director or even the head chef. The real stars are the revolving corps of male dance partners dedicated to women cruising solo. But to their detractors, these white knights in dinner jackets are nothing more than shameless gigolos—predators at sea, feasting on wealthy women far away from home. Undeterred, these nautical nightcrawlers fend off the sneers and delight in bringing happiness into the lives of lonely cruisers.

A heavy dose of humility often accompanies selflessness. In

America's expanding food truck nation, you won't find many mobile vendors in *Bon Appétit* or on the Food Network. Nor are they likely to be found pitching cookbooks on QVC. But that suits these unknown epicureans just fine.

In Honolulu, former celebrity chef Iva Kinimaka has no problem trading in his popular bricks-and-mortar restaurant and catering business for his Hawaiian Grinds food truck. Not only does he prefer the independence and simplicity of meals on wheels, but he is especially proud of his ability to offer healthy, affordable eats to those on the go. For him, sidewalk success in his cramped van beats the limelight of high-profile chefdom.

Other hidden gems are eager to shun the trappings of professional standing. Some seek to avoid the nerve-racking demands and remorseless striving of the winner-take-all economy; others find the lack of privacy at the top to be a major negative.

Even though Judy Greer has appeared in more than sixty films, the perennial co-star remains behind the scenes to most moviegoers. That's the way she likes it. Besides enjoying a steady stream of bulging paychecks, the self-effacing actress is able to sidestep the Hollywood syndrome and the paparazzi. "I'm like a normal person," she beams. "Every once in a while there will be a random person who will say, 'Hey, Judy!' But no, I don't have to deal with that problem."

Grit and high energy are other characteristics shared by our heroes. We wonder where some of them find the strength and determination to persevere. Although not physically imposing, Nepal's fearless Sherpas have been doing the heavy lifting on jagged Himalayan peaks for years. Their legendary might, exceptional endurance at high altitudes and cheerful smiles have been an integral part of extreme mountaineering for years. Defying danger in the service to Western climbers, these high-altitude heroes continue to put their lives at risk in the world's most perilous profession. They, and other relentless bravehearts, don't crumble in the face of adversity. They don't let obscurity erode their confidence. They have the tenacity so important in accomplishing anything of value.

One of Steve Jobs' mantras at Apple was "Real artists ship." So, too, does our supporting cast. They are men and women of action, not reflection. "Sometimes you don't even notice these people," writes David Brooks in his best seller, *The Road to Character*. "They radiate a sort of moral joy. But they get things done. They are not thinking about themselves at all. They just recognize what needs doing and they do it."

During World War II, more than 5,000 American pilots and crew flew 130 blimps, derisively called "rubber cows" or "poopy bags." They "shipped" every day in support of convoy protection, antisubmarine warfare and rescue missions. Although blimps were uncomfortable and difficult to fly, lighter-than-air pilots endured dangerous missions of up to fifteen to twenty hours a day throughout the war.

Because their lumbering contraptions were mainly out of sight, these aviators and their crews had no cheering sections. Few people understood their importance, or gave them much thought. The exceptions were the lucky survivors of America's merchant ships who vociferously shouted, "God Bless Our Blimps!"

As you might expect, camaraderie is another important attribute of hidden heroes. Whether it's to deflect ridicule or reinforce a common sense of mission, they understand that collaboration is not simply desirable, it is inevitable. Ultimate team players, they realize that they are powerless without the support of their peers.

Recall the Marine Corps' enduring culture that screams togetherness: Semper fi. Esprit de corps. The few, the proud. Our examples have their own special brand of esprit. In a lifetime of losing night after night to the celebrated Harlem Globetrotters, the Washington Generals always came to play. No easy task for testosterone-fueled athletes raised in a must-win culture. But the Generals' founder and owner Red Klotz created tight-knit team unity where his players could find comfort in losing, while making audiences laugh. He taught them to put their teammates first. In the process, Klotz transformed his hoopsters into consummate winners who often maintained lifelong friendships.

Besides "sharing salt together," as Aristotle put it, our unsung heroes often forge a subculture of their own. They learn to communicate with words, winks and silence. Overworked adjunct professors, for instance, band together to eliminate what, for many, can become "a bridge to nowhere." No longer defenseless, they are forging alliances to lobby everyone from organized labor to Congress for better wages, decent benefits, greater job security and resources to do their work effectively—reversing decades of dispirited existence and demonstrating that a battered heart can still beat strongly.

Similarly, America's community colleges are joining hands to becoming more than two-year way stations to a four-year degree. After years of flying under the radar, they, too, are beginning to play to their strength, putting quality education within reach of those like actor, producer, director Tom Hanks, who says of his distinguished career: "I owe it all to the community colleges."

❖ ❖ ❖

Routinely called upon to do the heavy lifting and forgo the credit, what then are the rewards for the hidden hero? For starters, many find enormous satisfaction in serving a cause they believe in. They seek to improve people's lives, not diminish them. Certainly, nurturing future generations of Tom Hankses and providing transformational experiences for others—at affordable prices—motivates many in the community college system. For others, their work has many of the qualities of social reform, and self-sacrifice is the price they are willing to pay for it. Night after night, the Washington Generals' no-name players had their pants pulled down by the fan-favorite Globetrotters to advance not only the globalization of sports, but also a better understanding of African-American culture.

Another frequent source of satisfaction is to revel in interesting, albeit often exhausting, work. Toiling an average forty-eight weeks a year, comic magician Harry Maurer takes great pleasure in his craft, showcasing his illusionary talents as the opening act for some of the world's leading headliners. During rare moments of downtime, you'll find him perfecting his skills and exploring new ways to bamboozle audiences.

In much the same way, backup queen Lisa Fischer loves operating in the shadows in support of other artists. She likens her role to that of a tuning fork, blending and harmonizing the voices of other entertainers. "My happy is different from your happy," she says of her underdog status. "Some people will do anything to be famous.

I just want to sing."

Intrinsically motivated, top-notch cohorts are buoyed by the belief that what they are doing is important. They ache to do good work—even though they may be exploited or underappreciated. Adjunct faculty often experience both. As we shall see, part-time teaching can be educational purgatory. Yet, every day, thousands of them march off to multiple gigs at different institutions. Among them, Nicole Beth Wallenbrock, an adjunct professor of French literature. Though living on food stamps, she remains true to her profession. "I love teaching, researching and writing," she says. "I haven't given up on the dream yet."

To keep their dreams alive, hidden heroes understand they can't always change the cards they are dealt, just how they play the hand. Many often pay a price: Their work is difficult, sometimes dangerous, and thankless service can be overwhelming. Make no mistake, there are definite hellholes out there, treacherous situations resembling what C.S. Lewis called "shadowlands," places of disappointment and faded dreams. Regrettably, some people strike a Faustian bargain, giving up their identity in exchange for an unworthy person or cause. In the process, they sacrifice soul and substance. Savvy stalwarts, on the other hand, know when to sidestep disaster and walk away. Remember, even Don Quixote, in his rational moments, recognized when he was tilting at windmills.

"No one is happy all his life long," warned Greek philosopher Euripides. Hidden heroes, like all of us, should expect speed bumps on the road to happiness. Yet happiness comes only from a life of sacrifice and service. "Putting others first and leading from the heart needs to emerge from every corner of American life," says Howard Schultz, a long-time proponent of servant leadership. The Starbucks chairman and CEO vividly recalls the image of Pope Francis, shortly after his election, kneeling and washing the feet of a dozen prisoners in Rome in a pre-Easter ritual. That said, it is hard to imagine strong-willed individuals like Donald Trump, Sumner Redstone, Rupert Murdoch or the Kardashians shunning the limelight in service to others. It's not in their DNA; they reject subservience in any form. It's hard to change from self-centered to self-effacing. Hence, prima donnas need not apply.

Exercising one's talents in support of others is a far more

reliable source of satisfaction than battling to become the center of attention. Albert Einstein had priceless counsel on this matter. "Try not to become a success," he said, "but rather try to become a man of value." Hidden heroes define "value" not in terms of being famous, but in terms they can influence. They find work that they love and do it well. In the most visceral way, they find people and causes they can believe in and serve them with all their hearts. They give their love and their energy to enterprises that improve people's lives, not diminish them. They find ways to savor all of life, not just the rewards of work.

The rallying cry for servant leadership is even more important in the age of millennials, who just last year passed baby boomers as the nation's largest living generation. Virtually every commencement address today offers invectives for putting others first. We can't necessarily make ourselves into the next Bill Gates or Oprah Winfrey. But even if we reach only modest heights, we can find ways to live well. Indeed, it is the hidden heroes who "dare to push the envelope, who dare to take risks, and who dare to be different," says Chad Griffin, president of the Human Rights Campaign. "In doing so, [they] prove the pessimists wrong and push the world forward."

In this new, more egalitarian view of the galaxy, we can no longer let the stars define us. It isn't just a matter of style; it's a question of survival. As the book of Ecclesiastes cautioned, the race goes not always to the swift, nor the battle to the strong. Similarly, the pope preaches that we should view the world from the bottom up, not the other way around. We need more givers than takers; more Davids, fewer Goliaths.

Over the years, the United States has shown the ability to respond successfully to similar challenges. A pragmatic resiliency is deeply ingrained in the American psyche. It has served as well in the past. If we so choose, it will serve as well in the future. The following chapters offer a forum for thinking about our hidden heroes—in clear, unemotional terms.

❖ ❖ ❖

For sixty-three years, the Washington Generals played the foil for the fan-favorite Harlem Globetrotters.

CHAPTER 2

HOOP DREAMS

"Show me a good loser and I'll show you a loser."

—Vince Lombardi,
Hall of Fame football coach

PROFESSIONAL SPORTS ARE ABOUT VICTORY. "Winning," as the legendary Vince Lombardi famously remarked, "isn't everything. It's the only thing." Sports headlines reflect that, whatever the contest, the only players who matter are the victors. But there is another legion of contestants that have a significant, if less heralded, impact on the course of events—the losers. In an age when winding up on the wrong side of the win-loss column can do grave damage to your athletic cred, there are hidden heroes: gritty competitors who have stuck with the program, survived injuries and abuse to emerge better men and women.

"My heroes are the losers," attests author John R. Tunis, who penned popular sports books for children in the last century. Losing, he argues, isn't the end of the world.

No professional team is a better testament to the virtues of second best than basketball's Washington Generals. In their sixty-three-year history, they would become the sorriest team in the history of sports. Their spectacular losing streak against the world-famous Harlem Globetrotters exceeded *16,000* games. They lost in front of kings and queens, and popes. They lost in front of Nikita

Khrushchev and Barack Obama. They lost on an aircraft carrier, in bullrings, in an empty swimming pool, in a prison and in a leper colony. They lost in arid deserts, tropical jungles and steamy rain forests. They lost in 122 countries on six continents—*all* to the same team. Their last victory over the heavily favored Trotters occurred on January 5, 1971, when the Generals' forty-nine-year-old owner-coach-player, Red Klotz, hit the game-winning shot in a 100–99 overtime thriller. Since then, the Generals endured a forty-four-year losing patch.

Undaunted, the iconic ninety-three-year-old Klotz, who died in 2014, often brushed off his Generals' losing legacy. "Losing's a part of life," he once explained. "You can't lose if you are striving to do your best. If you tried your best and didn't score the most points, you still won."

In a lifetime of losing to the Harlem Globetrotters, these undiminished hoopsters won over the world. Playing the role of the victim, the foil, the loser for six decades, the Washington Generals emerged as hidden heroes, providing many fans around the globe with their first-ever basketball experience, while helping to break down longstanding cultural and social barriers. Simply put: When the Generals lost, everyone won.

The top dogs in this peripatetic tandem began as a quintet of all-black basketball players who, in the 1920s, set out to conquer the court. The Globetrotters were the brainchild of Abe Saperstein, a twenty-four-year-old Chicago social worker turned businessman. The London-born son of Polish Jews who emigrated to the United States when he was five, Saperstein acquired an existing basketball club, the Savoy Big Five of Chicago, and changed its name to the Harlem Globetrotters to let people know they were black. Consequently, the Trotters are often mistaken for a team with its roots in Harlem. Their first game was on January 27, 1927, in Hinckley, Illinois, forty-eight miles west of Chicago. The Globetrotters won; their purse, a whopping seventy-five dollars.

Back then, white athletes dominated sports, but black athletes had gained prominence in football, track and field and especially basketball. Saperstein sensed the opportunity to develop an equally dynamic sports environment for his hoopsters. All it needed was someone to spearhead the movement. Never did he—in his wildest dreams—envision the long and historic road the team would eventually follow.

As the Trotters' owner, general manager, coach and trainer, Saperstein literally carried the team office in the sweatband of his hat—driving his players to games in a rusty Model T and serving as the team's sole substitute. With boundless energy and uncanny marketing skills, the five-foot-three-inch dynamo and his five black players barnstormed the country, playing in front of sparse crowds in tiny gyms, in sleepy, comatose towns and whistle stops seven nights a week and twice on Sunday. Traveling up to 40,000 miles a year, Globies lived hand-to-mouth—receiving just ten dollars a game, plus five dollars for expenses. In many cases, they had to steal out of town in their uniforms, sleeping in Abe's car because either they couldn't find another place or they were denied accommodations.

"By far the worst aspect of their travels was the fact that they were seldom allowed to forget their color," wrote team historian Chuck Melville. "Most hotels, motels and restaurants were off-limits to blacks. In many parts of the South, they had to play two games per day: a matinee for black fans and a night game for the whites."

Despite the hardships of segregation and bigotry, the Trotters feasted on a series of cupcake opponents, winning a gaudy ninety-five percent of their games. Along the way, they introduced black hoops and culture to thousands of mesmerized spectators. Playing night after night, the team's five starters often ran out of gas. (Saperstein, the lone sub, had hung up his uniform in the mid-1930s.) To afford his players a breather, Abe introduced the now-famous ball-handling routines that allowed one player to showboat, while his teammates took a much-needed break. To liven things up, he added a host of time-tested tricks: fancy dribbling and difficult long-distance shots plus numerous jaw-dropping comic routines, or "reams," to the games. All this to the toe-tapping music of "Sweet Georgia Brown," the Trotters' signature song. Crowds across the country ate up their roundball razzle-dazzle, and Saperstein told his players to keep clowning around—but only after they had achieved a big lead.

Make no mistake, the Clown Princes of Basketball, as they were known, were a seriously competitive team. In 1940, they defeated the Chicago Bruins to win the World Professional Basketball crown.

Several years later, Abe's troupe—featuring the ball-handling wizardry of Marques Haynes, Goose Tatum's deadly hook shots and Nat "Sweetwater" Clifton's fierce defense—won added respect, beating the Minneapolis Lakers of the newly established National Basketball Association (NBA) two years in a row, in 1948 and '49. No longer dismissed as a bunch of undisciplined clowns, the Globetrotters had reached the mountaintop. They were not just the most entertaining team in the nation, but the best.

"All over America," wrote professor Ben Green of Florida State University, "black families raised up the Trotters as heroes to the race." The days of living hand-to-mouth were over. The team was drawing huge crowds in the largest arenas across North America and, later, in Mexico, Cuba and Hawaii.

By the end of the '40s, the Globetrotters' popularity transcended basketball. Saperstein was turning down 300 booking requests a year. As a result, the Trotters were able to attract the best black talent in the country. Making the team, however, was akin to surviving boot camp. Players invited to training camp could expect to compete against 100 hopeful candidates for spots on one of now two traveling squads. In 1953, Saperstein added two more teams. That same year, Abe's warriors set world records for attendance. In May, the Globetrotters embarked on their maiden voyage to Europe and North Africa, making the team live up to its name. The team began its reign as one of America's most effective propaganda weapons at the height of the Cold War. Everywhere they went, the reaction was overwhelmingly positive. With seventy-three smash appearances under their belt, the Trotters returned as America's ambassadors of goodwill and kings of the sports world.

But back home, something extraordinary had happened. In 1947, Jackie Robinson, after an apprenticeship in the minors, joined the Brooklyn Dodgers, becoming the first African American to play major league baseball. That opened the door for other sports to integrate. Three years later, the NBA broke the color barrier by drafting the first black ballplayers in its history. Three signees—Chuck Cooper, Sweetwater Clifton and Earl Lloyd—had been Globetrotters. Saperstein slowly began to see more and more of his stars defect to the new league where players saw more opportunities, less travel and better pay. "Given the opportunity to play fewer games for more money with no clowning required, the best black players shunned the Globetrotters," explained NBA great and former Trotter Wilt Chamberlain.

Despite the competition, the team's star continued to rise. In 1951, Columbia Pictures produced *The Harlem Globetrotters*, a full-length feature starring ten of the players. The publicity added excitement to the Trotters' second world tour, where they entertained more than 50,000 fans in Rio de Janeiro and a world record 75,000 in Berlin (among them, a special guest, Jesse Owens, who, in 1936, in the same stadium, won four Olympic gold medals). Three years later, the Globies' profile got another lift with the opening of a second major movie, *Go, Man, Go!*, featuring a relatively unknown actor, Sidney Poitier. Riding this wave of popularity, the Harlem Globetrotters became a merchandising marvel. Fans around the world could buy Trotters T-shirts, autographed photos, pendants, "Sweet Georgia Brown" records and other goodies.

By the mid-1950s, however, the team's star began to fade. "Seeds of discontent, dormant for many years, would germinate, and like a lowly weed that forces its way through a concrete slab, send out wiry tendrils that would crack through the walls of Abe's business empire," wrote Ben Green. Not only was Saperstein's monopoly on black talent ebbing, but he lost his two most famous players, Marques Haynes and Goose Tatum. In 1956, the longtime icons joined the Harlem Magicians, a fledging Trotter rival co-owned by Haynes. As the result, the Globetrotters found beating both NBA and leading collegiate teams increasingly difficult. These events, in turn, forced Saperstein to rely more heavily on the entertainment side of basketball—and the team's selfless foil, the Washington Generals.

Years earlier, Abe began to appreciate that the Trotters' viability depended on creating a credible relationship between his all-black all-stars and a truly competitive counterweight. With the era of big bands and rumble seats fading, audiences no longer were content to watch the Globetrotters obliterate a series of badly outmatched opponents. So, in the tradition of the Lone Ranger and Tonto, Sherlock Holmes and Dr. Watson, Saperstein turned to Red Klotz to create a partnership that is largely responsible for the organization's remarkable durability.

The diminutive, five-foot-seven-inch Klotz had carved

out his playing career in the City of Brotherly Love, where the sharpshooting guard led South Philadelphia High School to city championships in 1939 and '40. That earned him a scholarship to Villanova, where he starred for two years, until World War II erupted. During the war, he was a key performer on the US Army Transport team. After the war, he joined the American League–winning Philadelphia Sphas, a pre-NBA pro team, before hooking up with the Baltimore Bullets, the NBA champs in 1948. "It was a thrill to be a champion," Red said at the time. "But in the off-season, we all wanted raises, so they canned us."

In 1949, Klotz, twenty-eight, returned as player-coach of the Sphas, who were contracted to play a two-week exhibition series against the barnstorming Trotters. Electric on offense, the underdogs humbled the favorites by twenty-five points, with Red dribbling out the clock, Globetrotter-style, to seal a rare victory. After the game, Trotter great Goose Tatum approached Klotz, waving a finger in his face. "That'll never happen again," said Tatum. Klotz responded, "Why not?" The next night, the Sphas won again. Later, Red led other teams over the Globetrotters a couple more times.

Duly impressed, Saperstein eventually called, and told Red: "I want you to get a really good team together to play us every night." Klotz said: "I'm going to beat you." And Abe responded, "You're going to try." In 1952, with the help of a $1,500 loan from Saperstein, Klotz formed his own team, the Washington Generals. "Ike [General Dwight D. Eisenhower] had just tromped Adlai Stevenson, and generals were pretty popular at that time," he told *Sports Illustrated*. "I thought the name might win us some fans."

Respond they did, as the Globetrotters—and the underdog Generals—became global sensations. Klotz, for his part, had carefully assembled a troupe of seasoned professionals. His roster was stocked mainly with underappreciated overachievers—the anonymous castoffs of elite programs. To supplement these diamonds in the rough, Red added a bevy of top-line players. Among them: seven-foot center Bill Spivey. The University of Kentucky All-American had led his Wildcats to a national collegiate title and seemed destined for professional stardom. However, he was unjustly accused in a point-shaving scandal and banned for life from the

NBA—only to be rescued by Klotz and his Generals.

From this apparent mishmash of talent, Klotz's gritty competitors always came to play, forcing the Trotters to be at their best. But never once were the Generals asked to take a dive. "Absolutely not!" Red insisted. "We play our best and keep it as close as we can. We never try to lose. It just works out that we do."

Klotz knew why fans came to their games: to watch the Globetrotters, not the Generals. His players also understood their supporting role and never upstaged the fan favorites. "Night after night, they have their shorts pulled down or the ball tucked under the back of their jerseys, which do not have their names on them," wrote John Branch. "They patiently watch the confetti-in-the-bucket trick and gamely play defense. When the game ends, they slip away from the court practically unnoticed."

Over the years, Red Klotz was the Globetrotters' greatest ally. He devoted himself to making the Trotters look invincible and his Generals formidable. With a sly grin, he once said, "Like Fred Astaire had Ginger Rogers, the Harlem Globetrotters have always had a dance partner, but I've always been dancing backwards."

"One part of coaching is pushing players to do things they don't necessarily think they can do," wrote Jonathan Mabler of *The New York Times*. "Another part is showing them how to lose. Not in the simple, good-sport way, but in how to take a loss and make something of it." In recruiting players, the Generals had to eliminate those constitutionally unable to handle defeat—repeatedly. Candidates had to sublimate their competitive fires and get past the need to win. No easy task for testosterone-fueled athletes raised in a "must-win" culture. But as Phil Jackson, the most successful coach in the history of American professional sports, notes: "The goal of success is surrendering to what is."

Yet Klotz refused to let the Trotters' showboat diplomacy take its toll. A stickler for precision, he made sure his hidden heroes could always hold their own on the court. "When you watch them play," wrote Tim Kelly, author of *The Legend of Red Klotz*, "they're doing everything fundamentally precise. They can all shoot. They all know how to hit the open man. They don't turn the ball over. They can't afford to make mistakes...[because] they have to keep it close."

Skills aside, "I tell my players that our first priority is always laughter," said Klotz. "We're the straight men. Laurel had Hardy, Lewis had Martin, Costello had Abbott, and the Trotters have us. We're not stooges, we're not losers at heart, but let's face it, who got more glory? Abbott or Costello."

Besides the laughs, Red took great pride in launching the careers of hundreds of players and coaches. "I owe him everything," said the late Gene Hudgins, the first well-known black player on the Generals who later joined the Trotters. "He's an icon. He's as important to the Globetrotters' tradition as the Globetrotters. He was like a father to me." Today, similar testimonies can be heard the world over from diverse former Generals, including US Air Force Chaplin Father Tim Hirten; Doug Stewart, assistant coach at the University of Nevada-Reno; and New York state judge John Elliott. Moreover, an important part of the Klotz legacy was his ability to transform apparent losers into winners.

❖ ❖ ❖

You're a prodigious prep star, amassing record numbers for your school. A whirlwind on the court, you go on to star in college—scoring points, distributing the ball and playing tight man-to-man defense. You're a coach's dream, always sacrificing for the good of the team. Now, you await the call from the NBA.

But the call never comes. Their rosters are loaded. How, you wonder, did this happen? How, all of a sudden, did the basketball get so heavy? Like hundreds of other neglected players, you're out on the street, looking for work. Driven by rejection, you need another option—and fast. For some, it's the NBA's Development League; for others, it's overseas, playing for a foreign team.

Then you recall watching the world-famous Harlem Globetrotters as a youngster. You were dazzled by their basketball hijinks: fancy passing and dribbling, rim-rattling dunks and acrobatic stunts. You joined thousands of the other fans, tapping your feet and clapping your hands to "Sweet Georgia Brown." The memory of their performance never faded—an unforgettable moment. So you get your first-ever passport and pack your bags. You certify that you've completed your NCAA eligibility. You take a deep breath and send your references and game footage to the Trotters' headquarters. Weeks later the call comes. But it's from the wrong team: the Washington Generals.

There are worse ways of passing a decade, and beggars can't be choosers. You're told competition for spots on the team is intense. While the pay isn't much, you know that many Generals wind up supplementing their income with off-season jobs. But the opportunity to visit exotic locales and play the game you love for an established, nationally recognized organization seems well worth the sacrifice. In addition, there is the potential to make contacts with other professional teams both in the US and abroad, as well as the possibility of securing a coaching or administrative position. If it works out, you reckon you'll become more polished, more committed, more mature—valuable lifetime lessons.

In their years of recruiting players, Red Klotz and his staffers consistently looked for young athletes who could find comfort in losing and in making the audience laugh. "I need players who—number one—have a sense of humor," he told ESPN News. "You're playing the Harlem Globetrotters. They've got everything in the world going for them. There's no disgrace in losing."

Character, too, counted. Not only did Generals get used to being publicly pilloried by Trotter fans, but they also handled the nomadic existence, traipsing around the globe for most of the year. Those inclined to act selfishly or put themselves ahead of their teammates were excluded, and the club's strict, zero-tolerance policy eliminated anyone prone to the temptations of a life on the road.

In the face of overwhelming odds, Klotz and his round ballers hit the road, night after night. One of Red's favorite stories occurred after a 1953 game in the Middle East. The Trotters were leaving for Istanbul, but their plane was overweight, so Saperstein ordered Klotz, two Generals and two Trotters to get off. They had to drive 100 miles to Beirut to catch another flight. En route, they were stopped at the Lebanese border. "Everybody's running around like crazy with machine guns," Klotz told *Sports Illustrated*. "They're ready to go to war with Israel for the umpteenth time. I'm trying to identify myself by pretending to dribble and shoot. But the guards just kept looking at my visa list that had forty-two, not thirty-seven, names on it. They wondered where the other thirty-seven guys were. It didn't help much that the first two names on the list were

Saperstein and Klotz."

In his heyday, Red Klotz was perhaps the greatest long-range shooter on the planet, combining textbook form with an exquisite touch. In one shootaround, though still in his seventies, Red sank twenty-one straight from behind the old NBA three-point arc. "He had one of the best three-point shots I'd ever seen," according to Trotters' lead funnyman and twenty-four-year veteran, Meadowlark Lemon. "He was tough in his day, even though he was this little midget among the giants. It was like David and Goliath, except David wasn't winning."

Then in 1971, David trumped Goliath. On January 5, in the dinky college town of Martin, Tennessee, Red and his Generals would extract their revenge. That fateful day, the Generals, masquerading as the New Jersey Reds, veered off script and upset the unbeatable Trotters, ending their 2,495-game winning streak. No one expected the night to end in any other way than with loss No. 2,496.

"I remember it like last week," Klotz recalled. "It was a terrific ball game." His perennial losers were up twelve points with two minutes to play, but the Trotters stormed back to take a 99–98 lead with thirty seconds to go. Red called a timeout and told the team he wanted to take the last shot. With about twelve seconds left, the forty-nine-year-old deadeye hit a twenty-foot textbook set shot— swish!—to beat the Trotters. Kids cried. Klotz rushed his players off the court as fans booed and cursed mercilessly. We were assailed "for killing Santa Claus," Red later said. "I loved it."

In their tiny locker room, his "never say die" hoopsters hoisted Klotz on their shoulders and showered him with orange soda because, let's face it, who could afford champagne? Afterwards several of the Globies snuck in to offer their secret congratulations to the victors.

The Generals never tasted victory again. The Globetrotters paid them back for the last forty-four years. That said, the Martin, Tennessee, loss symbolized the Trotters' decaying basketball skills. After Saperstein's death in 1966, they went through a string of owners and defections of more longtime stars, including Meadowlark Lemon. "Everything seems so heavy, almost like a blanket of doom cooling the atmosphere," lamented Trotter executive Joe Anzivino in 1980.

Over the next decade, the once-proud franchise continued to flounder. In 1991, the team's owners declared bankruptcy. The Trotters were forced to slash their schedules and traveling expenses, while reducing the team to one unit. The Generals, too, suffered—experiencing a ten percent cut in their fees and a three-year suspension of players' pension funds.

In 1995, former Trotter Mannie Jackson purchased the Globetrotters, becoming the first African American in US history to own a major sports franchise. In an effort to restore the team to its former glory, Jackson worked to improve the team's competitiveness, while developing corporate sponsorships and broadening the Trotters' community involvement. Training camps were toughened, fitness emphasized and players schooled on African-American history.

Although his Generals remained independent and separate from the Trotters, Red got the message. He was asked to upgrade his squad and "retire" the Generals name in favor of, first, the International All Stars, and then the New York Nationals. Jackson reportedly had insisted on the name change because of the volume of publicity showered on Red and his lovable losers. "We're still here and we're still pressing them to play their best," Klotz said at the time, reluctantly taking the team's lost identity in stride.

The New York Nationals era lasted a dozen years. But, in 2007, after Jackson sold the Trotters to Shamrock Capital Advisors, the new owners immediately changed the name back to the Washington Generals. "I brought back the Washington Generals," CEO Kurt Schneider told *The New York Times*, "[because] this is the team that has been playing against the Trotters since the early '50s and '60s and '70s. They are almost as big in pop culture as the Globetrotters, albeit for different reasons. One wins and one loses."

In 2013, though, Shamrock sold out to Georgia-based Herschend Family Entertainment, the largest privately held theme park company in America, for an estimated $75 million. Herschend CEO Joel Manby wants to expand the team's global reach (they already play in thirty countries a year). His chief goal: playing in China. At the time of this writing, he hadn't found the right local partner to crack the Chinese bureaucracy.

❖ ❖ ❖

Love basketball? Love comedy? Need a shot of both for you and your family? Buckle up for ninety minutes of high-flying action. That's the course a few thousand fans took on a frosty February afternoon as they crammed into Kean University's crackerbox gym in Union City, New Jersey.

By the time the Washington Generals in their familiar green-and-gold trunks make their appearance, the standing room only crowd have seen five tall, graceful black players in their blue satin warm-ups jog onto the floor. Met by thunderous applause, the Trotters form their famous Magic Circle and start whipping their red-white-and-blue ball around—behind their backs, between their legs, faster and faster. Performing to the beat of "Sweet Georgia Brown," they weave a spell of razzle-dazzle enchantment over the arena. There's a circus atmosphere in the air—one big family of touring entertainers, everyone a professional and each committed to making people laugh.

After the Magic Circle ends, the Generals go through their warm-ups, shooting layups and arching shots from thirty to forty feet. Then the action begins. For the first ten minutes, the Trotters race off to an early lead, making a series of thundering dunks along with a stunning display of ball handling, no-look passing and heading the ball into the basket. Next come the alley-oops in waves, bedazzling their immobilized opponents. Feeling comfortable now, the Trotters begin their sidesplitting antics—tugging Generals' shorts, bouncing balls off their heads, pulling the ball-on-a-string trick, taunting the referees and making impromptu visits into the stands. Never a dull moment. The fans are in a frenzy.

The struggling Generals play hard, panting and sweating as they approach their bench during much-needed time-outs. But, slowly, the underdogs find their spark. On the back of their own barrage of three- and four-point shots (the latter, thirty-five feet from the basket, was introduced six years ago), the Generals fight, scratch and claw their way back into the game, taking a 58–55 lead at halftime.

The second half gets rolling with a burst of scoring on both sides. The sharpshooting Generals continue to maintain their lead. By the end of the third quarter, it's Generals 89, Trotters 85. Clearly, it's an off night for the favorites, who fail to nail a single half-court shot. Repressing some of their zany shenanigans, the Trotters focus on basketball—no shows, no tricks, no clowning. They turn to scoring machines five-foot-nine-inch Ant Atkinson and female star T-Time Brawner to launch a comeback. By the end of regulation play, the game is tied: 106–106.

Despite the Trotters' size, speed and talent, the Generals are giving them all they can handle. The teams trade baskets as the hard-fought game pushes into overtime. Minutes later, the hidden heroes are charged with what, by all accounts, appears to be an ersatz technical foul. As if on cue, the Trotters summon Fred "Curly" Neal from the stands. The longtime legend, now in his seventies, calmly sinks the winning free throw. The final score: 111–110—another Generals loss. The outcome was never in doubt.

The Trotters' locker room remains silent. There isn't much to celebrate. The victors, somewhat humbled, hole up in the stands for longer than usual before returning to the court to sign autographs. Across the hall, the undaunted Generals, in a rare upbeat mood, dress, board their bus and leave town anonymously. In just five hours, they will return to the same gym once again looking for redemption.

Absent from the game was the ninety-three-year old Klotz. The first non-Globetrotter to receive the team's prestigious "Legions" award and have his jersey retired, he continued to coach and play well into his sixties, eventually turning the team over to his capable son-in-law, John Ferrari.

In his cozy beachfront home on the New Jersey shore, Klotz continued to play half-court pickup games well into his eighties. But eventually, a series of strokes slowed him down, and, in July 2014, he died from cancer at the age of ninety-three. Globetrotters CEO Kurt Schneider said that Klotz was "as much a part of the Globetrotters' legacy as anyone ever associated with the organization. He was truly an ambassador of the sport."

"Long before the NBA was bragging about its globalization, Red Klotz was the most prolific foot soldier in actually laying the foundation," says biographer Tim Kelly. "The NBA would not be composed of twenty percent foreign players, nor would it have such strong international appeal were it not for the groundbreaking work of the Globetrotters and Red's team, the Washington Generals." Klotz, for his part, earlier had said: "We helped pioneer basketball all over the world."

Success is one of the most seductive lures imaginable. And yet, much of the time, we allow success to be determined by others. In an era of galloping egos, especially in professional sports, Klotz altered conventional notions of winning and losing. He had a good life, a happy family, an exciting working environment and the respect of his players and peers. He bent his goals around his life, not the reverse. He defined success on his own terms.

In his earlier years, Red would get irritated when someone called his Generals "patsies," "stooges" or "punching bags." Later, he became more circumspect about winning and losing. Reflecting on life's slings and arrows, he decided success had nothing to do with the final score. Instead, it had everything to do with doing the job well, with making people laugh.

"We have a way in this county of worshipping winners," Klotz once told *Sports Illustrated*. "Kids today are taught from Little League on up that they must win. But only one team can win, so most of us are losers in a way." To be sure, everyone loses much of the time. Consequently, "winning is overrated," declared coach Al McGuire, who won a national basketball championship at Marquette. "The only time it's really important is in surgery and war."

Longtime Generals opponent and admirer Meadowlark Lemon offered a different spin: "You never lose when you bring joy to people, when you put a smile on their face that lasts forever. So if anybody calls Red a loser, they're missing the whole point. When a Globetrotter game is over, folks never remember the final score. People remember the laughter." Blending moxie with a heavy dose of laughter, Klotz and his hidden heroes made losing a winning strategy. As P.T. Barnum once said, "The noblest art is making others happy."

Entering the 2015 season, it seemed like the Globetrotters appreciated Klotz's remarkable legacy—officially dubbing their world tour, "Washington Generals Revenge," in salute to their longtime opponent. However, by midyear, Herschend Enterprises had an abrupt change of heart. After sixty-three years, the Harlem

Globetrotters decided to dump the Generals, presumably for business reasons.

"They just told me that that was it," Generals general manager Ferrari said, referencing a July phone call. "I turned to my wife and said to her, in disbelief, 'It's over.'"

As word began to circulate about America's best-known and most beloved underdogs folding, the fraternity of ex-Generals voiced their concerns. "I was shocked when I heard," Antoine Maddox told ESPN. "I just think the Harlem Globetrotters can't be the Harlem Globetrotters without the Washington Generals." Ferrari, the late Klotz's son-in-law, expressed equal dismay of the unceremonious end, adding, "I can't imagine if Red were around to see this. He identified so much with the Globetrotters and the Generals. I'm guessing it would have killed him." The hardest part for Ferrari was the way the partnership ended, with no sense of closure. "After all these years," he said, "we didn't even get to say goodbye."

The Generals played the Globetrotters for the last time on August 1, 2015, in Wildwood, New Jersey. Yes, they lost, 90–88.

❖ ❖ ❖

Pennsylvania Coach Bill Wagner's sprint footballers stand apart from the meat market of big-time sports.

CHAPTER 3

FOOTBALL-LITE

*"It's not the size of the dog in the fight,
but the size of the fight in the dog."*

—LONGSTANDING ATHLETIC AXIOM

AUTUMN. FOR SOME, it conjures up vibrant colors, the crunch of leaves and a chilly bite in the air. For others, it means football, big-time football, where devoted fans and old grads flock into huge stadiums to watch gigantic, beef-fed, Bunyanesque athletes engage in mortal combat.

Walking through the University of Pennsylvania campus in west Philadelphia—past founder Ben Franklin's statue, the prestigious Wharton School and the fabled Palestra—I was on my way to see the Penn Quakers do battle with Navy's Midshipmen. The venue: historic Franklin Field, the nation's oldest collegiate football stadium, constructed in 1895.

In this football-mad state where gridiron is the opiate of the masses, Penn has played more games than any other organized team in America—professional, college or high school. It's been kicking a football around since 1876, when the Red and Blue defeated the Princeton Tigers 12–0, before 12,000 fans. Forty-one years later, the Quakers appeared in the Rose Bowl, losing to the University of Oregon 14–0. Since then, Penn has given the game everything from the first placekicker and the flying wedge to the site of college football's first radio broadcast and first televised contest. Two of the sport's greatest collegiate awards are named after two of its grads: John Heisman and John Outland. Less we forget, Penn also produced Hall of Famer Chuck Bednarik, the last full-time, two-way (offensive and defensive) player in the National Football League, who held a part-time job selling concrete.

During its glory years, the nationally ranked Quakers successfully competed with the likes of Penn State, Wisconsin, Michigan, Army, Navy and other gridiron giants. In fact, the school had only three losing seasons from 1888 to 1952. Success, in turn, brought sold-out stadiums, with upwards of 80,000 screaming spectators. During the "Fabulous Forties," the Quakers led the nation in attendance, far outdistancing behemoths like the University of Southern California, Ohio State, Michigan and UCLA.

Mindful of Penn's storied history, I entered cavernous Franklin Field on a blustery October night to uncover a very different world: the niche world of sprint football. Formerly called lightweight football, sprint is a full-fledged varsity sport, now played primarily in the northeast. But unlike the conventional version of the game, which places a premium on body weight and strength, sprint squads emphasize speed and agility. Novelist and football fanatic F. Scott Fitzgerald called them "pony teams." Today, no player can weigh more than 172 pounds, and each gridder must maintain a minimum of five percent body fat (so as not to encourage eating disorders). If players don't meet both standards, they are ineligible to compete. Brawny 300-pound linemen need not apply.

Looking at sprint football teams, one might easily mistake the combatants for ball boys or managers. Not so. "These are superb athletes," says Cornell head coach Terry Cullen, who began his sprint football career in 1964. The decorated Vietnam vet and former Marine told me: "Many players are former stars in high school who come to us chiseled and in extremely good shape. They're gritty competitors who love the chance to continue to play the game. They just happened to be 'normal' or slightly undersized."

Because of their size, many sprint players were ignored by big-time programs. "All their lives, they were told they were too small, too slow, or couldn't compete with the big boys," says Jerry Izenberg, Hall of Fame columnist for the Newark-based [NJ] *Star-*

Ledger. "That just fired up their competitive juices."

"Sprint football is simply football with a weight limit. That's the only difference," says another Marine, former Navy coach Major Kavan Lake. He insists that sprint is just as tough, maybe a tougher version of the conventional game. To even the casual observer, it's much faster, more up-tempo, more hard-hitting. Putting their quick reflexes and athleticism on display, these tiny titans try to knock the snot out of their opponents. I liken it to boxing where the staccato-like punching of bantamweights puts the lumbering efforts of heavyweights to shame. In sprint, you'll often see a defensive tackle run down a speedy running back. When does that happen in a traditional football game?

A simple alpha-to-omega summary of the quirky sport's origins misses the mark. This unique brand of football-lite has had more gyrations than the stock market. Genesis is easy enough. In the early 1950s, university officials began to express growing concern about big-time athletics, especially football. From inflated coaches' salaries and excessive practice time to lax admissions standards and special treatment for athletes, some college presidents—in a blast of fresh air—sought to walk back the distortions surrounding major varsity sports.

Pennsylvania's President Thomas Sovereign Gates was the standard-bearer. "As soon as I took office," he told a reporter, "I saw something was radically wrong with the way we went about athletics." In short order, he slashed coaches' salaries, terminated training tables and athletic dorms, reduced spring and pre-season practices, eliminated post-season games and heightened admissions standards for prospective athletes. Harvard, Yale and Princeton already had adopted similar measures, but for football powerhouse Penn, many viewed the Gates Plan as draconian.

Nonetheless, Gates pressed on, seeking a more inclusive role for the game. "Consideration," he said, "will be given to the development of well-trained, 150-pound teams for competition with other universities or colleges having the same relative strength." Under the slogan "Football for All," Gates sought greater athletic participation for those students long excluded from the sport largely because of their girth—or lack thereof.

In 1931, Pennsylvania embarked on its first 150-pound football season, scheduling Yale, St. Joseph's, Georgetown and Villanova. Three years later, the Eastern Lightweight Football League—now known as the Collegiate Sprint Football League (CSFL)—was launched. Besides Penn, charter members included Princeton, Cornell, Yale, Lafayette, Rutgers and Villanova.

The Daily Pennsylvania, the school newspaper, hailed the development for affording "a student greater incentive to participate in the great fall pastime even though he is too light to play varsity ball." Since then, notable sprint players have included such diverse personalities as President Jimmy Carter (Navy), New England Patriots owner Robert Kraft (Columbia), former Secretary of Defense Donald Rumsfeld (Princeton) and rapper Hoodie Allen (Penn).

During the intervening years, fans and players slowly sensed that sprint football, by its very nature, was a peculiar beast. It gave the game a unique egalitarian spin that looked much like standard football, but with the slightly quieter clomp of cleats exiting the locker room. Eventually, pigskin's pooh-bahs have come to accept the hard-hitting efforts and warrior ethos of these often hidden heroes. Nevertheless, sprint players rarely experience the lofty dividends enjoyed by their "big-boy" counterparts on the flagship varsity team. No bonfires, pre-game pep rallies, marching bands or raucous crowds with thousands of cheering fans. No media coverage. No charter flights. Instead, lots of long bus rides, box lunches and subpar training facilities.

More often than not, these mighty mites scavenge for crumbs. On campus, they remain virtually anonymous, indistinguishable from the general student body. "Lack of recognition is probably the sport's biggest downside," Penn's two-year captain Mike Beamish told me. Yet, to their credit, Beamish and others have come to appreciate the virtues of their often-unappreciated sport.

To be sure, lightweight football has always had its ups and downs. Yale and Lafayette disbanded their programs in 1942 and 1943, respectively, and play was halted from 1943 to 1945, during World War II. In 1946, the Eastern League was resuscitated, with Penn, Princeton, Rutgers, Cornell and Villanova and, for the first time, the US Naval Academy. Eleven years later, Army's Black Knights entered the conference.

Earlier, in the aftermath of World War II, many universities experienced serious financial problems. Increasingly, their athletic programs not only were running whopping deficits, but were continuing to compromise the academic mission. The presidents of some of America's oldest and most reputable universities had long sought to de-emphasize sports—in effect, emulating the Gates Plan. In 1954, the landmark Ivy League agreement was signed by eight world-class schools: Brown, Columbia, Cornell, Dartmouth, Harvard, Pennsylvania, Princeton and Yale. Under the new rules, financial aid would be based exclusively on need, not athletic prowess, and prospective athletes were required the same grades and test scores as other entering students. Post-season play, too, was prohibited, and practices truncated. Academics would now control athletics.

Today, the Ivy League members of the CSFL—Penn, Princeton and Cornell—must comply not only with these standards, but other conference requirements:

- Seven games per season.
- No more than sixteen practice sessions prior to the first game in September.
- No spring practices, except for selected schools with roster concerns; for them, a maximum of five days (without equipment).
- No off-campus recruiting or on-site scouting.
- All coaches must remain on the field during the game (no press box assistance, and headsets are not permitted).
- Squads cannot exceed sixty-five players.
- Lastly, the rules on weight (172 pounds) and body fat (five percent or greater) apply.

The current CSFL includes a mishmash of schools. Leading the pack are the well-disciplined service academies, Army and Navy. For years, they have exerted a stranglehold on the league, winning or sharing the conference title for more than six decades. Next come the erudite Ivies—Cornell, Penn and Princeton. Then, there are the four eclectic latecomers. Mansfield University, a public college with a student body of 3,400, located in the hills of north-central Pennsylvania, joined the league in 2008. Two years later, Post University, a private, largely online school with 7,000 undergrads, based in Waterbury, Connecticut, came on board. In 2012, Ridge, New Hampshire-based Franklin Pierce University, with 1,400 students, was added. This year, smallish (900 undergrads) Chestnut Hill College, in northwest Philadelphia petitioned the league to field a team.

These recent additions have helped soften the loss of programs like Villanova, Rutgers, Columbia and others that bowed out over the years. "The newcomers could be the savior of sprint football," Cornell's Cullen told me. Threats to the game include constant pressures on colleges to balance their budgets, compliance with Title IX legislation (which requires equal resources for men's and women's sports programs), student apathy toward athletics and small crowds (typically only in the hundreds).

Pennsylvania's Bill Wagner, the seventy-six-year-old dean of sprint football coaches, has weathered these storms. On at least two occasions, he effectively lobbied university administrators not to drop the program. The New Jersey native came to the Quakers in 1970 and, this year, enters his forty-seventh season.

Coaches are usually former stars who understand greatness, or marginal players who understand the intellectual nuances of the game. "Wags" is both. He starred in football, basketball and baseball in high school and college, earning All-Conference honors at both levels. Later, he spent more than twenty years playing semi-pro baseball and served for thirty-four years as pitching coach for the Quaker baseball team, while juggling his football duties.

But it has been on the gridiron where Wagner has enjoyed his greatest success, mentoring more than 1,500 Penn student-athletes "to become a better person today than yesterday." In the testosterone-infused world of football, he has shunned the killer-ape mentality of many big-time coaches. Using a player-friendly style, he relies on his uncanny ability in finding and molding hundreds of overlooked, pint-sized players who can flourish in his system. No blue chippers here. Penn's rosters (and most sprint teams) are stocked with overachieving athletes, the unloved castoffs of marquee Division I and II varsity programs. From these cracked bricks, Wagner has built Quaker squads that—clawing and scratching—

produce handsome results.

Invariably, his hidden heroes may not be as gifted as their more celebrated "fat-boy" counterparts, but they almost always make fewer mistakes: fewer turnovers, penalties and misalignments. Far from the preening crowd of high-stakes football, Wagner has taken the road less traveled and shown that a small-sized (literally) program can have a big-time impact with modest talent.

Make no mistake, Penn's head play-caller doesn't mince words with his team, collectively or individually. He stands in sharp contrast to the slick coaches who often infest major college football. Honesty is his calling card, with a deft touch for keeping his gridders humble and grounded.

Using old-school values, without the aid of scholarships, Wagner's elevens have enjoyed considerable success, more than holding their own against conference major domos, Army and Navy. In 2002, the CSFL honored him with the William R. Wagner Trophy, which goes annually to the highest Ivy League finisher in the league. Last year, Penn's Director of Athletics and Recreation, M. Grace Calhoun, announced the endowment of the program's head coaching position in his honor.

"Bill Wagner has become an absolute legend among his players over forty-five years," Calhoun said at the time. "I am proud that this endowment will bear his name. It is important for the program as a whole, as it allows Penn Athletics to direct its resources to the team's general operations." Describing the gift as "a dream come true," Wagner thanked the alumni and parents for helping "secure the future of the sprint football program."

Entering the 2014 season, Wagner sensed that he had the makings of a well-rounded team that could break the service academies' lock on the CSFL championship. He returned the league's top offensive team, led by strong-armed sophomore quarterback Mike McCurdy. The previous season, the talented deep-ball specialist, a Penn premed major and a graduate of Saint Albans in Bethesda, Maryland, had hit eight of his fourteen touchdown passes for distances longer than twenty yards. During the off-season, he worked hard on improving his short passing game, as well as his speed and footwork.

Complementing McCurdy were a host of other bona fide

standouts, most noticeably five-foot-eight-inch Mike Beamish, more bulldozer than ballerina and Penn's leading rusher the last three seasons. Back, too, were highly regarded first team All-Conference performers, wide receiver Brendon Dale, linebacker Stu Helgeson and defensive lineman Ed Cai.

With this stockpile of talent, Wagner looked forward to a winning season—and more. "The championship is what's on everyone's mind," he said. "We've got the weapons on offense and defense."

The first test for the 2014 Quakers came from a seemingly unlikely source: former Pennsylvania players. Traditionally, Penn, Cornell and Army have used an alumni game as a tune-up for the varsity sprint squad. At Penn, it's part of the annual preseason Alumni Weekend, where current players have the opportunity to mingle with former Quakers in high places and discuss career opportunities in business, law, medicine, education and other areas. "It's also an important fundraising event for a program that's often overlooked, while giving the old guard a chance to relive their gridiron glory days," writes Dave Zeitlin of *The Pennsylvania Gazette*. Recently, alums and other boosters stepped in to renovate the players' locker room and coaches' offices and refueled the sprint endowment program, which now approaches $3 million.

On September 6, 2014, a record fifty old-timers suited up for the contest. Among them: J. Matthew Wolfe, class of '78, who returned for his eighteenth alumni game. Strapping on his helmet, the fifty-eight-year-old lawyer revels in playing tackle football against twenty-year-olds. "It's the highlight athletically for me," said Wolfe, who lives within walking distance of Franklin Field.

Since few alums can make the 172-pound limit, offenders must donate a penalty, two dollars per pound, for exceeding the weight. For safety sake, oldsters must also bring a medical waiver with them to the game.

That day, the current Quakers downed the former Red and Blue greats, 31–14, the youngsters' fourth victory in the last five years. Major contributions came from their up-tempo offense, featuring junior receivers Henry Mason and Jack Epstein, who scored twice. Linebacker Helgeson also returned an interception for a score, and sophomore Patrick Boyle booted a thirty-nine-yard field goal.

In early October, Penn entered the crucial Navy game coming off its best start since the 2010 CSFL championship season. With victories over Mansfield and Cornell, the Quakers confronted a conference titan that had perennially stymied them. The Midshipmen had dominated the series between the two schools, winning fifty-five of sixty-five meetings, and matchups were often lopsided. Undermanned Penn, with forty-five or so players versus Navy's league max of sixty-five, typically ran out of gas during the fourth quarter. However, Wagner hoped that the school's newly instituted conditioning program would boost his players' stamina until the final gun.

Before a modest crowd of 382 sprint diehards, the well-oiled Navy machine got off to a fast start when its star running back, Eric Wellmon, rushed for his first touchdown in the second quarter, followed by a forty-two-yard score in the third quarter. In this seesaw battle, Penn responded as quarterback McCurdy shook off defenders and connected with sophomore Mario Del Cueto for two touchdowns. As the game progressed, there was plenty of physicality. The intensity of the hitting increased, with successively resounding tackles on both sides. However, Navy wide receiver Matthew Hite's sixty-two-yard TD reception at the end of the third quarter iced the game. The final score: Navy 21, Penn 19.

The Quakers showed grit and toughness in defeat. "The defense played good enough to win," Coach Wagner told me. "They only gave up two big plays the whole game. They never packed it in and played hard enough to stop Navy's high-powered offense."

The double-digit underdogs had taken the heavily favored Midshipmen down to the game's final seconds. Reflecting on the heartbreaking loss, Wagner remained sanguine about Penn's chances for a conference title. "To think about being a title chaser," he reminded his players, "you've got to beat at least one of the service academies."

The good news for the Quakers was that the Army game would offer a second chance. The bad news was that the reigning champion Black Knights showed no signs of slowing down.

"I'd give a year off my life to win," said Hall of Fame football coach George Allen, who in his earlier days served as an assistant coach of the University of Michigan's now defunct 1947 sprint team.

In many respects, Bill Wagner felt the same as his Quakers hosted Army just three weeks after the Navy game.

Over the years, the fast-paced Cadets had also dominated their Philadelphia rivals, winning forty-eight of fifty-two contests. "Army plays to a different beat," Wagner warned. "They play with a mission to win a battle, because they're getting ready to win real battles. They bring that to the field. They're hard to beat, they're well coached, and they've got a lot of talent. Their game plan: Win at all costs."

Heading into the game, Army led the CSFL in scoring and offense. Their explosiveness was on display from the opening kickoff. The Black Knights fired on all cylinders, gashing the Quakers for big plays throughout the contest. At the same time, the Army's ferocious defense smothered the Red and Blue offense all night, sacking quarterback McCurdy six times, intercepting him twice and blocking a punt that led to a safety. When the last whistle blew, it was a genuine shellacking: Army 47, Penn 7.

Despite the losses to Army and Navy, Penn sprinters managed to salvage a winning season, but not in the way the Quakers expected. The Red and Blue were scheduled to face beleaguered Princeton on Halloween, but the Tigers forfeited the game because of the lack of healthy players. "Princeton's had a tough couple years," Wagner explained. "The school is so demanding. Their coach is trying to build his roster, but they've just run out of bodies."

With the win, Penn finished the season with a 4–3 record, third best in the conference. By emphasizing unselfish play, the Quakers placed nine gridders on the All-CFL team. "It's been an incredible experience playing this brand of football," said senior offensive lineman Alex Smith from Auburn, Maine. "We were all really passionate about the game and always had each other's back," echoed Captain Mike Beamish, a four-time All-CSFL first team selection. "I couldn't be more thankful for sprint football," the brainy materials science and engineering major added. "More than the game, this team is like a family."

This unique strand of esprit de corps sets lightweight football apart from the meat market of Division I heavyweights and its darker side: the hypocrisy of big-time coaches, false promises of a professional career, rampant academic fraud and players' frequent emotional meltdowns after sports.

"When you talk about sprint football, it reflects positive qualities of the game. It's defined by the speed of the players and the open nature of the offensive and defensive schemes," said former league president George VanderZwaag. "We offer something truly unique in the world of intercollegiate athletics."

Probably nowhere is this uniqueness more on display than in the Pride Bowl, where the CSFL's two top-ranked lightweight teams vie for the championship. More often than not, it pits America's future generals against its future admirals. Army versus Navy—generally considered the greatest rivalry in sports.

The Pride Bowl is "a real blood vendetta," says New Jersey sportswriter Izenberg. "You'll never see hitting any harder than in this game."

"The old guard always asks, 'Did you beat Navy?'" says Army coach and former sprint football star Lieutenant Colonel Mark West. "You never want to have to answer, 'No.'"

In 2014, both academies entered the contest unbeaten. Army had won twenty games in a row and had not lost since the 2011 title game against Navy. But on a late October evening, the Midshipmen smashed the Black Knights 27–7 to secure the league title.

Putting the defeat to archrival Navy in greater context, Army's star running back Marques Burrell said: "Sprint football allows us to be a part of something bigger than yourself and still be part of a team. No other sport prepares you as well for combat—or life." Burrell's mother shares his enthusiasm, motoring up from their home in West Virginia to watch every one of her son's games.

Reflecting on his own coaching and playing experience, Army coach West calls the sport "a great leadership laboratory," where players push their bodies to the limit and sacrifice themselves for the good of the team. "The sprint game means everything to me," says the 1991 West Point grad and Iraq veteran. "I wouldn't have graduated without sprint football, and many of today's players would say the same thing."

In a profession often filled with nakedly ambitious coaches and silver-tongued mercenaries who live on a career ladder, climbing as they toil, always seeking a better job and more money until they reach football's upper echelons, sprint coaches like Mark West,

Terry Cullen, Bill Wagner and others remain an aberration.

"I'm not a money guy," Wags told me. Before Penn endowed his position, he earned an estimated $40,000 a year as head coach—a far cry from his $3,500 starting salary for coaching two sports in 1970. Annual budgets for most sprint teams rarely exceed $250,000.

Yet "money is what makes the veins pulse for a lot of folks," novelist Carl Hiaasen reminds us. "Certainly it warps values, it destroys lives." In the strange biosphere of big-time coaching, one wonders whether the stresses and strains are worth it. Talk about a hot seat. The job comes with a torrent of workplace nightmares. Besides the endless pressure to win, big-time coaches are confronted with recruiting wars, barracuda boosters, reality-deprived expectations, call-in shows, acrimonious websites and the lack of job security.

"The job description includes criticism, doubts, frustration, anguish, heartbreak, anger, disappointment, tensions, exhaustion, Himalayan heights and Death Valley lows," writes *USA Today's* Mike Lopresti. A Division l coach "can watch his life devoured, like a shark gulps a seal."

In this pressure-packed profession, top-tier coaches are defacto CEOs with multimillion-dream operations, dozens of employees and more than 100 players. "They must win," says Andy Staples of *Sports Illustrated*. "They must recruit. They must make sure their players don't start bar brawls. They must schmooze with boosters and raise money. They must make sure their players graduate. *They must win!*"

In 2010, Vanderbilt coach Bobby Johnson decided to get off the hamster wheel. Just three weeks before the start of fall practice, the highly respected fifty-nine-year-old, with no health issues, called it quits. "Big-time football consumes your life," he said at the time. "You only have so many lives to live. Some guys will coach with one foot in the coffin." In retirement, Johnson can be found whistling past the graveyard. He is the exception in the money-soaked atmosphere that surrounds high profile football. Yet, more and more men seem willing to trade off these arduous jobs for the bucks—big bucks.

Once upon a time, Paul "Bear" Bryant insisted that his head coaching salary be one dollar less that the University of Alabama president. No wonder Alabama fans thought he walked on water.

Nick Saban, who has won three national titles for the Crimson Tide, walks instead on a sea of green. He makes a whopping $7,160,187, plus myriad other creative benefits; at last count, the university's president was earning $670,000. In the big-money culture of college football, coaches now rank above governors as the highest-paid public employees.

Welcome to the million-dollar fraternity. Today, the average salary for a Football Bowl Subdivision coach is roughly $1.95 million—up from $950,000 in 2006, according to research compiled by *USA Today*. Last year, twenty-seven major college coaches racked in at least $3 million. Their pay has climbed faster than corporate CEOs in the past eight years. In addition, performance bonuses, annuities, life insurance premiums, low-interest loans, housing and other special arrangements can drive these figures further north.

Recently, however, these inflated benefits—as well as the fantasy of the "student-athlete"—have drawn increasing criticism from those inside and outside collegiate sports. "I think we've sold out," longtime Kansas State football coach Bill Snyder told the media last August. "The concept of college football no longer has any bearing on the quality of the person, the quality of students. It's no longer about education. I don't fault TV and whoever broadcasts games. But athletics, it's sold out."

The straight-shooting seventy-six-year-old's remarks carry considerable weight in coaching circles. On two occasions, Snyder orchestrated the so-called "Miracle in Manhattan," transforming a perennial loser into a national championship contender. In 1988, his first year on the job, he earned $90,000—peanuts compared to the $2.9 million package he received in 2015.

"Football is a game played with arms, legs and shoulders, but mostly from the neck up," said legendary Notre Dame coach Knute Rockne. A major challenge for both the Ivy League and service academy sprint coaches is casting a wide enough net for the small pool of terrific athletes who can juggle a rigorous academic schedule. At Cornell, for example, close to 100 prospective student athletes apply for admission each year. Less than fourteen percent get in. Fortunately, Cornell and Penn have large undergraduate populations (in excess of 10,000), which work to their advantage. Smallish Princeton, though, with only 5,000 or so entering students and a tight-minded admissions office, is perennially short on numbers and talent. (At the time of this writing, Princeton's sprint program was under review.)

Despite their own lofty entrance requirements, the service academies have some unique advantages. "Depth is a major plus," former Navy coach Stu Helgeson told me. Both schools are able to tap into their respective preparatory schools for recruits. In addition, every entering student must participate in a sport—varsity, club or intramural—but varsity athletes like sprinters can avoid mandatory Thursday marches. As a result, Army and Navy typically attract sixty to eighty plebes to sprint tryouts, with twenty to twenty-five of them winding up on the sixty-five-man roster.

Ironically, CSFL newcomers—Mansfield, Post, Franklin Pierce and Chestnut Hill—view fielding a sprint football team as a catalyst for attracting more undergraduates. State-supported Mansfield, for instance, was looking for a full-fledged varsity sport to replace its conventional heavyweight team, which was dropped in 2006 for financial reasons. In their search for low-cost alternatives, university administrators concluded they could add sprint football on a relative shoestring—thanks to smaller rosters, cheaper coaching staffs, less travel and no scholarships. As important, Mansfield bigwigs hoped "to corner the market on smaller young men who want to play football but can't afford—or can't qualify academically for—the other schools in the league," wrote *The Wall Street Journal*'s Adam Thompson. Franklin Pierce, Post and Chestnut Hill have similar aspirations, hoping their sprint programs will call more attention to their schools.

Looking ahead, sprint football has its challenges. For one thing, the sport has yet to connect with the growing ranks of foreign students that make up a growing proportion of undergraduates. In addition, there is substantial evidence that youngsters today are shunning football (Think: concussions). Conversely, other contact sports—particularly hockey, lacrosse and rugby—are gaining in popularity. Then, too, there are diversions like fraternities and "e-sports" (video game competition) that appeal to students who simply want to "veg out" rather than engage in athletic participation.

Acknowledging that the CSFL almost folded a decade ago, sprint coaches like Wagner, Cullen and West are drumbeating expansion.

"We're aggressively reaching out," says Army's West. "I'd like to see sixteen teams in the league. But I want to make sure we're selective. Any newcomers must share our academic values and mission statement."

In the topsy-turvy world of big-time football—with its flamboyant coaches, vociferous fans and gigantic players—the sprint game demonstrates that you can't measure competitive spirit by size. Despite their lack of stature, these hidden heroes offer an inspirational tale of hard work and determination. "Sprint football is what football should be," says columnist Izenberg, who has followed the sport for half a century. "Players play the game for the right reasons—for the love of the game."

Pennsylvania's Wagner agrees: "Playing the game for the love of competition and the camaraderie between teammates and coaches remain the driving force that has made our sport the most genuine varsity sport in the country." As for its future, Wags remains optimistic: "We've survived the test of time and set the standard for future generations of student-athletes."

The Quakers' feisty septuagenarian, for his part, shows no signs of slowing down, of taking a knee. His competitive juices still rage. For the time being, Wagner will continue to coach his undersized athletes to their ultimate potential—getting them to believe there are no limits to what they can do. Let the games begin!

❖ ❖ ❖

Comic magician Harry Maurer, here with wife Carol Ann, is
unmatched in setting the stage for top headliners.

CHAPTER 4

SUPPORTING ACTS

*"The most difficult instrument to play
in the orchestra is second fiddle."*

—LEONARD BERNSTEIN,
COMPOSER AND CONDUCTOR

"T HE HUMAN BRAIN," comedian George Jessel once remarked, "is a wonderful device. It starts up the moment we're born and never stops until we stand up to speak in public." While most folks are tongue-tied when called upon to make a public presentation, Harry Maurer is the exception. For the better part of three decades, the loquacious comic magician has found sanctuary as a successful opening, backup or supporting act (he prefers the latter term), setting the stage for stars such as Joey Bishop, the Supremes, Frankie Avalon and Rosie O'Donnell. His quick-witted stage presence and ability to prop up leading headliners in venues ranging from Biloxi to Brunei win him numerous kudos as a premier leadoff man.

One spring, I witnessed Maurer's sleight-of-hand and zany antics onboard the luxurious Regent *Seven Seas Voyager*. Harry joined the swanky ship in Borneo for four shows over eleven days. His assignment: Serve as an appetizing intermezzo for the liner's feature attraction, Jean Ann Ryan Productions, a full-service troupe specializing in Broadway musical revenues and cirque-style aerialist performances. But in short order, audiences came to appreciate that second banana Maurer was no second-rate spear-carrier.

The fifty-something magician enjoys a very good living introducing showbiz stars. It's a role that Harry has evolved into. As a child, he was determined to be a magician, much like *The Tonight Show*'s legendary Johnny Carson, and soon proved that magic was more than a childhood fantasy. At age thirteen, the New Jersey native performed the first of his many nightclub shows. He was an instant hit. By the time he had reached high school, Harry managed to rearrange his classes to leave school early to perform matinee and evening gigs at a Jersey Shore club. Later, while juggling jest and studies at Rutgers University, he began a longstanding run—more than 1,300 shows—at the Playboy Club in New York City. That followed a series of opening acts for Bishop, Jack Vernon and other big name comics before sell-out houses. Since then, Maurer has never stopped working—spending an average forty-eight weeks a year performing in theaters, casinos, comedy clubs, college campuses and, as in this case, on the world's leading cruise ships.

"Good evening, ladies and gentlemen. From the entertainment capital of the world, welcome to the comedy and magic of Harry Maurer," booms the emcee's voice over the PA. "Remember, no cell phones or electronic recording of any kind is permitted. Thank you. Now enjoy the show!"

The house lights flicker before going dark. The cozy, perfectly tiered 500-seat showroom grows hushed. A flash of light hits center stage, followed by a puff of smoke. Maurer steps through the cloud wearing a perfectly tailored blue tux jacket, his recently graying hair combed back.

"Good evening—and welcome to my show," he says. The applause is generous. Harry, after all, has become a magic-comedy favorite to generations, spanning from retirees to college students. For the seriously minded, his cunning stagecraft today is endlessly discussed on websites, chat rooms and special forums. This scrutiny would overwhelm most performers. Not Harry Maurer. It's just another night to showcase his special illusionary talents.

"It's one of the first rules of magic," Maurer says. "People see what they want to see." For the next hour, he does everything an illusionary wizard should do, with liberal doses of humor thrown in. "Sorry to wake you up, sir," he calls out to one slumbering octogenarian. "I didn't realize I'd whipped you up into a coma!"

Heroic Harry is huge on audience participation, which lends an effective sharing atmosphere to the show. He'll do a guillotine joke here, a card trick there. Objects appear, disappear, are burned and made whole, without any visible clue to where they went. Before disbelieving eyes, his lovely blonde assistant (wife Carol Ann) is transformed into various forms. Harry is a master of exploiting nuances of human perception, attention and awareness. By now he is batting a thousand. Afterward, everyone compares notes about what they saw and didn't see—to try to make sense of it all. "But, as all magicians know," says Maurer, "audiences never really see anything."

Like other great magicians—Harry Houdini, the Amazing Dunninger, Blackstone, Ching Ling Foo and David Copperfield—Harry Maurer takes chances. He tells me he can't always predict how each show will come out. Although it's risky, he's discovered that's why people come to see him work. They want to experience something impromptu and unique, and Harry never disappoints.

"Are there ever flubs?" I ask him. "Sure," he admits, "but you have to move on—and quickly. Most important, you *never*, *ever* want to close on a mistake!"

This night, like most, is flub-free. The resulting ovation is long and hard. A fully enthralled audience is revved up, waiting for the next act. Satisfied with his performance, Maurer understands that his role is to set the stage, not to outshine the Jean Ann Ryan dancers, who headline the *Voyager*'s three-month cruise.

Although his illusions and quick wit are second to none, his special gift is "energizing, warming up an audience for the leading man or lady." "I'm just better at it," he says of his supporting role. But it's anything but easy. "Tourist venues like Las Vegas or Atlantic City are friendlier," he explains. "Folks come in already loosened up, maybe after a few drinks. They want to be entertained, to have a good time." The mood has already been established. "But conventions and corporate events can be much tougher," he says. "Often attendees are troubled, stressed out or skeptical, particularly about magic acts. They need a lot more convincing. You have to win them over quickly, very quickly. Opening acts usually run only five to twenty-five minutes, so it's imperative to be compact, to keep to a strict deadline."

"What about the dangers of stealing the show from the featured star?" I ask. "That's way overblown," Harry says. "Any experienced headliner lusts for the opening act to have the audience as heightened as possible, at fever pitch. Even the most difficult prima donnas are comfortable in their ability to transfer that energy into their own routine. The worst thing they want from an opener is to leave the audience flat."

"We can do as partners what we cannot do as singles," Daniel Webster observed. In Maurer's case, wife Carol Ann supports the supporting star. The couple met on a cruise ship in the early 1980s when Harry was performing and Carol Ann, a trained nurse, served in the infirmary. During one of Harry's performances, an elderly gentleman in the first row passed out. Carol Ann was immediately dispatched to the theater, where she quickly determined that the man was dead. To avoid upsetting the dead man's wife—not to mention spoiling the show—Carol Ann told her they would need to assess her husband's condition in the ship's medical center. In the interim, Harry continued on with his wisecracks and sleight of hand, with the just-widowed woman still in attendance.

Later that evening, Harry accompanied the woman to the infirmary to gauge her husband's status. To make things easier on the wife, Carol Ann had placed the old gent on a respirator, informing her that although her husband's condition was very serious, she would spend the night by his side and advise her in the morning. The next day, Carol Ann told the woman that her beloved had "passed away quietly in the night." An hour later, the grieving widow left the ship with the body in tow.

Once Harry understood the details, he began to actively court the unflappable, attractive nurse. Although Carol Ann had vowed never to get involved with an entertainer—let alone a magician—she succumbed after a seven-year relationship. Twenty-five years later, they remain partners on and off stage.

When the Maurers aren't touring the world, they retreat to their comfortable Houston area home, which is crammed with an enormous collection of magic tricks and stage illusions. In his spacious second-floor office, Harry continues to perfect his skills and explore new ways to bamboozle unsuspecting audiences, while organizing future bookings and responding to fan mail. When I last left him in Singapore, he was scheduled to disembark a few days later for an upcoming series of country club appearances on the US East Coast, culminating in a gala event in one of New York City's tonier restaurants. The odyssey, it seems, never ends. There's one magic trick Harry's never figured out: How to stop time.

Hidden heroes like Maurer understand the spoils of second place. They find activities that they love and do well. In mixing prestidigitation with sidesplitting comedy, Harry remains thankful that he gets to improve people's lives, not diminish them. In sharing the limelight, the comic magician has defined success on his own terms.

❖ ❖ ❖

"I am not a movie star," nimble comedienne Judy Greer insists. "Chances are when you saw my face, you knew I looked familiar. Maybe you know I'm an actress, but you just don't know my name since I've had as many different jobs and played so many characters." Even though Greer has acted in more than sixty films, the refreshingly honest, perennial co-star remains anonymous to most moviegoers. But, for nineteen years, she has been one of the hardest-working women in show business, as befits her hardscrabble upbringing in suburban Detroit.

Greer has played an ape in *Dawn of the Planet of the Apes*, a bearded lady in *My Name is Earl* and a high school guidance counselor in *Miss Guided*. She was J. Lo's ditzy best bud in *The Wedding Planner* and Lily Tomlin's girlfriend in *Grandma*, Jennifer Garner's foil in *13 Going on 30*, the file clerk in *What Women Want*. Add to that her nineteen minutes of fame in *The Descendants*. Since 1998, the self-deprecating character actress has been stealing scenes at every turn from some of Hollywood's biggest stars, including Ashton Kutcher, Nicolas Cage, Jeff Bridges, George Clooney and Sigourney Weaver.

That's just the movies. Then there's television. If you tuned in on *The Big Bang Theory*, *ER*, *Modern Family*, *House* or *Two and a Half Men*, you would encounter the willowy, five-foot-ten-inch supporting actress. And don't forget her directorial debut in AOL's film *Quiet Time* or her recent memoir, *I Don't Know What You Know*

Me From: *Confessions of a Co-Star*.

All in all, not bad for Greer, who grew up in Livonia, Michigan, far removed from the glamour of Los Angeles. Her mother had been a nun for eight years before she met Judy's father, a mechanical engineer. Raised a Catholic, Judy studied classical ballet at Winston Churchill High School, followed by acting lessons at DePaul University's Theatre School. Then came stints as a telemarketer and oyster shucker. In 1998, she moved to the City of Angels to pursue an acting career.

Legendary actor Jimmy Stewart claimed that the secret to longevity in show business was all about staying on the bus. If you get on at the start, you should sit up front. Then, as time passes, you can shift to the middle. Later, when you're fully established, you can afford to move to the back. The key, Stewart asserted, is to never get off the bus.

Since arriving in Hollywood, Judy Greer has stayed on the bus. To do this, she has mastered the art of making herself up as she goes along. Today, the forty-one-year-old actress continues to reinvent herself. From breaking into movies as the ultimate best friend to serious dramatic roles, she remains focused on staying engaged. "I'm diversified," she says of her multifaceted roles. "I remember learning in acting schools that 'work begets work,' so I have always just tried to stay in motion and keep working. Now I'm busier than ever. Slow and steady wins the race. That's how I've always thought of my career."

Building a tortoise career in a town full of hares brings its own array of special benefits. Besides a steady stream of ever-expanding paychecks, playing second banana allows Greer to sidestep the paparazzi. "I'm like a normal person," she told *The Wall Street Journal*. "Every once in a while there will be a random person who will say, 'Hey, Judy!' But no, I don't have that problem."

In addition to avoiding the shutterbugs, Greer gets a kick out of seeing Hollywood's best-known celebrities at 5 a.m. with no makeup, finding out what size shoes they wear and what they eat. But her all-time favorite perk as an under-the-radar actress is listening to them pee. "I have peed next to several *very* A-list celebrities, and every time I hear the tinkle of celebrity pee, I giggle," she confesses in her tell-all book. "I have no idea why." Among her favorite potty mates are Jennifer Lopez, Heidi Klum and Debra Messing.

Though revealing some endearing quirks in her book, Greer is all business about the importance of propping up one's leading man or lady. "One thing I've learned from playing sidekick characters is to be direct and honest," she explains. "There isn't a lot of time to beat around the bush. You don't want to get edited out, and you're responsible for a lot of exposition."

In addition, the talented actress roils against the industry axiom that there are no small roles and no small actors. "There really are small roles," she insists, "but when you get a lot of them in a row, you can become a pretty successful actress, and that's what I've done." In short, Greer has stayed on the bus.

As for dark places, she professes some insecurities, particularly "the fear of it all ending and regretting having wasted any small opportunity I might have had. But most of the time I'm happy with where I am—a bright co-star, a steady co-star, a co-star you can depend on if you're lost, flipping channels in the night."

Obviously, Judy Greer refuses to suffer the curse of the understudy. She understands that if you are overly concerned about taking center stage, you are paying too much attention to something other than the task. "There's a lot of peaks and valleys in the life I've chosen, but my mission statement reminds me to focus on what matters most," she says. "When life is awesome, it keeps my head from getting too big, and when things are shitty, it reminds me that my life is still awesome. I've been very lucky."

To industry pooh-bahs, the clever comedienne hardly goes unnoticed. Five years ago, she was honored with the John Cassavetes Independent Spirit Award, the first actress to receive the tribute. Yet her willingness to serve as a subordinate runs contrary to Hollywood's starstruck conventions. Greer accepts that the genius of a first-rate performance is truly collaborative. She provides an egoless commitment to teamwork from start to finish.

Truly exceptional supporting players like Judy Greer need unusually healthy egos. That's a paradox really, because it would seem that they would need less ego strength than the star. But, especially in a business obsessed with celebrity, it takes extraordinary self-confidence to buttress the No. 1. No matter how great an effort a gifted supporting actress or actor makes, the majority of credit is going to accrue to the headliner. That's just the nature of showbiz.

As impressive as Judy Greer's selfless accomplishments are, they are not unprecedented. Indeed, writer Roger Rosenblatt captured the spirit of other great adjuncts in a wonderful tribute to the late George Burns. The cigar-smoking comic made a career of working in the shadow of his marvelously ditzy wife, Gracie Allen. Like other successful co-stars, Burns understood the personal and professional rewards that come only as a result of collaboration.

As Rosenblatt wrote, "The essence of the straight man is that he gives. He gives the best lines, the stage, the spotlight. By giving, he creates the show—the entire show, including all the performances... And he gets by giving. It takes a certain kind of person to do that— one who is willing to diminish his part for the good of the whole."

The generosity of the great supporting player is grounded in a profound understanding that we are all in this together. No wonder satisfied co-stars don't care about the credit. They are having too much fun creating the show. In a great partnership, everybody wins.

❖ ❖ ❖

"Music is spiritual. The music business is not," warned singer-songwriter Van Morrison. Longtime entertainment attorney Mark Bernstein also cautions newcomers about the vagaries of this often-cutthroat industry. "To become a real star," he told me in a recent interview, "you need three things: (1) Aptitude, (2) Attitude and (3) Luck. The last two factors far outweigh aptitude, or raw talent, in importance." There's an extremely shallow pool of truly great singers—Luciano Pavarotti, Barbra Streisand and Tony Bennett— who can make it on their vocal cords. What's absolutely critical to achieve stardom is a killer instinct plus a heavy dose of circumstance or destiny. Successful musical careers, Bernstein reckons, are usually preceded by unforeseen accidents.

Hollywood Walk of Fame actor and singer Jim Nabors is a case in point. Born and raised in rural Alabama, he attended the University of Alabama, where he began acting in skits. After graduating, he moved to New York for a short stint as a typist with the United Nations. Then, it was back down South, to Atlanta and

Chattanooga, where he was introduced to the television industry as a film cutter. Because of asthma, he moved to Southern California.

While working as a film cutter for NBC, he began moonlighting at the Horn, a Santa Monica gin mill, winning over audiences with his hillbilly characters and rich baritone voice. His efforts soon caught the attention of comic Bill Dana, who landed him a brief stint on *The Steve Allen Show*. Not long afterward, another high-profile TV performer, Andy Griffith, caught his club act and asked him to audition for a new role on *The Andy Griffith Show*.

Despite his success on stage, Nabors had trouble seeing much of a future in acting. "I was from a small town and, God knows, I had no experience in acting," he told me in his palatial Diamond Head home, with its panoramic view of the Pacific Ocean. "The only thing I could possibly think of was possibly becoming a character actor in a Western or something. I never had any thoughts about going into the acting business."

Nevertheless, incorporating his golly-mouth patois into the part, Nabors nailed the role of the addlebrained, but lovable, country bumpkin Gomer Pyle, whose signature phrases, "gawwlee" and "shazzayam," helped rocket him to fame. In 1964, after two seasons as the goofy gas station attendant, CBS made Pyle the star of a spinoff sitcom, *Gomer Pyle, U.S.M.C.* Despite its run during the Vietnam War, a time of growing disenchantment with war and the military, *Gomer Pyle* remained popular and ran for five seasons. In fact, the show is credited with boosting Marine Corps recruitment and re-enlistment by thirty-five percent during its run. That, in turn, led to Jim's hosting his own variety and talk shows in the 1970s.

Weary of "the prime time TV grind," Nabors abandoned television for an extended series of nightclub and concert engagements, headlining in leading venues across the country. Later, he relocated to Hawaii. "When I first walked off the plane in the '60s, I knew this is where I wanted to be," he recalls. "It was the air and the friendliness of the people. I love this place and everything about it." For a time, he stepped away from the stage completely and concentrated on managing his 500-acre Maui ranch with more than 20,000 macadamia trees.

After a five-year hiatus from show business, Nabors returned to performing, primarily in Reno and Las Vegas. Eventually, however, another case of "bright lights burnout" coupled with some life-threatening health issues convinced him to downshift and devote himself to charity work and community service. He is particularly revered by the US Marine Corps, which made him an honorary sergeant a few years ago.

Ironically, the happiest days of his illustrious career were as the wacky sidekick in *The Andy Griffith Show*. "I absolutely loved it," the eighty-five-year-old retired actor and singer told me of his one and only supportive stint. "I didn't have to carry the show—working 24/7 with writers, directors, the cast and others. There was much less pressure, much more fun." Perhaps as a result, the country boy from down South has always considered his supporting players as "co-equals, *never* anything less." Impressive, too, are the showbiz luminaries who later opened for him in Las Vegas, Reno and Lake Tahoe. They include Jay Leno, Joan Rivers, Rosemary Clooney and Kay Starr.

❖ ❖ ❖

Jim Nabors' close friend, entertainer Carole Kai, also understands the challenges of supporting and starring. "I've been on both sides and know how things work," she told me. The youngest of three children, Kai grew up in Hawaii. Her mother was a single parent who owned her own business in Honolulu, the Kapiolani Barber School.

The family hovered on the brink of poverty, but Carole and her siblings never knew it. "We always had food on the table and decent clothes," she says. "But I didn't join the Girl Scouts, because my mom couldn't afford to buy me the uniform."

After high school and a music degree from the University of Hawaii, Carole took a detour to Japan to work as a model. In the late 1960s she returned home and began working the entertainment circuit as a singer and dancer. "Those were Hawaii's golden years," she remembers. "There were over forty bands in Waikiki, working every night and all making good money." In time, the bright lights of the Las Vegas/Reno/Lake Tahoe circuit beckoned, where she quickly found work as an opener and slowly began to build her brand. In 1974, she was named Vegas' "Most Promising Newcomer of the Year," serving as the tantalizing warm-up act for Shecky Greene ("a great guy"), Don Rickles ("horrible, a real jerk"), George Carlin ("an absolute lecher") and other notables. Yet, Carole was miserable.

Her exotic Suzie Wong looks attracted the worst from both headliners and entertainment heavyweights. "Basically, they all wanted to go to bed with me," she says. "'Female singers, especially sexy Asian girls like you, are a dime a dozen,' one hotel owner told me. But I was a born-again Christian. Our values just clashed, and I got very depressed."

A close friend and influential newspaper critic who had positively reviewed her acts listened to her frustrations, and then shook his head. "You're not the kind of person who has the killer instinct," he said. "All the girls I know who became stars here had to claw their way up, and they would do *anything* to succeed. You're more of a flower. You should go back to Hawaii and find happiness there."

Looking back, Kai says, "He gave me very good advice. Although I was making $5,000 a week, good money in those days, I just wasn't comfortable there, and headed home with my reputation intact."

Initially, boomeranging back was anything but easy. She toiled away as an underpaid newspaper reporter, then invested heavily in a failing restaurant. Eventually, though, the pretty, pert, ebullient entertainer persevered. She restarted her Hawaii career, headlining her own shows, making numerous TV appearances (*Hawaii Five-O* and *Magnum, P.I.*) and co-hosting *Hawaii Stars*, the most popular locally produced TV show of its kind in the Islands. Clearly, the dame still had game.

Serendipity struck in 1974, when Kai discovered that philanthropy was her true calling. She founded the Carole Kai Bed Race, an annual event benefitting the Variety School for children with special needs. Twenty years later, she teamed up with a Honolulu cardiologist to launch the 8.15-mile Great Aloha Run, one of the largest road races in the Islands, attracting 22,000 runners annually. Now in its thirty-third year, the popular event, supported by 4,000 volunteers, has raised more than $11 million for a wide variety of local charities.

"I'm not just proud of the race," Kai beams. "I'm proud of the volunteers who labor for seven months as committee members. I couldn't do it without them." Dozens of businesses have also stepped up, donating money, manpower and merchandise to make the event a major milestone.

What fuels her philanthropic spirit? Carole Kai attributes her work ethic and devotion to community service to her mother. "Mom taught me you have to give back to the community so the well doesn't run dry. You can't keep taking from the well. You have to put something back."

Johann Sebastian Bach perhaps put it best. Asked about the true contribution of music, he claimed: "Music's only purpose should be the glory of God and the recreation of the human spirit." He believed sanctification and service underscore life's purpose. Carole Kai's career reflects these values.

"I'm grateful every day that I live," the seventy-one-year-old former songbird says with a sparkle in her eyes. "Every day, I thank God and ask Him to do the right thing. If I can inspire just two people to help fill the well in our community, then I'll be happy."

❖ ❖ ❖

"The hell with critics," singer Ethel Merman once bellowed. "I know when I'm good." So, too, does vocalist Lisa Fischer. You probably know her by voice if not by name. At fifty-eight, the New York City native is the music industry's reigning backup queen. She has toured with the "world's greatest rock 'n' roll band," The Rolling Stones, for three decades, where her popularity with the fans brought her to routinely duet with Mick Jagger on several show-stopping songs while performing onstage. In concerts or sound studios, Fischer has backed up Luther Vandross, Tina Turner, Chaka Khan, Sting, Beyoncé and Dolly Parton, among others. She has also recorded several albums with the Stones.

But the voluptuous vocalist hardly fits the background-singer stereotype. "If you're singing backup," writes *The New York Times'* Brook Barnes, "you're supposed to hunger nonstop for one thing: the move to center stage. Performing lead is the prize position."

Fischer prefers singing backup. "I think background singing is like being cradled, like being loved and supported," she says. "It's sacred to me." She also rejects the notion that backup singers are second-class citizens. "I just love supporting other artists," she says.

Her peers are quick to applaud her versatility. "Lisa's uniqueness is based on the fact that she is a chameleon, a vocal shape-shifter," says Robin Clark, another prolific background vocalist, who's sung for Aretha Franklin and Bob Dylan. "Lisa has the innate ability to become whatever or whoever is needed at any given moment. She transcends all genres."

Fischer's love for singing was encouraged by her mother, a homemaker; father, a security guard and warehouse worker; and two younger brothers, who all sang together around a piano, especially at Christmas. "Music has always been my friend from an early age," she says. "When I sing, I'm in my safe zone. It heals me and I never tire of it."

Eventually, she appeared in local clubs, recorded a couple of records and began singing backup for various artists. "But I was struggling," she recalls. "There were times when I couldn't pay for food or rent. But that changed when I met Luther."

In 1983, Lisa got her big break when she was hired to backup Luther Vandross (who also started as a backup). The superstar R & B singer immediately recognized the immense range and delicacy of her voice and took her into his orbit, schooling her in the subtleties and nuances of the music industry. That, in turn, influenced her to put her ego aside and mesh her identity with other singers. The partnership lasted until Vandross' death in 2005.

Another breakthrough came in the late '80s when Mick Jagger's publicist, Tony King, saw Fischer perform with Vandross at Madison Square Garden. That led to an audition with Jagger, which she aced. Lisa concedes that the "Stones could have asked anybody to sing with them. It was an honor to be part of this sound." That honor continues today—she's sung on every Rolling Stones tour since 1989.

Lisa, in fact, experienced an early bout of stardom in 1992, with a hit of her own. That year, she won a coveted Grammy for her first single, "How Can I Ease the Pain," beating out none other than the Queen of Soul, Aretha Franklin. But she never made another solo record after that, downplaying the need for the limelight. "I just didn't want to do it anymore," Fischer said in an NPR interview. "Stardom was war. It just scared me too much, especially the business aspect of it, the chess moves." Backup would remain her calling—singing her heart out, night after night.

"I've spent my whole life not being the nucleus, and that suits me perfectly," she told *Fanzine* reporter Marilou Regan. "Part of the beauty of [backup] is that you're invisible. It's not about you. It's about being selfless, and that to me is the most joyous thing."

Ironically, Lisa Fischer's anonymity was shattered in the 2013 Oscar-winning documentary, *20 Feet From Stardom*. Directed by Morgan Neville, the film delves deep into the often-ignored corner of the music business—the history, the histrionics, the heartache of unheralded female backup singers. The searing chronicle of the industry's exploitation and appropriation highlights the ups and downs of Fischer, Darlene Love, Judith Hill and other perennial background vocalists whose careers often went unnoticed. In many respects, Lisa emerged as the reluctant star of the film, largely because she was one of the few backup singers who professes not to seek stardom and remains quietly confident in the space she occupies. Tranquility, in fact, embodies everything Lisa Fischer does.

"Everyone's needs are unique," she says of her underdog status. "My happy is different from your happy. I just want to sing." Recently, she has stepped back—gingerly—into the spotlight, touring the country with her inventive new band, Grand Baton.

Not everyone has what entertainment attorney Bernstein refers to as the aptitude, attitude and good fortune to become a star. Those factors are unevenly distributed, and pipe dreams can often lead to disappointment. You can't make yourself into the next Beyoncé or Sting, but you can convert your talent into a form that will enrich the lives of others. If, along the way, you achieve stardom, so be it. But even if you simply support powerhouse performers, you have found a way to live well.

❖ ❖ ❖

The odd couple, Jack Lemmon and Walter Matthau, inaccurately portrayed dance hosts in the 1994 classic *Out to Sea*.

CHAPTER 5

PERFECT GENTLEMEN

*"It is better to die on your feet than
to live on your knees."*

—Dolores Ibárruri,
General Secretary of Spain's Communist Party

W HEN YOU THINK ABOUT the people who are crucial on a first-class ocean liner, who comes to mind? The captain perhaps. Maybe the cruise director or even the head chef. Well, with several hundred crew on a luxury liner, there are so many others laboring in the shadows—all committed to making the sailing experience a memorable one. But surprise, surprise: The unheralded stars of high-end "six-star" ships of sailing's golden age are the revolving corps of male dance partners dedicated to women cruising solo.

Dancing, dancing, dancing. That's the hook that convinced Leona Davis Wachtstetter, known around the world as Mama Lee, not only to become a serial sailor, but a permanent cruise ship resident. For the past eight-plus years, the lively eighty-eight-year-old widow has lived on the über-chic, 1,070-passenger *Crystal Serenity*, dancing day and night away. What sold her on the thirteen-year-old floating country club was its cadre of elegant, well-dressed, mostly retired gentlemen—armed with a handful of sophisticated dance moves and clever conversation.

"I enjoy dancing," Mama Lee explains, "and *Crystal Serenity* has the best dance hosts." From 1962 to 1989, while living in Florida, the retired nurse took cruises with her banker husband. "But Mason didn't dance, just didn't like to," she says. "So he encouraged me to dance with the hosts. Before he died, sixteen years ago, he made me promise to keep cruising—and dancing."

Nowadays, Mama Lee sticks to her strict regimen, dancing seven nights a week—rumba, samba, foxtrot, waltz and cha-cha—before and after dinner. She also trains with the ship's dance instructors. With a mind-blowing 200-plus voyages under her belt, the elegantly coiffed dowager rarely bothers going ashore, because she's most likely already been there several times. "I don't get off the ship," she told *The Honolulu Star-Advertiser* on a recent stop. "I just dance— dance my way from port to port."

While few ladies have the brass, or the bucks, to jettison life on land for residence aboard a posh cruise liner, many grannies are sold on twirling the nights away on the arm of a perfect gentleman— spiked with at least a touch of titillation. For instance, Australian mother and daughter passengers Rose and Kate Chaney had never heard of these hidden heroes when they signed up for a recent cruise. "We thought we'd like to go and see what the dancing was like," says Rose. "And it was great. We sat down perhaps thirty seconds and someone came up and asked us to dance. They were very charming—not oily charming—just fun and nice." Fully satisfied, the Chaneys plan to book more voyages, largely because of the attentive male escorts.

Professionals in the cruise industry, which is expected to exceed $40 billion in revenues this year, can't afford to ignore the sea changes that are affecting their passengers, particularly elder, single or unattached women—who typically outnumber men three to one. Many lively ladies are no longer content to sail through their senior years solo—even temporarily. Savvy cruise executives know that their core female clientele will have a much better time kicking up their heels with an experienced gentleman host. More important, a good time on the dance floor often guarantees another lucrative booking. Another plus, Mama Lee explains: "Most wives don't want to share their dancing husbands with a harem of single ladies."

That cruise ships would have to engage male escorts to satisfy their most precious passengers—unaccompanied females—seemed highly unlikely when the industry came to life years ago. The Peninsular and Oriental Steam Navigation Company first introduced passenger service in 1844, advertising Mediterranean voyages from its Southampton homeport. The latter half of the nineteenth century saw a rapid rise in luxury travel, although most passengers were restricted to Europe's aristocracy. In 1900, the German Hamburg-America Line dedicated the first luxury liner for a more inclusive market. Several years later, a handful of other European companies competed for the transatlantic trade. The ill-fated *Titanic* and *Lusitania* offered Edwardian-era elegance, including fine dining, impeccable service and richly appointed staterooms.

However, the advent of large passenger jet aircraft in the 1960s sent the cruising industry into a death spiral. The then-clunky ships were plagued by high fuel consumption, an inability to enter shallow ports and windowless cabins. The noticeable exception: Britain's Cunard Line (now in its 176th year), which, not unlike the Harlem Globetrotters' makeover described in Chapter 2, shifted its focus from pure travel at sea to turbo-charged entertainment. Its *Queen Elizabeth 2* engaged top-flight celebrities to perform cabaret acts onboard, advertising the seven-day crossing as a vacation in itself. The ship also inaugurated "one-class cruising," where every *QE2* passenger received the same quality berthing and facilities. These changes revitalized high-end cruising and were soon mimicked on both sides of the Atlantic.

Later, the sappy TV series *The Love Boat* and the affectionate overtones of Cary Grant and Deborah Kerr in *An Affair to Remember* popularized cruising as a romantic haven for both singles and couples. But until the mid-1970s, most lines continued to offer cramped cabins, shuffleboard, deck chairs and drinks with umbrellas—all of which went out with Baked Alaska and the midnight buffet. During the past thirty years, though, the sea-faring industry has upgraded dramatically.

"I remember selling cruises and actually making the point that the porthole opened up in the room," recalls Richard Sasso, chairman of the Cruise Line Industry Association (CLIA), which represents ninety-seven percent of all cruises sailed by Americans. "But, now, we have everything under the sun. It's been an extraordinary achievement."

Indeed, the efforts of cruise lines to satisfy growing consumer expectations has been driven by new, larger capacity vessels and ship diversification, more local ports, more destinations and new onboard and onshore activities. The modern cruise industry now counts more than 400 ships offering travel to an estimated twenty-four million passengers this year, up nearly one million over two years ago.

Over the next three years, up to thirty additional vessels are scheduled to be launched. The industry's commitment to adding new capacity is based on its tremendous growth potential. For starters, only twenty percent of US adults have ever taken a cruise vacation. Yet, Americans represent almost sixty percent of the market. Therefore, there is a major upside for more domestic passengers. In addition, enormous opportunities abound for other cruisers, especially Europeans and Asians, to experience "cabin fever." Although the number of Chinese who go cruising is small, roughly 700,000, their numbers are climbing rapidly—thirty-five percent a year, with no ceiling in sight. Carnival Corp., for example, is doubling its cruise lines in China. Yet if all the cruise ships in the world were filled to capacity, all year long, they would only amount to less than one-half the total number of visitors to Las Vegas.

Besides the improving economy, the cruise industry also benefits from swelling consumer confidence. Although bookings fell after the grounding of Carnival's *Costa Concordia* in 2012, a tragedy that killed thirty-two people, and *Triumph*'s loss of power at sea the following year, cruising continues to garner consistently high ratings. A recent British survey revealed that a whopping ninety-four percent of voyagers were satisfied with their time at sea, and would book a future trip. All good news for the industry, which now represents the fastest growing tourist segment.

To be sure, seafaring travelers have an extensive array of vacation opportunities at both ends of the spectrum, boutique and behemoth. Among the latter are the $1.5 billion, 6,600-passenger, city-sized vessels with a theme park's worth of amenities, from sky-diving simulators to swings over the side of the ship for panoramic views from 300 feet above sea level. By contrast, there are the smaller, specialty lines that offer "expedition cruising" to exotic locations, such as Antarctica and the Galapagos Islands, or river cruises that often weave historical themes that highlight a destination's special features.

Straddling both worlds is a handful of super-luxury brands, whose midsize 300- to 700-passenger ships cultivate the image of classic elegance. Among the most prominent: Crystal Cruises, Regent Seven Seas Cruises, Silversea Cruises and Cunard, where competition has reached a fever pitch. Due to their stance on formality, these lines happily host formal nights on a regular basis. Their demographic is decidedly older and richer than guests found on the above-mentioned ships. It is on these top-tier vessels that handsome and charming male dance hosts earn their keep— sweeping single female passengers off their feet, while leaving their troubles at home.

From the moment they step aboard a luxury cruise ship, their every desire is anticipated. A seasoned hero is at their arm offering tantalizing appetizers and a glass of Cristal champagne, while a capable room steward hefts their carry-ons to an elegant suite that will be their home away from home for the next several days or, in Mama Lee's case, years. After their things are stowed away, they emerge to get the lay of the luxury liner. As they walk the decks, friendly crewmembers greet them by name—recalling their previous sailings. Everybody bonds.

First-class personalized service is just one of the hallmarks of the high-end lines. Guests can also expect exotic itineraries, fine wines and spirits, gourmet meals, as well as unusually high crew-to-passenger ratios. That being said, luxury ships have a country club feel that affluent seniors especially enjoy. Well-heeled cruisers can stroll the polished teak decks, chat with their newfound friends, flip through the latest best seller or engage in every imaginable amenity, from taking one-on-one tech classes and French lessons to tai chi and Zumba dance sessions. And they are more than willing to pay for all of this: sail, sip and savor.

A typical two-week stay on an upmarket cruise costs about $30,000 per passenger for a 350-square-foot suite to $70,000 for a 1,500-square-foot master suite, including food, drinks, gratuities, onboard activities, shore excursions and round-trip, business class airfare. Round the world travel, lasting approximately three months, can easily broach $250,000 a head.

British Prime Minister Benjamin Disraeli once said: "The delight of opening a new pursuit imparts the novelty of youth even to old age." For these premium prices, wealthy travelers can expect total physical and emotional rejuvenation while at sea. Nowadays, more and more health-conscious guests recognize that inactivity is the enemy of longevity. They aren't ready to clock out. Rather than vegetate, these adventurous elders want to remain as physically and socially engaged as possible. But, for women in particular, dancing remains the activity of choice.

"Dancing has always been especially important on ships," says Doug Jones, owner of Fort Lauderdale-based Sixth Star Entertainment & Marketing, which supplies polished dance hosts, as well as entertainers and lecturers to many leading lines. "In particular, cruises want to attract older, single passengers with disposable income—and these women like to dance." Sixth Star currently lists 388 agile escorts in its database. Their Distinguished Gentlemen—typically single men between fifty and seventy-five—operate only on one-month assignments, and are prohibited from doing back-to-back cruises. On average, the firm places about 450 gents on the best ships annually. Most hosts, in turn, average three or four gigs a year.

For their placement efforts, Sixth Star extracts a twenty-five dollar a day fee. In return, it completes a background check and carefully interviews each applicant to ascertain that "they love dancing and can schmooze," says entertainment coordinator Carol Sussman. "If these men weren't on onboard one of our client lines, they would be at their local ballroom. They absolutely love dancing and, quite literally, must do it day and night. They are required to be present at every dance, during lessons (although they do not get involved in instructing) and for any special singles events. Hence, they better be in very good shape." Every Distinguished Gent must be proficient in the foxtrot, swing, rumba, waltz and cha-cha.

At cross-town rival Compass Speakers and Entertainment, the criteria are much the same. Tracy Robison, director of onboard programs, taps into 425 single men for assignments for a range of luxury lines, including Cunard, Silversea and Regent Seven Seas. The firm's website indicates a preference for "Forty- to sixty-eight-year-olds who are still young at heart; good minglers, kind, honorable, smiling, community-minded volunteers; and always *dancers.*" Graciously hosting a dining table, assisting with shore excursions and lifeboat drills and being visible in the daytime to chat with guests are other expected duties. But "Dancing Every Dance" is Rule No. 1!

If you're dapper and a great dancer with Fred Astaire flair, you, too, could become a dance host on a luxury liner. Many footloose and fancy-free bachelors are lining up for the opportunity to twirl their way around the world. For them, it's a great gig. Although they aren't paid, hosts travel in the pinnacle of seaborne luxury. While they are considered volunteers, they get to share a first-class room, delicious meals, with most of their bar tab covered, shore excursions and access to a state-of-the-art fitness center. In return, they must quickstep with the ladies and abide by a strict dress code—a tuxedo or dinner jacket for evenings and a blue blazer during the days, replete with name tags and badges. Jeans and elastic waistbands are verboten. And, of course, impeccable manners are a must.

"Just a generation ago, the male host phenomenon didn't exist," says travel writer Bob Morris. Sometime in the late '70s, with the rise of feminism, older women who were widowed, divorced or just didn't happen to have a traveling companion began demanding a better time during the wee hours of oceangoing. Phyllis Zeno, a travel industry professional, introduced her Merry Widow cruises for various ships, offering one male dance host for every four women. That, in turn, inspired Lauretta Blake, another industry vet, to establish the Working Vacation in 1987, her business designed to identify and dispatch unsalaried escorts to leading cruise lines. Although Blake sold her business to Compass Entertainment a few years ago, she is credited with establishing the strict criteria and lengthy set of rules that govern the field. She meticulously screened potential hosts as dancers and conversationalists before they were ever allowed to wear a dinner jacket. She also cautioned them not to get too personal with the ladies. Today, hosts never dance with the same partner twice in a row and avoid women who are traveling with a male companion unless they are invited to do so.

"We're here for the fifty-plus women seeking dance partners," says sixty-one-year-old Alan Benedict, a seasoned host from the Compass stable. "Women understand that our role is to circulate and not pair off with just one person." With so many waiting ladies, there's only one ride per customer.

Diane Zammel, who ballroom-danced on cruises for twenty years before opening her own entertainment company, agrees. "There can be no favoritism," she says. "Hosts can't dance with one woman more than others. They have to be on their best behavior, and behave like gentlemen." That means no hanky-panky.

Really? "Really," says Benedict, with more than two decades of hosting experience. Although the old sea dog professes to have received many romantic overtures from interested ladies, he knows that sex with a passenger "would cost me my job" and could lead to serious legal trouble. "I'm not saying that intimate relations haven't happened in the past," adds fellow escort Omar Ales. "But a gentleman would be out—just like that."

Still, there's something about a cruise—the moonlight, the chilled champagne and caviar, the white dinner jackets, the lull of tranquil waters, your grandfather's music—that encourages romance, says *Travel and Leisure*'s Morris. In *Out to Sea*, the hilarious high-seas adventure featuring Walter Matthau and Jack Lemmon, carefree Charlie (Matthau) cons his widower brother-in-law Herb (Lemmon) into joining him as dance hosts in search of lonely ladies with big bank accounts. Under the watchful eye of a tyrannical cruise director, the twosome break every rule in the book.

"Think of yourselves as butterflies, gentlemen, and the guests are flowers," the cruise director tells them. "Your job is to pollinate the flowers with hospitality," which means refrain from showing favoritism. In short order, the two men find themselves in rough water and are thrown off the ship.

Hijinks aside, making sure that you're kind of a moving target every single night is no easy task. "When you have 150 single women and just ten hosts, that keeps us busy," says escort Peter Drew, who lives in New York when he's not at sea. "It's almost like a bakery line." Clearly, three-minute dates with a buffet of fashionable ladies is not all fun and games. Yet, this nautical version of speed dating has its own rewards. "I think I bring happiness into the lives of other people," says Bill Rolfing, a seventy-four-year-old widower from Southampton, Pennsylvania, who battled his own loneliness after his wife died. "That's the main reason I'm doing it."

"The important thing is to make the ladies feel they're the most important person in the world," explains another longtime host, Jack Ross from Nova Scotia. Such unflagging attentiveness separates the perfect gentleman. That's no problem for Ken Hickey of Kissimmee, Florida. "It's an endless fun time," he says of the at-sea lifestyle. "I love to be in a crowd of people and love to be social. Plus, I get to smell some of the best perfume in the world."

Interestingly, squiring the ladies draws a surprising variety of talented men. "I've had presidents of companies, doctors, even an ex-astronaut," says former booking agent Ronne Infeld. "These are very interesting, wonderful gentlemen."

In the interest of full disclosure, I've traveled on several luxury cruises as an "enrichment lecturer" and (gulp!) a paying passenger—and have been uniformly impressed with the caliber of single men who attend these unaccompanied ladies. On a recent *Crystal Serenity* sailing from Rome to Istanbul, I encountered a talented quartet of hidden heroes: Rob Nostrand, John Farrell, Jack Moya and Harry Norton—each accomplished in their respective fields.

Seattle native Nostrand is a lawyer and certified public accountant, practicing tax and business law. Mostly retired, he still maintains a portfolio of clients and, in recent years, has been involved in Chilean and Peruvian mining projects. Sensitivity to international business and cross-cultural relations makes him a shipboard favorite.

Philadelphian Farrell spent most of his career in the travel industry, while also teaching ballroom dancing part-time for Arthur Murray, Fred Astaire and independent studios. Now relocated to Tampa, Florida, the retired executive still enjoys teaching dance classes three days a week and attending ballroom competitions. His favorite vacation combines his love for dancing, making new friends and cruising the high seas.

Moya is a native Californian, born, raised and educated in Los Angeles. Recently retired from Loyola Law School, he works part-time for a Whittier-based tax service. Moya told me he's been dancing for thirty-five years...and still loves it.

But of this capable crew, few stand out more than Harry Norton. For the past dozen or so years, the Hamilton, Ontario, native has been the dance partner and social companion for scores of single divas. He had been cruising as a passenger since 1980, when he discovered *The Love Boat*. "In 1999, I saw an ad in *The Los Angeles Times* for Ambassador Hosts and applied to Crystal," the Royal Canadian Air Force (RCAF) veteran told a number of us as we sailed through the Mediterranean Sea. "I sent them a video of my dancing skills. They wanted to see my foxtrot, rumba, cha-cha, swing and waltz—and I got the job." A month later, he was en route to South America to join a luxury liner.

Actually, Harry came to dancing the hard way. When he was a teenager, a girl asked him to dance. He liked her and said yes. But he had a problem: two left feet. He didn't know how to dance. Subsequently, he signed up for lessons at a nearby Arthur Murray studio. The rest is history: Ladies have never asked him to stop steering them safely across the sea of parquet.

In the intervening years, Harry did a five-year stint with the RCAF, followed by a thirty-one-year career with oil giant Chevron. Unmarried and retired, he continued to hone his dancing skills at the Pasadena Ballroom Dance Association. Nowadays, Harry, who's eighty-two, can be found waltzing with one of several female partners in Crystal's stabilized ballroom with a nine-piece orchestra or, perhaps, escorting a single woman out onto the ship's deck to admire the evening sunset.

"Above all, you have to be an excellent dancer with good social skills," he says. Like his fellow Ambassador Hosts, Harry also has to thrust himself into card games, intimate lunches and dinners, often with a number of people who don't speak English. Then, there are the requirements to attend dance classes, chaperone land excursions and lend an ear—or an arm—to single ladies past their prime. Heroic Harry never forgets the old axiom that the longest walk on a ship for a solo woman is the walk from her suite to the dining room.

Every summer, Harry and the other experienced escorts get sent a choice of available cruises. By October, they know where they'll be heading on their next bucket list adventure. "I normally do three cruises a year," he says. "It's a great time." Since joining Crystal, Harry reckons he's done fifty cruises—and counting. When he's not on the high seas, he lives in Valley Glen, California, outside Los Angeles, where besides ballroom dancing, he keeps himself in shape with golf and health club workouts.

Camaraderie among Harry and the boys is critical. Published manuals tell dance hosts to be supportive team players in their efforts to rescue ladies without partners from wallflowerdom. "Hosting is not the arena for self-centered, competitive/aggressive, or inflated ego behavior," warns vanLee Hughey in *You Could Be at Sea Dance Hosting*, a self-published primer. This means "getting along with your fellow hosts both socially and on the dance floor without hostility or envy." Indeed, many hosts develop their own esprit de corps. "It's not unusual for our escorts to stay in close touch for years," says Compass Entertainment's Robison.

Yet, when the passengers disembark, dance hosts are on their own. A comprehensive rating form is left in each guest cabin—feedback used by the cruise line to evaluate every escort. What's more, these ratings are submitted by all guests, not just the ladies with whom hosts had the opportunity to twirl away. Hence, there are literally thousands of eyeballs watching an escort's every move. Even if a dance host acted as a perfect gentleman, he can expect the occasional bad grade. "Women get jealous," explains Tom Goodale, a retired Philip Morris executive and highly regarded Gentleman Host for Silversea Cruises.

Whether it's mollifying elderly matrons with daggers in their eyes or not feeling appreciated by the ship's cruise director, dance hosts must be prepared to navigate choppy waters. In their efforts to deliver elegant escapism to sometimes lonely ladies, they and their partners are often subjected to stinging criticism on several fronts.

"It's a shame women of a certain age are stuck with these kinds of men to socialize with," says one blogger. "If I were to hang out with hired men, I would expect them to be young, hot and hung." Jamie Hayes adds: "As a single woman, who often travels alone, I find [hosting] appalling. These women must be so desperate for the attention of a man that they settle for someone who is being paid to service them. Yuck!!!" Not to be outdone is another bitter blogger: "I am a reasonably attractive and successful woman in my early 50s. I'd choose to forgo a cruise and simply tie the anchor around my neck if I had to rely on a 'host' for male attention and companionship."

But "Let the Little Girl Dance" say proponents of older gals looking for *La Dolce Vita*. "I've been on several different cruises with my husband," says Rosemary Hirsch, "and often saw what were single, nice looking gentlemen dancing and talking with older women who were alone. I thought it was a great idea. The 50-plus women wanted male companionship, to dance, an innocent flirtation. There is nothing wrong with that." Fellow advocate Fran Platt also touts the merits of hosting. "Hire some handsome old hippies," she tells cruise line execs. "And sign me up!"

Dance hosts themselves also suffer from a range of opinion, mostly positive. To their critics, they are shameless gigolos—predators presented with a veritable smorgasbord of wealthy women to exploit far away from home. High-minded male passengers, in particular, often sneer at hosts, wondering how and why any self-respecting man would descend into the world of chaperoning at sea. To others, however, cruise escorts are white knights in dinner jackets, who provide much-needed companionship and a human touch for the genteel set. Ironically, their biggest fans are lead-footed husbands eager to outsource their dancing duties to attentive hosts, allowing them to escape to the roulette wheel or cigar bar.

No doubt, the misperceptions surrounding these nautical nightcrawlers relate to their myriad duties and often unclear role. Since the days of the Phoenicians, ships have been consummate hierarchies. At the helm, of course, is the captain, typically an ancient mariner, with years experience on the bridge. Second in command is the staff captain, overseeing safety, security and environmental matters. Next come the general manager, chief engineer and cruise director, followed by a series of other officers dedicated to deck, engine or hotel responsibilities. On their heels are "staff," primarily entertainers and musicians. Further down the pyramid and living, literally, three levels below the waterline are the "crew"—from waiters and bartenders to cabin attendants and able seamen, who do the grueling, repetitive work and often labor on three- to eleven-month contracts in what have often been described as "sweatshops at sea."

Excluded from this mix are the world-renowned guest lecturers and Broadway-style performers, who operate under independent contracts, which, depending on the individual, can be very lucrative. They rank significantly higher than dance hosts. Because escorts are unpaid, noncompany employees, passengers and crew are often confused about where they stand in the ship's pecking order and, hence, how to treat them. On most luxury lines, they are considered de facto guests, while enjoying many officer-level privileges.

Looking ahead, most industry observers predict that, with the aging global population and groundswell of retiring baby boomers, there will be growing opportunities for male escorts. Others, however, suggest that increasing interest by first-time, younger travelers, especially millennials, as well as more multigenerational and affinity-group travel, could make the dance host an endangered species. Cruise lines, like airlines, are hell-bent on eliminating every nonrevenue expense, particularly free cabins and meals. For these reasons, Holland America discontinued its host program a few years ago.

"There is nothing so desperately monotonous as the sea," wrote twentieth-century American poet and diplomat James Russell Lowell. Farsighted cruise companies today are determined to obliterate any smidgen of monotony. As long as the Mama Lees of the world want to dance with the stars, luxury liners will supply them with perfect gentlemen.

❖ ❖ ❖

Devoted adjunct faculty such as accountant Robert Hatanaka teach a growing number of American college students.

CHAPTER 6

DISPOSABLE DONS

*"A teacher affects eternity. He can
never tell where his influence stops."*

—HENRY BROOKS ADAMS

WANTED: SUPERHERO. *Dynamic teacher to carry
onerous course load. Must be prepared for long hours,
low pay, no benefits, no job security and no possibility of
tenure. Minimal access to office, secretarial, library and
computer support. Limited interaction with faculty and staff. Must
show immediate progress or face termination.*

❖ ❖ ❖

Why would anyone take such a tough, thankless job? Yet
more than seventy-five percent of America's 1.6 million-employee
academic workforce—with their ranks steadily rising since the
1970s—toil daily in this educational purgatory. That's the devil's
bargain made by many adjunct professors, or faculty without a
permanent position or tenure.

"The job can kill you," says one adjunct. "Literally." On August
16, 2013, Margaret Mary Vojtko, an eighty-three-year-old adjunct
French professor, learned this the hard way. After twenty-five years
of teaching at Pittsburgh's Duquesne University, she was summarily

discharged. Homeless, impoverished and cancer-ridden, Vojtko suffered cardiac arrest and never regained consciousness. She died two weeks later, and was buried in a cardboard box.

In the days that followed, Vojtko's undignified death became a rallying cry for many in academia and beyond. To them, it was inconceivable that a dedicated teacher could be so shabbily treated by a Roman Catholic school of nearly 10,000 students founded by Spiritan priests. Besides touching a nerve, fellow adjuncts saw shades of their own future in Vojtko's apparent abandonment.

"The situation, in the long term, is what a lot of us ultimately face," according to Robin J. Sowards, another adjunct professor at Duquesne. "When your employer is done with you, you get tossed to the curb."

On virtually every American campus, Vojtko's shameful death inspired outrage. A picture of vulnerability, she was elderly, fired from her job and suffering from cancer. Although she had worked at the university for the better part of three decades, her take-home pay hardly covered food and clothing. Nor was she entitled to health care or severance pay, let alone a pension. Her situation drew renewed attention to the woeful working conditions of these "disposable dons," the thousands of university instructors who labor off the tenure track. "No contingent faculty is ever more than 15 seconds away from total humiliation," says longtime adjunct activist John Hess. And, in many respects, Vojtko's passing symbolizes one of universities' dirtiest little secrets, and "everything that is wrong with the economics of higher education," writes *Slate*'s L.V. Anderson.

To understand fully the death of an adjunct, consider the life of Margaret Mary Vojtko. Born on January 15, 1930, to Catholic Slovak parents, "Margaret" or "Marge," as she was called, grew up in Homestead, Pennsylvania, just outside the Pittsburgh city limits. Her father worked in a nearby steel mill and later joined the United Steelworkers; her stay-at-home mom died when she was seven. After graduating from a Catholic high school, Margaret worked as a secretary at the University of Pittsburgh, while majoring in French and Italian literature. In 1967, she graduated cum laude at the age of thirty-seven. Three years later, she earned her master's, and went on to teach French and medieval literature at Pitt, Carnegie Mellon and Indiana University–Purdue University Fort Wayne. To make ends meet, she supplemented her income as a freelance editor and translator.

In the mid-1970s, Vojtko began working on a doctoral degree at Catholic University in Washington, D.C. But life does not always give one easy choices. She was forced to abandon her studies to care for an ailing brother. In 1988, she hired on as an adjunct at Duquesne, because her lack of a PhD made her ineligible for a tenure-track position. An accomplished linguist (fluent in five languages), violinist and licensed nurse who studied theology in her spare time, Vojtko taught both undergraduate and graduate courses in French language and literature for the next twenty-five years.

No one ever questioned her devotion to her students. "Teaching is not a profession or a career," she once told a campus magazine. "It's a devotion—a dedication. Too many people look upon it as a job, a source of income." Very little income, in Vojtko's case.

As a contract worker with no job security and no benefits, she earned between $2,500 to $3,500 for a three-credit course. As an adjunct, Vojtko was limited to a maximum of two courses per semester. As a result, she had a hard time making $25,000 a year—wages far less than those who came in at night to clean classrooms. In addition, she was forced to share an office with five other adjuncts. Despite being underpaid and underappreciated by the university administration, the well-respected instructor enjoyed solid student evaluations.

In the late '90s, she began a longstanding battle with ovarian cancer. Though she had Medicare, her out-of-pocket costs for treatment were high. In addition, the family home that she had inherited in Homestead fell into disrepair because of her lack of funds. So when the United Steelworkers began to organize Duquesne adjuncts in 2011, Vojtko enthusiastically signed on. She saw her father's old union as the salvation for better wages and health insurance. "You have to understand that I come from a very strong union family," she told friends.

Roughly eighty-five percent of the adjuncts on campus voted in favor of unionization. Yet Duquesne refused to recognize the union, claiming that it was exempt from federal labor law as a "church-operated school." At the time of this writing, the matter remains under dispute, although the National Labor Relations Board has ruled in other instances that Catholic universities can form a union. But in the absence of one, Duquesne slashed Vojtko's teaching load from three courses per semester to one—leaving her with less than $10,000 a year. "I am my sole support and have no other resources than Social Security, which covers my expenses for food, utilities and incidentals," she wrote in a subsequent complaint to the Equal Employment Opportunity Commission (EEOC). "I have no retirement income from previous employment."

Stress began taking its toll. Her reduced income, coupled with the effects of intensive radiation therapy, drained her energy. In the summer of 2012, she suffered her first heart attack. To worsen things, her house was literally falling in on itself. She was no longer able to maintain or heat it during the cruel Pennsylvania winters. For warmth, she sought refuge in a local restaurant, while catching a few winks in her crowded campus office. Eventually, university security guards booted her out of the building and escorted her off campus. Yet despite her delicate condition, Vojtko never missed a day of class.

On April 2, 2013, the near-homeless octogenarian was fired after being told she was "no longer effective in the classroom." As an alternative, the university offered her a tutoring job that paid fifteen dollars per hour for ten hours each week—two-thirds of her adjunct pay. Rejecting this, she was instructed to clean out her desk.

"More than the money, she felt hurt that they said, 'We don't need you anymore,'" says Daniel Kovalik, a longtime friend, adjunct professor at the University of Pittsburgh and union organizer. (It was Kovalik who helped Vojtko file a complaint for wrongful discharge with the EEOC.)

In the meantime, her cancer had seriously worsened. On August 16, she was advised by the Allegheny County's Adult Services Agency, which investigates reports of elder neglect, that she had been identified as a woman in need. She also was warned that if she didn't meet with a caseworker, her situation would be turned over to the Orphan's Court. "For a proud professional like Margaret Mary, this was the last straw," said a close friend.

Overwrought, Vojtko was returning home from a cancer treatment when she collapsed just yards from the two-story, yellow-brick home on Sylvan Avenue, where she had lived almost her entire life. On September 1, 2013, she died.

The funeral mass for the devout Catholic was held at Epiphany Church, only a few blocks away from the university. She was laid out in a simple, cardboard casket—devoid of any handles for pallbearers. "A sad sight," one attendee lamented, "but an honest symbol of what she had been reduced to by her ostensibly Catholic employer."

"Three things in human life are important," wrote Henry James. "The first is to be kind, the second is to be kind, and the third is to be kind." Did Duquesne University, the Catholic cathedral that employed professor Vojtko for a quarter century, offer such kindness? In response to the hailstorm of criticism surrounding her death, the university defended its behavior, asserting that "with great compassion, it had attempted to support Margaret Mary during a very difficult time in her life." Yet, in truth, Duquesne took her job away when her life was spiraling downward. At best, its outreach was woefully inadequate.

"I would not suggest that Duquesne University acted alone in killing professor Vojtko," argued Philip Nel, an ex-adjunct, turned tenured full professor at Kansas State University. "Duquesne had many accomplices. Exploitation of adjuncts has become the norm in academe. Even under the best conditions, they are second-class citizens."

"Adjuncting is a bridge to nowhere," contends Mary-Faith Cerasoli, a part-time professor of Spanish and Italian at Mercy and Nassau [NY] Community Colleges. "I would never recommend it to my students." Like the late Ms. Vojtko, she's also homeless, while battling a life-threatening thyroid disease that has left her deeper in the hole financially, adding unpaid medical bills to her student loans. Living off the generosity of others, the fifty-three-year-old woman drives a battered loaner hundreds of miles a week between teaching gigs that average $2,000 to $3,000 per course. Before taxes, her salary last year was $22,000—just about the poverty line for a family of four. Also, she's ineligible for public assistance because she's considered to be on a "full load."

In today's academic workplace, there is a distinct caste system: permanent, full-time professors and "disposable dons," adjuncts or part-timers. They live very different lives despite the fact they may be teaching the same courses at the same schools. Those on tenure track are the fairly compensated stars; contingent faculty, on the other hand, find themselves toiling like migrant workers in our nation's academic fields. How, then, did adjuncts wind up getting the short end of the stick?

In 1970, roughly eighty percent of the faculty on US campuses were full-time employees with the prospect of tenure. Adjuncts then represented thirty percent of university faculty, who were well-educated part-timers employed on a contract basis to help the university expand its course offerings or to share their expertise in a particular field with their students. In many instances, these academic temps populated the professional schools in particular, with no desire for a professorial career. For well-heeled retirees or those with "real jobs" in business, medicine, law or engineering, the attraction of teaching an occasional course or two at a prestigious university carried the day. They taught for noneconomic reasons. Although these "contingent-haves" may still be found at almost every American university, their numbers pale in comparison to the "have nots"—the castaway Vojtkos and Cerasolis of the world. Yet, taken together, adjuncts are indispensible: They teach more than half of the undergraduate courses at public universities and three-quarters of the remedial courses at community colleges. Consequently, tenure-track faculty now represents just one-third of those teaching on US campuses.

"This shift to part-time employment started in community colleges," explains Adrianna Kezar, director of the University of Southern California's Delphi Project on the Changing Faculty and Student Success. "But it spread across four-year institutions and research universities, private and public."

Critics of this trend—the vanishing of full-time professors and the rise of adjuncts—blame the "corporatization" of academia. For the past few decades, the private sector has been contributing to the so-called "flex" or "gig" economy. Driven largely by globalization and technology—the two most powerful forces of our times— businesses across the country have been slashing costs and hiring temporary workers rather than traditional employees. The labor force participation rate—the share of the population that is working or looking for work—has dropped dramatically to a thirty-six-year low, 62.8 percent, down from sixty-six percent in 2008.

Enter the rise of independent workers, pejoratively referred to as "the throwaway workforce." A business survey conducted by Ardent Partners, a management consulting firm, found that about thirty percent of corporate personnel are now made up of part-time employees, up from ten to twelve percent five years ago. What's more, Ardent predicts a thirty percent growth in the independent workforce over the next three years. While some say this trend won't outlive a robust economic recovery, most pundits believe it represents a fundamental shift in the American labor force.

Simply put, firms today want more flexibility and more agility to remain globally competitive. A more adaptable workforce helps them scale production up or down to meet demand. "It's all about getting our workforce to the right size for the business we are doing today," explains Carlos Migoya, president and CEO of Miami-Dade County's Jackson Health System. Don't forget, too, the passage of the Affordable Care Act, commonly known as "Obamacare," has also caused employers to replace full-time staff with part-timers to avoid having to pay for health care coverage.

Interestingly, though, many folks in the private (and even nonprofit) sectors are more than willingly foregoing full-time jobs in order to work as temps. Thanks to space-age technology, thousands of Americans are opting out of semi-permanent work for greater work-life balance. At the click of a mouse, millennials in particular are more selective in the type of job they want and the venue in which they do it. In fact, fifty-nine percent of freelancers said they made the switch from full-time completely by choice.

High-flying Nate Ginsberg is one such convert to the flex economy. The twenty-something Internet marketer travels the world, earning $2,500 to $3,000 a month and growing his business through Google Adwords and Bing Ads. "I would do anything possible *not* to get a traditional job," he recently told *The Christian Science Monitor*. "I really enjoy this lifestyle."

Not so giddy, however, are America's so-called "task takers," the roughly seven million of the temporary workforce that will take any kind of work a company offers them. "It was great at the time," says one mid-fifties manager, who recalls accepting a part-time assignment at a relatively small, Los Angeles-based company. But eight years later, he still has the "job no one else wants to do. I get glowing reviews," he says, "but there has been no movement toward making me full-time. I'm beginning to feel a bit embarrassed when friends ask: 'When are they going to make you full-time?'"

For most Americans, going temp does not lead to a platinum lifestyle. While some people are making the move to gain greater control over their lives, others are scrambling for whatever short-term assignments they can find, trying anxiously to find a permanent position. Look for more winners and losers as part-time America continues to grow.

"We're at a pivot point," says Sara Sutton Fell, CEO of FlexJobs, a website for people looking for alternative work arrangements. "Things are changing, but it's not going back to the way it was." To many in the academy, these changes are absolutely toxic. Christian Pyle, an adjunct at Kentucky's Bluegrass Community and Technical College, blames universities' governing boards, often composed of business executives, for injecting a throwaway mentality on colleges and universities. "Today, the majority of teachers at any given college tend to be adjuncts, not traditional professors," he says. "The practice of depending on a disposable workforce is sad enough in corporate America. But in universities, it's obscene."

Nevertheless, this slide to corporatization is inevitable. "Schools have no choice," argues Terry Hartle, a senior vice president at the Washington-based American Council on Education. "The pressures on colleges and universities to maintain or prevent tuition hikes are extraordinarily high." Adjuncts, he says, reflect the market realities and provide schools with the flexibility "they need to stay in business." Part-timers are productive and less expensive. So why, many ask, should schools change?

What we are left with, contends Carnegie Mellon professor Jeffrey Williams, is "the era of the Great Stratification." "The American university," he says "has adopted a harsh class structure: the mass of contingent faculty struggling at the bottom, tenure-stream professors in the middle class speaking for the university's intellectual values and productions, and superstar faculty and administrators in the upper class setting its direction and taking the greatest rewards." In this winner-take-all world, adjuncts, who now account for almost three-quarters of all college teachers, are the hidden heroes.

Loading up on brainy part-timers is unquestionably beneficial to a university's bottom line. But from every other perspective, it's shortsighted. Contingent faculty, often called the "working poor," suffer gross inequities on several fronts. On the financial side, they juggle multiple part-time jobs, earn little-to-no-benefits and often depend on public assistance. That's certainly not what French professor and single mother Nicole Beth Wallenbrock had in mind when she began teaching. But she's now working part-time as an adjunct, offering just two courses at the City University of New York, making $2,800 a class, though she's more highly rated than almost all her full-time peers.

"I had this idea that I could get a job with a good income to support my son, but it didn't work out that way," she says. "I'm now a precarious worker, with no job security and living on food stamps. It's depressing. It makes me feel like a failure in a lot of ways."

That's the same conclusion reached by Joseph Fruscione, a longtime adjunct at George Washington University. "I entered academia with an idealistic sense of it as a place of knowledge and intellectual inquiry," he told *The Chronicle Review*. "Being essentially cheap, renewable labor has made me feel cynical and a little angry about how universities are knowingly overusing contingent faculty, while adding more administrators, provosts and the like."

Frustrated after fourteen years teaching English, he's saying adios to academia—shifting to freelance writing and editing. "All the [teaching] experience I've gained hasn't gotten me any kind of meaningful tenure-track position," he says. "I've decided that my way of fixing all that is leaving the system." Fruscione also acknowledges that he's "very, very, fortunate to have a wife who's the primary breadwinner."

Rebecca Schuman, who teaches world literature at the Pierre Laclede Honors College of the University of Missouri at St. Louis, also sees academia losing its sheen. She discovered "that teaching itself was not the independent source of magic I'd thought it was." What's more, "my years as an adjunct are an indelible stain on my CV, making me tainted, engendering whispers of: 'There must be something wrong with her.'"

No doubt the magic wears off when one also considers the

dearth of "hygiene factors" confronting adjuncts. For starters, their on-campus privileges are pathetic. Forty-seven percent report having limited access to copying machines; forty-five percent for library services and twenty-one percent for curriculum guidelines—all essential for getting ready to teach students. In addition to missing out on these basics, adjuncts are often denied basic technology. Another survey found that forty-one percent of them had no campus phone, while little over half had access to a computer. But what particularly galls them is the lack of office space to prepare for class and to meet with students. According to the Coalition of the Academic Workforce, sixty percent of part-time professors have access only to a joint office. For instance, Betsy Smith, an adjunct at Cape Cod Community College, shares hers with as many as eighteen other adjuncts. "Some of my colleagues post office hours, but I refuse to," she admits. "I'm a second-tier faculty member, and those in my classes are second-tier students."

Sascha Flanders, a pseudonym for an adjunct who teaches at two colleges, also avoids after-class meetings. She simply doesn't have the energy or the time. "I'm paid to teach, and that's all," she insists. "No person in the system is to blame, but I can't help thinking that the students are getting shortchanged. Sooner or later they're going to realize what they're missing, and they're going to opt out."

"Don't my students deserve to meet me between classes in a private office?" asks Bluegrass adjunct Pyle. "They're paying the same amount to take my course as a full professor. Yet, I'm in a constant hunt to find a quiet place on campus."

Or take the case of William and Barbara Shimer, adjunct professors at Northeastern University. In all, they have been averaging eleven classes a semester—with no office. "We used the trunk of our car as our office, rushing back between classes to dump one set of books and materials and get what we need for the next class," Mr. Shimer told *The New York Times*. "Then one day, our office got towed." There and then, the couple became adjunct activists.

Besides the push and pull over office space and the basic necessities of teaching, adjuncts are constantly pressed for time. Many are cobbling together multiple gigs at different institutions to make ends meet. When the bell rings, these "ghosts in the classroom," as one critic calls them, belt off on the freeway to their next assignment. "Many adjuncts are unavailable to their students," says the departing Fruscione. "It's virtually impossible to give students the kind of attention they deserve."

Yet the poverty-level pay and shameful working conditions haven't stopped adjuncts from returning to the academic job market, usually at their own expense. Despite the fact that they are marginalized on campus and often teach more than twice the number of classes taught by tenured professors each semester, they seem to do a better job of it. That's the conclusion reached in a 2013 report of the National Bureau of Economic Research. At Northwestern University, researchers found "strong and consistent evidence that faculty outside the tenure system outperform tenured and tenure-track professors in introductory undergraduate classrooms." They also discovered that students who were relatively less qualified academically fared particularly well when they were taught by these hidden heroes, especially in courses where high grades were generally tougher to earn.

As for student staying power, the report noted that "a non-tenure-track faculty member increases the likelihood that a student will take another class in the subject by 7.3 percentage points, and increases the grade earned in that subsequent class by slightly more than one-tenth of a grade point."

To be sure, Northwestern's adjuncts are somewhat atypical. They are relatively well compensated ($4,200 to $7,354 per course) and enjoy longstanding relationships with the university. Moreover, considerable anecdotal evidence suggests that many contingent faculty more than hold their own in the classroom.

"Respect yourself, and others will respect you," Confucius said. Unfortunately, a major complaint by adjuncts is their lack of respect from the permanent faculty class. "Adjuncts are frequently more qualified than our full-time colleagues, but always less respected," says Dennis Báthory-Kitsz, a Vermont-based adjunct professor of music. "This lack of respect filters upward to the administration and outward to the public." Indeed, contingent teachers' opinions are rarely solicited, nor are they included in shared university governance. A study of more than 100 research universities found that about two-thirds had faculty senates that were off-limits to adjuncts.

As part-time professors seek to improve their standing on campus, they often find that the people standing in their way are not administrators, but tenure-track faculty. "The janitor is going to be more our ally than some of the professors," laments David Wilder, an adjunct lecturer in art history at John Carroll University and co-chairman of the Ohio Part-Time Faculty Association.

That the "Age of the Adjuncts" has allegedly increased their workload may help explain the lack of support from permanent faculty. "More contingent labor means that the same number of committees have to be staffed, thousand or more students have to be advised, the same curriculum has to be organized—but there are fewer people eligible for the work," says Claire Potter, an associate professor of history at the New School for Public Engagement. "One feature of contingent labor is that what is cheaper for the university is more costly in time for the full-time faculty who have to hire, supervise and review the Adjunct Army."

Whether it's because they are overstretched or threatened by ubiquitous adjuncts, full-time professors generally have been either oblivious or unsympathetic to their cause. Faculty unions, for instance, have struggled to reconcile the demands of contingent educators with the demands of those either tenured or on a tenure stream. The American Federation of Teachers, for example, is pushing legislation that will mandate that at least seventy-five percent of university classes be taught by tenured or tenure-track teachers.

Many faculty unions are selling out adjuncts, claims A.G. Monaco, a senior human resources official at the University of Akron. "In negotiations, the first thing they want is a limit on adjunct hours," not improved conditions for them. Tenure-track faculty and their unions often refuse to help adjuncts, who are seen to be trying to take away their jobs. "Full-time faculty can no longer sit on their hands," Monaco warns. They "have to stop lying" and do more than pay lip service to the way adjuncts are treated.

"Those of us who have attained even a modest amount of institutional power need to speak up," agrees Kansas State's Nel. "We need to support organizations fighting for adjunct rights. We need to stop exploiting adjuncts. It's killing them—and it isn't good for us, either."

For almost three decades, these scholars have been on the wrong side of the supply-demand curve. Since the 1990s, the number of new doctorates has grown by more than fifty percent, yet the number of coveted full-time positions at colleges has shrunk as schools continue to face economic pressures. A recent Fidelity survey found that many tenured or tenure-track faculty aren't planning to retire anytime soon. Almost three-quarters of them hope to teach well into their golden years. Grappling with this aging workforce, more and more universities have been able to exploit platoons of underpaid and less secure part-timers.

"How does it feel it be an adjunct?" asks Christian Pyle. "A dead-end job is bad enough, but a dead-end career is a real soul-killer." Yet many critics of "adjunctivitis," as PBS correspondent Paul Solman calls it, blame the victim. "Nobody forces someone to become an adjunct," says Terry Hartle. "It's a very difficult way to make a full-time living. People who get PhDs owe it to themselves to think long and hard about the labor market that they're entering."

"What good is professional training for a job you are not likely to get after a decade of discipline, debt and deferred opportunity?" asks William Pannapacker, an associate professor of English at Hope College in Michigan. "Who are these people who think you can spend from two to ten years [of graduate work] with no realistic career goals in mind? They seem to assume that [they] will remain childless, will have no responsibility to care for elderly parents, will never have any health problems. It's a kind of infantile narcissism: placing one's desires above all the other obligations that adults generally assume."

Universities, too, are to blame. They are irresponsible for turning out hordes of PhDs into a job market where many of them wind up going on food stamps or Medicare. Our centers of learning could and should be more upfront about their placement success in securing permanent academic employment for their graduates. Without coming clean to their students and by preying on their naïveté, schools do a grave disservice to the profession.

"Stop training people for yesterday," adds Ohio-based blogger Maha Muslimah. "Focus more on tomorrow. Maybe it's not such a good idea to train legions of American studies specialists and

Egyptologists who won't be able to find quality employment when they graduate."

"A more honest and desirable course," says professor Pennapacker, "would be for universities to recruit graduate students with *no* expectations of an academic position." This group might be more prone to consider careers outside academe, rather than "previous generations who were taught to regard anything but the professional life as failure from which one could never return."

Stephen Trachtenberg, president emeritus of George Washington University, has also counseled adjunct faculty who, if they are not earning enough to support themselves, do something else with their lives. "Merely because you have earned a PhD," he says, "doesn't oblige you to take on a life of penury."

This, too, was the conclusion reached by outgoing adjunct SooJin Pate. Heeding Deepak Chopra's advice, she stopped chasing the carrot and let go of academe. "With this new definition of success in hand," she says, "I found a whole new world of possible career tracks opened up to me. I no longer wanted to be eaten alive by academe."

Also changing skins, former adjunct Ingrid Steffensen embarked on her own high-speed chase out of academia. As an eighteen-year-old romantic, she fell hard for university life. She went on to complete her doctorate in art and architecture, never intending to divorce herself from scholarly pursuits. Besides being frustrated that she couldn't earn a decent living, she became disillusioned "by the endless quest for validation that the eternal adjunct is forced to embark on."

Steffensen realized there was more "to life than the single-minded pursuit of a career that declined to return the favor." So she traded in her life on campus for a new home on the racetrack. After a year of high-octane training, she discovered that as a racecar driver she was "a different person from the scared ninny I was [as an adjunct]." Her mantra today: "Gimme a helmet, a fast car and a tank of gas!"

Of course, not everyone can be Danica Patrick. But other academics would do well to venture outside their comfort zone. "If you want to run with the big dogs, you have to get off the porch," urges Rensselaer's straight-talking president Shirley Ann Jackson.

Henry Ford, the automobile pioneer, put it somewhat differently. "Life as I see it," he said, "is not a location but a journey. Everything is in flux and is meant to be. We may live at the same number on a street, but it's never the same person that lives there." Proud breadwinners like Ingrid Steffensen are prepared to change addresses. They believe that lifestyles can, and should, be *elastic*, and that one of the true tests of happiness and personal development is the capacity to molt, to change skins, to take risks and move in new and exciting directions.

No doubt, making a smooth transition to alternative employment in today's sluggish economy is anything but easy, especially for those trained for a lifetime in the academy. "It's extremely difficult, if not impossible, to get a job that's outside your academic background," says one anonymous adjunct. "Most employers won't even look at your application, much less consider it. No one wants to take the time to completely train someone, no matter how smart they might be. I feel very much stuck."

Also stuck in the contingent conundrum is Nicole Beth Wallenbrock, the adjunct professor of French lit living on food stamps. "I don't know what other place there is in society for me," she laments. "I love teaching, researching and writing, so I haven't given up on the dream yet."

Considering all the resources that she and other adjuncts have put into their education, there must be a way to keep the dream alive. To turn what has become many professors' American dream into the American nightmare. But how?

"Only activism, organizing and effective shared governance can create and advance improved conditions for contingent faculty," argues retired professor Richard Moser, in his recent piece on the overuse and abuse of adjunct teachers in *The Chronicle of Higher Education*. He and many others feel that unionization is the only way to unleash these hidden heroes.

The Duquesne situation reported earlier refuted longstanding Catholic dogma that the proliferation of unions is "greatly to be desired." Over the years, this admonition by Pope Leo XIII in 1891 has been supported by the great majority of church fathers. "Catholic social teaching is quite explicit about the importance of labor unions," explains adjunct professor Robin Sowards, the

Duquesne colleague of Margaret Vojtko. "The church has an obligation to propagate them."

For this reason, Georgetown, the oldest Catholic university in the United States, opted to support an adjunct union when, in 2013, its part-time faculty unanimously voted to join the Services Employees International Union (SEIU). "The university was very constructive in its view," says David Rodich, executive director of Local 500. "Georgetown chose to adhere to the principles of Catholic social teaching, including the right to form a union."

Shortly after its recognition of SEIU, Georgetown even supported the academic freedom of an adjunct faculty member in its School of Foreign Service who had written indirectly about assassinating President Obama, according to *The Hoya*, the school's student newspaper. A university spokeswoman responded that "being committed to the free and open exchange of ideas does not mean that we approve of or endorse each and every statement made by members of our faculty."

Whether other campuses are as open-minded remains to be seen, but more universities are accepting adjunct unions. In the Washington, D.C., area, besides Georgetown, part-time instructors have formed unions at American University, George Washington University and Maryland's Montgomery College. Elsewhere, Tufts, Duke, the University of Chicago, the University of Minnesota and Washington University in St. Louis voted to unionize.

"The SEIU strategy has momentum right now," says the University of Southern California's Adrianna Kezar. "And we know that unionization leads to salary hikes and at least the beginnings of other benefits." A recent survey by the Coalition on the Academic Workforce found that universities with adjunct unions pay twenty-five percent more on average than those that were not unionized. The study also indicated that unions have been successful in securing health and pension benefits, job security and regular raises as well as compensation for non-teaching duties.

"Unionization is associated with getting people out of the working-poor category, and I think you can see that happening," says Gary Rhoades, director of the University of Arizona's Center for the Study of Higher Education. "There's now beginning to be a reversal as more and more adjuncts begin to organize."

There's still a long way to go, however. In their search for allies, adjuncts have found only tepid interest from full-time faculty. Joseph J. Fahey, a professor of religious studies at Manhattan College, brazenly denounces his cloistered colleagues as "gutless workers who sit in their little fiefdoms and ignore the needs of adjunct faculty members." Yet former adjunct Fruscione encourages part-time professors to keep the faith and "reach out in constructive ways to tenured or tenure-track faculty. Get them to do more than pay lip service to adjunct issues."

In any case, contingent groups are looking well beyond tenured or tenure-track faculty for support, demanding that they be paid at least $15,000 per course (up from the national average of $2,700 per class). Adjunct faculty are turning to everyone from hourly workers on campus, to tuition-paying parents, to students. Union organizers have been instructing adjuncts to join hands with service workers, janitors, cafeteria workers and other blue-collar types who share "a commonality of interests." But the results to date have been mixed.

Adjuncts have also been trying to win over parents, who are unaware of how poor working conditions affect student learning or that their huge tuition bills go to underpaid faculty who flip-flop between multiple campuses, with limited time or energy for their children. Limited progress, here too.

More effective have been adjuncts' efforts to enlist student support. Called "our most natural allies" by Ann Kottner, an adjunct professor of English at New Jersey City University, many students have been hell-bent on eliminating the image of adjuncts as second-rate nomads. Their organizations have been unmatched in attempting to improve working conditions for contingent faculty. The United Students Against Sweatshops, for example, has helped get students in several cities energized to eliminate adjunct exploitation. "We believe that this is an issue of quality higher education," says K.B. Brower, an organizer of the student movement.

These howls of rage are not enough, says Debra Leigh Scott, an adjunct instructor of humanities, who is helping produce the documentary film, *Junct: The Trashing of Higher Ed in America*. Even unions, she contends, affect only a limited group of people and can take years to organize. Better yet to lobby Capitol Hill for a more comprehensive workers' "bill of rights."

Representative George Miller of California, the senior Democrat on the House Committee on Education and the Workforce, has emerged as the standard-bearer of adjunct reform. Two years ago, he set up an online forum for contingent faculty to share stories about their working conditions. Not surprisingly, it generated a grab bag of all-too-familiar complaints.

"There's a huge lack of understanding of what it means to be in the adjunct world," Miller discovered. Among other things, "adjunct professors have taken on the task of educating the nation's future leaders, but they do as often with little, if any, administrative support from their colleges." Worse yet, he found that the colleges with the highest-paid presidents had the fastest growing share of their workforces made up of adjunct faculty.

"The buck stops with you," Miller urged college presidents. "Adjunct professors are your employees. You own their working conditions. You can keep defending the status quo and trying to excuse shabby workplace practices, but I respectfully suggest you change them instead."

Representative Miller's comments and his subsequent report, "The Just-In Time Professor," marked an important turning point for those trying to improve life for contingent faculty. With newfound Congressional support, the plight of adjuncts is "no longer an invisible problem," says professor Kezar.

"We have all this momentum and it's just continuing to build," agrees Maria C. Maisto, who has headed the adjunct-advocacy group New Faculty Majority since 2009. "When we first started out, we were just trying to get people to listen. Now we're not so easy to dismiss."

That said, universities are notoriously "a refuge from hasty judgment," Robert Frost once noted. Disruptive change goes against the grain. Although college bigwigs flaunt innovation, they are "a crushing force against it," says Arizona State University president Michael Crow.

Universities, in fact, have not changed much since students and faculty first gathered in Oxford and Bologna in the eleventh century. But times have changed, and the clock is ticking. Those in positions of power should know full well that colleges and universities, like other institutions, only get what they pay for. With their ranks increasing and the numbers clearly on their side, academia's hidden heroes are not defenseless boffins. They are beginning to stand up en masse to push universities to pay them a living wage, give them decent benefits and some job security and provide them with the resources they need to do their work effectively.

"First they ignore you," Gandhi observed, "then they laugh at you, then they attack you, then you win." Only by putting their talents in tandem can university leaders and their indispensable dons allow new dreams to be realized—and Margaret Mary Vojtko's tragic death be put to rest.

❖ ❖ ❖

Community college chancellor Erika Lacro and others take great pride in creating opportunities for underserved immigrant, first-generation and minority students.

CHAPTER 7

HALLS OF IVY

*"I have never let my schooling interfere
with my education."*

—MARK TWAIN

"OH, NO!" was Reuben Chong's street name—as in "Oh, no! Here he comes!" For a decade, the homeless ex-convict prowled Honolulu's Chinatown in search of funds to support his drug habit. Who could imagine that this thirty-four-year-old, street-smart thug would eventually find his footing at Leeward Community College, where he graduated as a straight-A student and student body president? He then went on to earn his bachelor's and master's degrees, again with honors, at the University of Hawaii's flagship campus in lush Manoa Valley.

Nothing in Reuben Chong's life came easily. Given up by his parents at birth, he was abandoned by his adoptive parents at age three. As a ward of the state, he shuttled between "at least a dozen" foster homes before fleeing an abusive "father" while in the eleventh grade. After a precarious year on the streets "learning to survive," Chong joined the Army and stayed for almost six years. There, he completed high school, but also encountered his first exposure to drugs and alcohol. At twenty-four, he mustered out of the service with an honorable discharge.

Broke and broken, with no family to call on, a demoralized

Chong lived for ten years on Honolulu's mean streets or in shelters. He was convicted for four separate felonies for theft and assault, and served almost five years in prison. There, he began to turn his life around after a substance-abuse program began to take hold.

"I wanted something, but I didn't know what," he told me over a pizza lunch. "I didn't want to fall into the same cycle of drugs and crime." Opting to delay his release from prison for almost a year, he entered a peer-counseling program, which stirred his interest in giving back to the community.

"A happy life," wrote Helen Keller, "consists not in the absence, but the mastery, of hardships." Heaven knows, a parentless man is hardened in many ways. Yet he will often search for a place to attach his loyalty and devotion. Chong found this place at Leeward Community College, an institution ready to embrace him when others turned him away.

After his release from prison, Chong was in a hurry to make up for lost time. In 1998, he enrolled at Leeward. He had taken the standard battery of placement tests in reading, writing and math—but failed most of them. Steered into intensive remedial courses and tutoring, Chong slowly began to assimilate. "But," he says, "nothing I experienced in jail or on the streets intimidated me more than going to school, sitting in a classroom and competing with all those bright young faces."

"You're smart, you're really smart!" Beth Kupper-Herr, director of Leeward's Learning Resource Center, told him. "Those words of encouragement did it," Chong recalls. "The lights came on, opening my eyes to my potential and the possibilities ahead."

"I was so impressed by how driven he was," Kupper-Herr recalls. "We rarely saw anyone with drive like Reuben's. He was truly exceptional." As a full-time student, Chong managed to excel in the classroom, tutor his fellow students, serve on a neighborhood board and make the mandatory visits to his parole officer. In his spare time, he read to the homeless in downtown Honolulu, counseled prison inmates and served as Leeward's student body president. For his academic accomplishments, Chong was awarded a Presidential Scholarship at the University of Hawaii, where he graduated with honors, earning his BA and MSW degrees.

In recent years, he has taken on a variety of challenging

counseling assignments for both the state and federal government. "That's my gift," he beams, "sharing my experiences, my hopes, with others. They may think I'm helping them, but I'm really the one who benefits." Today, at fifty-four, Chong serves as program manager for the nonprofit Community Health Outreach Work (CHOW) project to prevent HIV/AIDS. On every Hawaiian island, the devout Christian intends to make this world a better place.

"Leeward Community College opened so many doors for me, doors of dreams," he says. "It changed my life. It gave me opportunities that I never thought were possible." On balance, Reuben's life is good. "Oh, no!" Chong is now "Oh, yes!" Chong— helping others fulfill the American dream.

"The direction in which education starts a man will determine his future life," wrote Plato. Community, or "junior," colleges were created a century ago to provide that direction. Their mission: To offer open and affordable education in liberal arts and vocational training to a diverse group of non-traditional students, who, like Reuben Chong, could either enter the mainstream or fall back into a cycle of despair. Today, they serve almost half of all undergraduates, many of them juggling coursework with jobs and families. In many respects, these two-year, sub-baccalaureate institutions appeal to folks of all ages and backgrounds who can't afford four-year colleges because they lack the required grades and/or funds, or are looking for practically oriented courses that lead to a certificate and a career. Yet to many, these hidden heroes, America's community colleges, are derided as "schools of last resort." (Leeward Community College— LCC—is often called "Last Chance College.")

In academic circles, prestige remains the coin of the realm. "It's to higher education as profit is to corporations," points out professor J. Douglas Toma of the University of Georgia. "The primary goal of most schools is legitimacy through enhanced prestige."

Colleges are a mirror of the society they serve. The growth of inequality is reflected in higher ed, American-style, which has evolved into a caste system, "separate and unequal for students with different family incomes," says Cornell government professor Suzanne Mettler. At the top of the pyramid are private nonprofits, the Ivies and top-tier schools, such as Stanford, Duke and North-western. They carry a hefty price tag—up to $60,000 a year.

"The top colleges, shinier than ever, are Porsches," writes *The New York Time*'s Frank Bruni. "They can take you far and fast, but it's a lucky few who get behind the wheel. These hyper-competitive schools are crowded with the richest kids."

One step down the scale are the elite state flagships, notably those in California, Michigan and Virginia. They are followed by America's second-tier public universities and colleges. Where they perform well, they represent a reasonable-quality, lower-cost alternative to the research-intensive universities. Next come a growing number of for-profit "career colleges," including the Apollo Education Group (owners of the University of Phoenix), the Education Corporation and American Public University. Typically, these schools target low-income students and veterans, but are under increasing government scrutiny. On their heels are the newcomers, a bevy of "just-in-time" education providers, including Kahn Academy, General Assembly, Skillshare and Dev Bootcamp, among others.

"At the bottom of the status hierarchy are community colleges," contends John Quiggin, author of *Zombie Economics*. These underdogs of higher education, he alleges, "are failing badly." This criticism comes at an especially bad time.

For the American academy, the honeymoon is over. From the early 1980s to the end of the twenty-first century, our two- and four-year colleges and universities were on a roll. The economy was strong, endowments expanded and lavish amounts were expended on bricks and mortar. A robust job market made the "wage premium," the difference between college grads and those with only a high school degree, more enticing. Students flocked to campus— two million new ones in public institutions alone. A sheepskin was a VIP ticket to the middle or upper-middle class. By almost every indicator, universities and colleges were transforming higher education from a former bastion of privilege into a path toward the American dream.

The golden age ended a decade or so ago. The 2001 recession and the subsequent financial crisis hit campuses across the country like an economic tsunami. In the process, the wage premium plateaued, and a once-warm public turned cynical about the academy. Often blamed are skyrocketing tuitions, lack of accountability and transparency, uneven quality and poor graduation rates. The price of college has risen more than four times faster than inflation since 1978, easily outpacing doctors' bills. "Much of this cash," reports *The Economist*, "has been wasted on things that have nothing to do with education—plush dormitories, gleaming stadiums and armies of administrators." As a result, survey after survey indicates that colleges at every level have been steadily losing America's trust.

Today, our colleges and universities, once the envy of the world, face a cascade of dark clouds—from tighter budgets and declining enrollments to unruly faculty and greater government oversight. Higher education, long considered the great leveler, has put the American dream out of reach for all but the privileged few. "We are squandering one of the finest US accomplishments and historic legacies," laments Cornell's Mettler, "a system of higher education that was long characterized by excellence and wide accessibility to what seemed to be an even wider and more diverse group of citizens."

This loss of opportunity has led many Americans to conclude that college degrees are a waste of time and money. Few graduates say college led to career success. In a recent Gallup study of 30,000 college graduates of all ages across fifty states, just three percent reported having had the types of campus experience that some studies suggest can lead to career success and personal well-being. Besides, easy student credit has turned steep tuitions and fees into a dangerous bubble, with student-loan debt hitting a record $1.1 trillion—more than America's credit card debt. About two-thirds of college students graduate with debt, with the average loan of about $35,000. What's more, an estimated fifteen percent of these debtors default within three years.

The unpredictable job market hasn't helped either. Many recent graduates haven't improved their employment prospects. Almost half of them wind up in jobs that don't require a degree; a startling 115,000 graduates work as caretakers. Consequently, increasing numbers of prospective students are either gravitating toward career-oriented colleges and curricula or skipping college altogether to learn a trade.

Skipping college is not good advice for everyone, though. Studies indicate that declines in employment and wages fall much more heavily on those with less education. The premiums commanded by a college degree have risen. On average, a college graduate still earns almost $20,000 a year or $2.3 million over a lifetime, nearly $1 million more than a high school graduate. Moreover, the Pew Research Center recently found that "on virtually every measure of economic well-being and career attainment—from personal earnings to job satisfaction to the share employed full-time—young college graduates are outperforming their peers with less education." In the twenty-first century, one needs higher skills, whether welding materials or writing code.

Community colleges, it would seem, should be ideally positioned to meet these challenges. They have doubled in number since 1965, while their enrollments have exploded almost sevenfold over the same period. Though still serving as a stepping stone to a four-year degree, these hidden heroes do far more today than simply offer a ladder to the final two years of a university. In recent years, their mission has become more comprehensive, thanks to a gradual shift toward much-needed vocational education, job training and programs catering to the community. From crime scene investigators and video game animators to organic farmers and sustainability coordinators, cutting-edge two-year colleges provide a wide array of exciting career options. They also give eighteen-year-olds their first glimpse into the world of work and, at the same time, prepare retirees for a second or third career.

"I owe it all to community college," says actor, producer, director Tom Hanks. He describes his stint at Chabot College in Hayward, California, as "the place that made me what I am today." Chabot, in fact, inspired his 2011 film, *Larry Crowne*.

Community colleges also offer future Tom Hankses low tuition (typically, one-third less than a state university), convenient campus locations, open admissions and, as mentioned, a broad spectrum of flexible courses in emerging fields where the number of jobs are growing, not shrinking. Add to this heavy remedial lifting, since at least half of their entering students require additional catch-up courses, particularly those whose primary language is not English. No surprise then that the nation's two-year colleges have been referred to as "today's Ellis Island" or "America's democracy college" because they serve a disproportionate number of immigrants, first-generation citizens and minorities.

Despite their very full plate, community colleges are often treated as second-class citizens. Though their growth had been much faster than four-year colleges and universities, that trend reversed three years ago. One reason: The competition got much tougher. For starters, the Internet genie is out of the bottle, changing the expectations of a large number of students across the century. Today, dozens of upstarts, as well as big-brand schools, are offering more than 2,000 massive online open courses (MOOCs) and other forms of online learning to teach topics that students and employers both understand and value.

There are also the for-profit outfits, which now account for twenty percent of the two-year associate degrees granted in the United States, up from eight percent two decades ago. Generally more nimble than public sector community colleges, they can very quickly develop an appealing curriculum and hire the appropriate faculty. They also are more inclined to take risks on older students who might have had poor grades in high school, but are now more mature and ready to advance their education. For-profits "are adding to the supply," says professor David Deming of Harvard's Graduate School of Education. "They are reaching students in a different way, opening in places where there are no community colleges. They are filling in the cracks."

Four-year institutions also are becoming much more aggressive in appealing to traditional community college students, predominantly commuters with day jobs and children at home. Clever baccalaureate colleges are pitching them, highlighting cutting-edge technology, resort-grade amenities and strong links to employers—features that most two-year schools can't match. Students also are discovering that an associate degree doesn't carry the same weight with potential employers that it once did.

By portraying themselves as more than "two-year way stations," big-time universities are slowly winning over talented minority, low-income and first-generation students long considered the red meat of community colleges. As a result, two-year programs are in a fierce academic dogfight, squeezed between a dizzying array of learning options: online offerings, for-profit schools and elite universities.

In the teeth of tougher competition, community colleges remain academia's redheaded stepchildren. Tom Hanks aside, they continue to suffer from an image, or "brand," problem. By often serving ill-prepared, economically hard-pressed students—the Reuben Chongs of the world, if you will—even the best two-year schools draw snickers from an increasingly cynical public.

"The bias against community colleges—and, by extension, their faculty members—runs deep in our society, and not just among academics," reports Rob Jenkins, author of *Building a Career in America's Community Colleges*. "I've encountered a surprising number of people, from all walks of life, who naturally assume that professors at two-year colleges must be second-rate intellects who couldn't get a job at a 'real' college and whose ideas are, therefore, not worth considering."

Jenkins and other educators who have dedicated their careers to helping underserved students bristle at the suggestion that they—and their institutions—aren't up to the task. This charge sends a "pernicious message," warns Patricia A. McGuire, president of Trinity Washington University, a Roman Catholic institution located in the nation's capital.

Nevertheless, "beauty lies at the top of the mountain," as Mao Zedong observed. In most academic circles, America's two-year colleges—largely because of their tightly defined mission to serve all members of the community—have yet to scale higher ed's upper echelons. For one thing, newly minted PhDs, with research in the veins, often are turned off by what they consider to be an immature, unprepared and apathetic audience. At teaching-intensive community colleges, there is usually no research support. Likewise, sabbaticals, release time, summer grants and travel assistance are hard to come by.

"Teaching is the ponderous portion of the profession, the burden to be carried," according to Arthur M. Cohen and Florence B. Brawer, two longtime observers of the community college scene. Typically, the teaching load is non-negotiable; everyone teaches the same number of courses (usually three to five a semester).

No surprise then that some in academia consider the community college career choice "a loss of equity of their PhD training," says professor Matthew Tuthill, a whip-smart molecular biologist at

Hawaii's Kapiolani Community College. "At worst, they call it 'career suicide.' Some believe that junior college positions are for those who aren't capable of competing in a traditional research setting."

Having landed a job at one community college, SooJin Pate found faculty life far different from research-intensive University of Minnesota, where she received her doctorate. "The campus environment and the workload—teaching five writing-intensive courses each semester—created havoc on my body and spirit," she recalls. "So I quit." Another turnoff is the heavy dose of remedial courses that faculty must teach to help students advance to either a four-year institution or a career-oriented certificate.

There are also the so-called "dual enrollment" programs that require junior college faculty to descend into high schools to offer a host of courses. Conceived to accelerate the college experience and, hence, reduce student debt, these initiatives—financed largely by both private and public funds—allow sixteen- and seventeen-year-olds to earn dual credit and get on the higher ed track earlier, building up momentum toward a college degree ahead of schedule. Nevertheless, these dual-degree programs turn off faculty interested in serving a more mature clientele. Think *Sixteen Candles*!

Finally, don't expect big bucks. Although community college professors have a much greater teaching load than their university counterparts, their salaries are considerably lower—one-third less in the Maryland system, for example. Nationally, a full professor at a two-year school earns roughly the same as an assistant professor at a four-year institution, according to recent data from the American Association of University Professors. (Presidents of community college systems, too, typically receive one-quarter to one-half the compensation afforded their counterparts in public universities.)

Still, these hidden heroes serve nearly half of the nation's undergraduates who generally come from lower-middle income families, for whom education is the route to upward mobility. Though they handle the lion's share of college teaching, they have long been burdened by rising costs, falling enrollments, anemic alumni donations and dwindling state support. While spending per student has risen over the past decade at every kind of four-year institution, it has remained all but flat in community colleges.

To survive, financially strapped two-year schools have cut labor costs by replacing full-time professors with part-time instructors, who typically have no health or pension benefits and are often abysmally paid, earning in the vicinity of $3,000 to $3,500 per course. These adjuncts, the subject of the previous chapter, far outnumber full-time faculty on most community college campuses. As we saw in the last chapter, many part-timers bolt from campus the moment class ends. They tend to be less likely to participate in instructional activities such as advising or tutoring, which can benefit underserved students. Without engagement, the prospect of academic success can seem slight. Yet, on virtually every campus, there is an increase in the use of part-time faculty and a decrease in full-timers.

To worsen things, community college students, whose life histories and social disadvantages make them the most likely to need academic guidance and counseling, are largely left on their own. Student-advisor ratios in the two-year sector are abysmal in many schools; they can run as high as 1,500 to one, reports *The Atlantic's* Ann Hulbert. "A surer formula for widening the gap between the haves and have-nots would seem difficult to achieve." Add to that the often substandard library, computer and athletic facilities.

For decades, the community college sector expanded almost automatically as it helped educate an increasingly diverse population at reasonable costs. But waiting for students to show up is no longer enough, says Peter S. Bryant, a senior vice president at the educational consulting firm Noel-Levitz. "There's a growing realization," he says, "that there has got to be a more strategic approach." This, too, was the conclusion recently reached by the American Association of Community Colleges. The watchdog group recommended a broad transformation of its members to meet the future needs of their students and the economy.

President Barack Obama, the Bill and Melinda Gates Foundation, other higher ed associations and individual states would like to jumpstart this transformation. Among their stretch goals: doubling the number of students who earn a certificate or degree and transfer to a college or university; reducing by half the number of students who enter college unprepared; closing the achievement gap across diverse populations; and accelerating workforce training in vanguard industries.

In 2015, Obama announced $600 million in grants to help train Americans for jobs in specialized industries, such as information technology and advanced manufacturing. Around $500 million will go toward increasing coordination between community colleges and businesses. The result will be used to expand apprenticeships across the country. "It's a great model for transferring skills from one generation to the next," says John Ladd, director of the Department of Labor's Office of Apprenticeship. Ninety percent of apprenticeships will be given jobs with average starting salaries of more than $50,000 a year, yet the United States has far fewer apprenticeships than European nations (one-fifth those of Germany).

Mindful that practical, vocational training is where America is weakest, savvy community colleges are listening to what the government and others want—offering much more in the way of formal training and on-the-job coaching to bridge the gap. Aided by various grants, farsighted two-year colleges are partnering with employers in offering apprenticeships in not only high-growth industries, such as biotechnology and nanotechnology, but also traditional fields from baking to banking. For example, Virginia Community College and Cisco Systems have established high-tech training centers at more than twenty-five campuses, while Birmingham-based Lawson State Community College has partnered with Microsoft and Novell in information technology. Caterpillar, too, has linked up with schools in North Carolina and Georgia, donating factory equipment and steering young people toward manufacturing and helping overcome the stigma of working with your hands.

Other two-year programs are gaining newfound respect by offering a mix of important services. Besides job training, they rent space and equipment, sell research and provide paid consulting advice. Iowa's Muscatine Community College, for instance, is helping local start-ups with patents and business plans; firms needing a high-tech 3-D printer can rent one at Wisconsin's Fox Valley Community College.

Two-year colleges are also helping tamp down college costs. In 2013, Obama unveiled the "college scorecard," which tells students the cost and graduation rate of the course they have chosen. He and others are calling for double-digit increases in quicker completion rates to lessen student debt. This is forcing community college leaders to overhaul remedial education, among other things. Florida, for instance, is one of several states adopting a novel approach to determine whether incoming students are prepared to move on to college-level coursework. In many instances, remedial courses have become optional, thanks to a state law that lets students decide whether they really need them. In their place are alternatives, such as pre-orientation counseling, summer bridge programs, peer mentors, backup learning in credit-bearing classes and accelerated courses that compress remedial classes into tighter formats.

With universities' record sticker prices and mounting student debt, a number of two-year schools also are presenting themselves, as a more affordable, fast track path to a four-year degree. For high achievers right out of high school determined to save money, the prospect of living at home, attending a nearby and less-expensive community college and knocking off one's undergrad prerequisites carries great appeal. Last year, the average cost of tuition and fees for one year at two-year public college was one-third of that paid by an in-state resident at a public four-year college, according to the College Board.

"As tuition has been going up more steadily in four-year institutions, community colleges are an increasingly attractive alternative for savvy kids who want to save money," says Sacramento State University professor Nancy Shulock. "They know what they need, know how to get it and don't need a lot of the student services that community colleges are struggling to provide. They can get through in two or three years—and transfer." Therefore, parents should try to "shift the goalposts" for their children, says Kevin Fudge, the manager of government relations and community affairs for American Student Assistance, a watchdog nonprofit focused on college expenses.

Fortunately, there's a new breed of community college students and their parents who know how to navigate the system, with considerable savings. The Jack Kent Cooke Foundation, among others, provides scholarships of up to $30,000 to talented transfers. Amherst, Cornell, the University of Michigan and the University of California, Berkeley are among the big-name schools receiving funds to assist community college transfers. Separately, Florida, Hawaii, Virginia and California also have created special incentives to accelerate the transfer process and keep student fees down.

Perhaps more enticing are the growing number of states considering no-cost community colleges. Tennessee now offers free tuition; Oregon and Mississippi are considering similar measures. The Tennessee Promise, for instance, affects 26,000 residents at an estimated cost of about $35 million a year. Students must attend full-time, take at least twelve credit hours per semester and maintain a 2.0 grade point average to receive a tuition waiver. They must also complete eight hours of community service and have a mentor. The program's objective, says Governor William E. Haslam, is to strengthen the state's workforce and attract outside investment.

The idea of free community college is winning converts. "Because they are generally more affordable and are perceived as less liberal than four-year colleges, community colleges have a bipartisan appeal," says Stephan G. Katsinas, director of the University of Alabama's Educational Policy Center.

Clearly, President Obama got the message. Last year, he announced a bold plan to make community college virtually free. His proposal would waive tuition fees for students who attend two-year programs at least half time and maintain a 2.5 GPA (a C-plus). Washington would pick up seventy-five percent of the tab, conservatively estimated at $60 billion over ten years—while states would cover the rest.

Critics, however, argue against these freebies. "I won't ever back giveaways," says John Morton, who oversees the University of Hawaii's vast community college system, now in its fiftieth year. "Students must have some skin in the game," he adds, noting that community college tuitions are already deeply discounted.

Besides competing on price, many community colleges are trying to improve their brand. In the past decade, some forty colleges have gone so far as to drop "community" from their names. "Shedding the word 'community' is an important step toward attracting a broader cross-section of students," argues Richard Kahlenberg, a senior fellow at the Century Foundation. But opponents view these efforts as "institutional aggrandizement," which compromise schools' long-standing and carefully defined goal to serve the broader community.

"I'm against it," says Hawaii's Morton. "Rebranding means straying away from our core mission of decades past to serve all members of the community. 'Community' is what defines us. It's what makes us special."

In a related move to generate more academic uplift, other community colleges are shifting to four-year status. Private junior colleges, in particular, have concluded that their finances are too shaky for them to survive solely on two-year programs. Hampshire-based Chester College of New England, for instance, scrapped its associate degrees in a switch to becoming a four-year institution. Others, like Indiana's Holy Cross College, award both bachelor's and associate degrees.

Public community colleges also are trying to move upstream. California, for instance, is following the lead of twenty-one other states in seeking authority for many of its two-year colleges to award four-year degrees in some fields. Constance M. Carroll, chancellor of the San Diego Community College District, calls herself a "card-carrying" advocate of the baccalaureate proposal, which she says is driven by workplace demands. The nursing profession, for instance, is moving to require a bachelor's degree rather than the associate's degree offered by many community colleges. It makes sense, Carroll contends, to broaden the charter of her schools and help both students and employers.

Motivations aside, the pecking order in higher education remains ostensibly the same. "Authorizing the community colleges to offer the bachelor's degree does not change public perceptions of their relative merit," argue professors Cohen and Brawer. "It merely establishes a bottom stratum of former two-year colleges among senior institutions."

These overly ambitious measures are "like putting lipstick on a pig," one university administrator told me. He and others worry that strategies like institutional rebranding and emphasizing bachelor's degrees don't enhance prestige, and detract from the central mission of community service. "Maybe it's a natural evolutionary move," concedes George Boggs, chief executive emeritus of the American Association of Community Colleges, "but I hate to see us lose any feeling of being in touch with the community and trying to build a sense of community."

Blurring the lines between what has historically differentiated the role of two- and four-year institutions seems hard to contain. Yet keeping up with the Joneses or "mission creep," is ill advised. The prestige race not only squanders scarce resources but "encourages a one-size-fits-all model where our increasingly diverse student body demands more differentiation among colleges," says Arizona State professor Jeffrey Selingo.

"We tried to be all things to all people," Robert Agrella, a former community college president, chimes in. "We can't afford to do that any longer." Rather than straying from their core mission, some community colleges are refocusing on what they are already doing rather than trying to stretch upward.

For example, insightful two-year colleges are attempting to better prepare their students for four-year university life. At Honolulu-based Kapiolani Community College, students are discovering that high-level science is now an important career option. Kapiolani's professor Tuthill works with two-year students to manufacture complex monoclonal antibody-producing hybridoma cell lines. To prepare for this work, students enroll in research-intensive molecular biology, tissue culture and protein chemistry-immunology courses.

"Not surprisingly," says Tuthill, "research platforms like these enable our community college students to compete successfully with students from four-year schools at local and national scientific conferences. This work contradicts the dogma of the traditional role of community colleges and the reputations of their scientific staffs." (According to the American Association of Community Colleges, nearly a quarter of science and engineering faculty members currently populating two-year campuses hold doctorates.)

Several miles away from Kapiolani's picturesque campus on the slopes of Diamond Head, scholars at Honolulu Community College (HCC) also are ramping up their twenty-first-century skills. The state legislature recently allocated $38 million to build an Advanced Science and Training Center on campus. Leading the charge is HCC's feisty chancellor, Erika Lacro. The forty-three-year-old high-flyer, with a doctorate in communications and information sciences, seems more like a hotshot CEO than an ivory-tower leader.

Back on the US Mainland, mathematics professor Robert A.

Chaney, winner of an earlier Professor of the Year award, looks for practical applications of his discipline to motivate students at Sinclair Community College in Dayton, Ohio. Especially effective has been his robotics project, in which students write functions to program robots to walk or interpret data. "If students find early success," he says, "they wind up enjoying math." Administrative support to attend conferences and write grants, as well as the school's state-of-the-art Math Science Technology Center, has helped Chaney's hands-on approach to winning hearts and minds.

Ironically, faculty success in the hard sciences and liberal arts brings its own problems. Two-year college instructors, particularly those in the hands-on technical and vocational areas, are sometimes threatened by those committed to the more academic disciplines that dominate the university track. Striking the right balance between this cultural divide is a major challenge for community college leaders.

"It's huge," says the straight-talking Lacro. "The more practical, hard-trades faculty often take offense of their peers with advanced degrees, who, in turn, don't want to be 'dumbed down' by those offering supposedly less rigorous coursework. What's worse, students become aware of these tensions.

"As a result, I spend a good deal of my time bringing these two, often segregated, groups together," she adds. "In many cases, I have to force a solution."

Differences aside, I found both sides, and their leaders, committed to what one community college instructor called "an overpowering feeling of success." For the most part, faculty accept that America's two-year colleges are not selective, residential collegiate institutions. They know, too, that all higher education, at the end of the day, is career-oriented. "The poverty-proud scholar attending college for the joy of pure knowledge is about as common as the presidential candidate who was born in a log cabin," argue Cohen and Brawer. "Both myths deserve decent burials."

After years of flying under the radar, these hidden heroes of higher education are beginning to play to their strengths, putting quality education within reach of anyone willing to strive. "We are now out of the closet," says Terry O'Banion, president emeritus of the community colleges' League for Innovation. "This is an Andy

Warhol moment."

The ability to open doors and create opportunities for the Reuben Chongs of the world is enabling many community colleges to achieve their fifteen minutes of fame—basking in the spotlight switched on by the recent Obama proposal. Nationwide, faculty turnover is low, and the desire to move to a flagship university, never great, is even less appealing. "I never thought I wanted to be anywhere else," beams Sinclair's award-winning professor Chaney. "I see my work making a difference in so many lives. Working here has truly been a dream come true."

❖ ❖ ❖

Despite few cheering sections, more than 5,000 naval aviators
and crewmembers flew blimps like this on important
World War II missions.

CHAPTER 8

UNDERDOGS OF THE AIR

"Aviation is a game—an amazing game, a game of adventure, of countless thrills, of soul-stirring excitement, a game in which courage and daring achieve honor in life... glory in death."

—Captain Jacques De Sieyes (in 1918)

MAN'S CONQUEST OF THE AIR began with flight in a balloon. Today, in skies filled with jet aircraft, some traveling at supersonic speeds, it is hard to conceive that man first flew in lighter-than-air (LTA) craft—balloons, blimps and great dirigibles. To some, these unconventional airships are stately galleons of the skies. But to others, they are windblown oddities—plump, sluggish vessels—often ridiculed and nicknamed "rubber cows," "poppy bags" or "playful pachyderms." These underdogs of the air continue to suffer from their inherent silliness. Even the name "blimp" sounds silly—by one account, coined in World War I by a British naval officer from the sound of a finger striking the airbag.

"There's a certain giggle factor associated with them," admits one former airship executive. "But there's an ineffable quality that makes people like them. It's like a sunset. You just sit there and watch them."

It didn't start that way. The forerunners of today's Goodyear blimps were supersized, rigid dirigibles that floated high above the world so majestically that many thought that they—not fixed-wing airplanes—would end up ruling the air. No one ever thought we'd see anything larger in the skies. They were four times as long and more than twice as wide as the current blimps (or airships without a rigid structure). Nor will passengers ever fly in such comfort as they did during the glory days of spacious airships. Like luxury cruise ships, they offered attractive sleeping quarters, with comfortable beds furnished with soft, light blankets and linen sheets and shower baths. There were smoking rooms, lounges with grand pianos, well-stocked wine cellars, cocktail bars and gourmet meals served on real china.

During their reign, "all work on the ground stopped, traffic ceased to move, and thousands crowded into the streets to watch their majestic passage," wrote historian Douglas H. Robinson in *Giants in the Sky*. From 1900 to 1940, these aerial leviathans announced the attainment of man's dream of exploring the farthest reaches of the earth, connecting the nations of the world in peaceful commerce through the air. Regaled in postcards and advertisements, the sleek, cigar-shaped airship was the embodiment of future air travel.

While LTAs may have been slower than airplanes, they were quieter, more energy efficient and logistically simpler. They could also liftoff silently from a city, rather than an exurban airport. At the time, they could carry more passengers than airliners. But a litany of intervening events—from slow-motion, stomach-churning crashes to second-class treatment from policy makers—scuttled these gigantic airships. In less than fifty years, they became the byword for doomed futurism, an Icarus-like symbol of industrial hubris.

❖ ❖ ❖

All flights are naturally three-act dramas: takeoff, flight, landing. Similarly, the evolution of LTAs is a journey of triumph, setback and, perhaps, redemption.

The United States' entry into World War II saw a resurgence of these lumbering contraptions, whose descendants dot the skies today as airborne billboards pasted with corporate logos. During the war, Goodyear manufactured approximately 130 blimps for the US Navy. Operating out of airbases stretching from Massachusetts to

California, they escorted thousands of convoys and assisted in the damage or sinking of several German U-boats. Similar patrol duty was undertaken in the Caribbean, Brazil, the Mediterranean and North Africa, as well as in the Pacific against the Japanese. With one possible exception, no Allied ship was sunk under their watchful eyes. As important, only one blimp and one airshipman were lost due to enemy action.

Airships played an important, but often overlooked, role in the war. Nonetheless, most Americans, even those in the Navy, failed to appreciate their accomplishments. Because blimps were mainly out of sight, involved primarily in unglamorous convoy protection, these hidden heroes had no cheering sections. The exceptions were the officers and men who manned our merchant ships and who vociferously voiced their sentiments with "God Bless Our Blimps!"

Throughout the war, LTA units were often treated like stepchildren. Carrier aviation and flying boats remained the major focus of naval aviation. Senior officers were heavier-than-air (HTA) pilots, inclined to discount the needs and accomplishments of their inflated competition. "Accordingly, scant effort was made to find a place for airships and their crew in naval aeronautics," contends William F. Althoff in his *Forgotten Weapon*. "Airship opponents did not act out of sheer perversity; it was a very expensive machine... and there was an honest conviction that the airship was unreliable, its utility marginal, and funds could be applied [elsewhere] with quicker and more certain results."

By the end of the war, these unsung heroes saw their welcome withdrawn, and faced rapid demobilization. From fifteen squadrons patrolling an area of three million miles, there were only two LTA squadrons by the end of 1946. Military blimps, for the most part, were scrapped, sold or put into storage. Although there was a brief revival in the mid-1950s as the Cold War heated up, the Navy remained pre-occupied with heavier-than-air aviation and nuclear submarines. In 1961, military and political bigwigs decided to deflate these unglamorous "gas bags." On August 31, 1962, the last flight of a military airship took place at Lakehurst, New Jersey. In predictable fashion, there was no official ceremony, no speeches, no fanfare of any kind to mark the occasion.

In subsequent years, numerous proposals to revive the airship as a tool of war and peace have surfaced, but, until recently, few evoked more than a passing interest. Space-age technology, though, could rescue blimps and their crews from the dusty relics of aviation history.

❖ ❖ ❖

In most of the world, airships are also known as "dirigibles," from the French *diriger* (meaning to direct or steer). The first were called "dirigible balloons." Over time, the term "balloon" was dropped because, as any savvy aeronaut knows, balloons are held captive to the wind, not engine power. Unlike lighter-than-air craft that are both powered and steerable, free-floating balloons are extremely difficult to control and are highly sensitive to changes in weight, temperature, humidity and pressure. Aircrews soon discover that the atmosphere is not a homogeneous medium, and their ship is seldom in an absolutely stable condition. A seaman's eye, therefore, is essential to survive.

Despite the risks, a pioneering generation of eighteenth- and nineteenth-century European and American balloonists paved the way for dirigible dreamers. Alexander Charles, a French physician, made the first non-tethered, human flight in 1783. While soaring in a hot-air balloon 500 feet above Paris, he declared: "Balloons give the first physical glimpse of a planetary overview. There is something both exotic and magnetic about balloonists. They are artists of the air." Nevertheless, the Frenchman admitted to being "utterly terrified" of his upper atmospherics, and chose never to fly again.

On Charles' heels, squadrons of scientists and adventurers became captive to the early days of "balloonacy." Gripped in a wave of folly, they quickly found out how low the ceiling of the world is. Five miles up, you enter the "death zone." The sky really is the limit. In addition, the awkwardness of balloons—inflating and deflating like lungs, bumping up against the limit of the breathable world and subject to the vagaries of weather—demonstrated the dangers of unassisted flight.

In 1819, Sophie Blanchard, who overcame crippling nervousness to become Napoleon's official balloonist, was, in flight, "a provoking exhibitionist in a low-cut dress, daring to the point of recklessness."

She fell to her death when her balloon's hydrogen-filled bag exploded. Then, there was the American aeronaut John Wise, ferrying US mail, who was last seen blowing in bad weather over Lake Michigan. Add to the list of crazies, James Glaisher, a British meteorologist, who during an 1862 ascent passed out at 29,000 feet, while taking notes of the temperature and barometric pressure. Fortunately, he had a copilot.

Perhaps most dramatic, however, was balloonist Salomon August Andrée's ill-fated polar expedition to reach the North Pole. The nautically trained Swedish engineer had claimed that he could pilot a balloon as easily as a boat. However, Andrée's adventure ended in his death on the ice in 1897, though it was another thirty-three years before anyone found his frozen bones alongside those of his frozen companion.

Precisely because every balloon flight was an adventure—because no one had figured out how to steer them reliably—the age of the free-floating gasbag was passing. Leave it to a cast of dogged visionaries, starting with Brazilian Albert Santos-Dumont, to take up the LTA baton. In 1898, he was able to demonstrate engine-powered dirigibility, using a combination of a propeller, steering rudder and two sacks of ballast. Riding in his hydrogen-filled airship, he reached of altitude of 1,300 feet, commanding "a view of all the monuments of Paris." A few years later, his exploits often culminated in his dangling from a tree or a high building, with shredded gas bags draped around him like a shroud.

After Santos-Dumont, the Germans took the lead. At the turn of the century, "Crazy Count" Ferdinand von Zeppelin initially focused on blimps—non-rigid, free-flying airships that had no internal framework, but kept their plump form by the pressure of their lifting gas. But because of blimps' unstable hull, which could kink in the middle when overpressure was insufficient or when maneuvered too fast, the brilliant inventor turned to semi-rigid and rigid dirigibles of enormous size, light metal frameworks and hydrogen gas-filled interiors free to expand or contract inside fabric-covered hulls.

Zeppelin mania soon consumed the German public, and dirigibles—blimps, semi-rigid and rigid—became synonymous with the inventor. Despite their mixed results in World War I, the Germans, along with the British, Americans, French and Italians, competed aggressively to explore their peacetime use, yearning to see who would be the first to cross the Atlantic.

Given the still primitive state of the aeroplane, the first airmail delivery arrived in the United States via airship from Britain in 1919. Two years later, energetic Admiral William A. Moffett became chief of US naval aviation and emerged as the nation's most powerful airship cheerleader. He tirelessly shaped an ambitious dirigibles program predicated on achieving aviation supremacy. The admiral's interest in rigid airships dated back to the Great War, where he noted their proficiency in naval reconnaissance. No other craft could match their speed, cruising range or endurance. Some were more than 750 feet long and could even launch and recover small scouting airplanes.

Moffett also knew that only the United States possessed vast reserves of nonflammable helium for use as a lifting gas. Conversely, European nations still had to fly their ships with highly flammable hydrogen, and wartime experience had proved that a craft inflated with hydrogen was "a grotesque instrument of aerial warfare." At Moffett's urging, the US Congress authorized a major rigid-airship program in 1919.

Operating out of an enormous shed, at the time the largest enclosed space in the world, the newly built Lakehurst Naval Air Station stood in the pine barrens of nowheresville New Jersey. Inside was the pride of the new fleet, the 682-foot *Shenandoah*, Native American for "daughter of the stars." It was the first airship supplied with inert helium.

Misfortune plagued the *Shenandoah*—and America's airship ardor—from the start, when the craft took off on a poorly planned publicity flight into a severe thunderstorm. It crashed on September 3, 1925, killing fourteen of its crew. Eight years later, the *Akron*, a 785-foot dirigible, encountered a violent storm that sent it plunging tail-first into the Atlantic, killing seventy-three of seventy-six aboard—the deadliest airship disaster on record. Among the casualties: Admiral Moffett. Finally, the *Macon*, christened by the admiral's widow, was lost after a structural failure off the California coast on February 12, 1935, claiming two lives.

While they operated from 1923 to 1935, the Navy's rigid airships dominated the smaller, sluggish, non-rigid blimps. "In the heyday of the big airships, blimps attracted little attention and held little appeal for naval aviators," writes J. Gordon Vaeth in *Blimps & U-Boats*. "The Navy used them mainly for training officers preparing to fly the rigids; pilots were required to make twenty flights in blimps, for minimum of twenty hours."

After the *Macon* was lost, America's dirigible dreams were put on hold. What's more, giant flying boats produced by Boeing Aircraft for Pan American Airways were taking shape, soon to dominate transatlantic travel. "Despite all the politicking about airships in America, governmental influences did not intervene to save the rigid dirigible either from later disasters or from competition with heavier-than-air machines," wrote Henry Cord Meyer, a historian at the University of California, Irvine.

Germany, though, continued to press ahead aggressively with dirigible development. The Zeppelin company, with a deep reservoir of talented engineers and a powerful citizenry of builders and maintenance personnel, remained intoxicated about building superior airships for global travel. The *Hindenburg* was that ultimate zeppelin, an intercontinental cruiser built for both today and tomorrow. With the ultimate support of Adolf Hitler and guaranteed government subsidies, the *Hindenburg* was the largest airship ever built, 804 feet long and 135 feet wide, able to hold seven million cubic feet of highly flammable hydrogen. It could carry fifty-two passengers in luxury, travel at seventy-seven miles per hour and fly 8,750 miles in a single hop. During the 1936 season, the ship, filled to capacity, flew between Germany and New York ten times. That year, *Town & Country* boasted that the *Hindenburg* was "the climax of all aerial efforts since Icarus."

"It was twice as fast as the fastest transatlantic ship," Dan Grossman, an Atlanta-based airship historian, told *The Washington Post*. "It was definitely the Concorde of its times." Since 1912, German zeppelins had transported 48,778 passengers over 20,877 hours and 1,193,501 miles of flight without a single fatality or serious injury.

But the so-called "golden era of the airship" came to a ghastly end on May 6, 1937, when the *Hindenburg* burst into flames attempting to land at the Lakehurst Naval Air Station. Within thirty-four seconds, this flying behemoth was reduced to smoldering ruins, killing thirty-five of the ninety-seven people on board, plus one person on the ground. Radio broadcaster Herbert Morrison vividly described the scene: "It is a terrific crash, ladies and gentlemen. It's smoke, and it's in flames now; and the frame is crashing to the ground, not quite to the mooring mast. Oh, the humanity!"

Subsequent investigations failed to explain the cause of the disaster. Conspiracy theories abounded in Germany, but no conclusive evidence of sabotage was ever uncovered. Most knowledgeable experts concluded that the explosion was a combination of human error, structural failure and natural phenomena. However, says historian Althoff, "one fact is indisputable: the fire could not have occurred if the *Hindenburg* had been helium inflated. Hydrogen would never again be used to carry passengers. Without [helium], the commercial transoceanic airship was finished." Germany soon scrapped its airships program, after pocketing 500,000 British pounds—$81 million today—in insurance proceeds from the disaster.

"The dirigible age came and went far too quickly," according to C. Michael Hiam, author of *Dirigible Dreams*. "The brief epoch of the airship...was charged with incredible potential, it consumed nations and imaginations, and for an exciting period in aviation history, it represented the future of human flight."

However, predictions that the *Hindenburg* crash meant the end of airships failed to materialize. The phoenix that would rise from the ashes was the tortoise-like blimp. These smallish, non-rigid craft would soon reinvigorate LTA flight, establishing impressive records of performance and safety.

By the late 1930s, only two US blimps remained in inventory, and most of the American public and Navy opposed spending more on "the big ships," or rigid dirigibles. The cliché that forty seaplanes could be purchased for the price of one rigid airship was constantly put forward. The offensive-minded Navy, too, was not interested in oversized scouting airships, which had neither significant attack nor carrier capabilities. In short, airships failed to meet the needs of the fleet and were, in the eyes of one high-ranking officer, of "undemonstrated value." Worse yet, President Franklin D. Roosevelt, a longtime "nonbeliever" of big airships, had extended only minimal support for the LTA movement.

Leave it to a feisty airship proponent, Admiral Charles E. Rosendahl, who had served on every American dirigible from the *Shenandoah* to the *Macon*, to ask: "Are there any basic reasons why airships—and particularly American airships—cannot succeed? Are American brains such as those which designed and built the Douglas airplane, the Martin and Sikorsky flying boats, the Holland Tunnel, the Washington Bridge and the Boulder Dam, stumped by the problems of airships?"

No one, especially firebrand Rosendahl, questioned the safety, usefulness or reliability of blimps. Although these smaller craft were faring only marginally better than their larger cousins, in 1938 the Navy authorized the construction of two blimps a year, to be produced by Goodyear, whose popular advertising airships had much to do with the award. The following year, however, the European war began, accelerating America's mobilization and rearmament. In 1940, the Congress called for a "10,000-plane program," including forty-eight non-rigid airships for the Navy. But LTA units remained at the bottom rung. They "floundered in the bureaucracy," wrote Richard G. Van Treuren in *Airships Vs. Submarines,* and were denied essential equipment and material until very late in the conflict.

Because protecting critical sea lanes would be the blimp's primary mission, funds eventually were provided to expand to six additional bases in diverse locations, ranging from South Weymouth, Massachusetts to Richmond Naval Air Station in Florida. Active-duty naval aviators were encouraged to request assignment to lighter-than-air, while naval reservists, including a number of Goodyear pilots, were recalled. The naval aviation cadet program was also expanded to include airship training, eventually cranking out more than 5,000 pilots and air crewmen.

During the war, Goodyear produced approximately 130 blimps, or K-ships, for the Navy. Called "sentinels of the sky," these smallish, 250-foot, non-rigid airships were used primarily for convoy escorts, antisubmarine warfare, rescue missions and mine-spotting operations. They were, however, anything but easy to fly. In the air, K-ships rolled and pitched; their behavior was more like a ship's than an airplane's. As a result, they often deviated from their prescribed flight plan.

"The real test of an LTA pilot's skill was the ability to fly in turbulence and gusts yet maintain altitude within reasonable limits and with minimal pitching," observes William Althoff in *Forgotten Weapon*. Landing, too, could be an adventure, particularly in inversions, weather conditions in which low-lying air is colder than the air above. "Unmitigated hell" is how one seasoned pilot described it. As for takeoffs, the cardinal principle was: "Do not take off with a nose-heavy ship." Doing so spelled disaster.

Among other things, K-ships also were uncomfortable. They were noisy, since there was no soundproofing, which would have added weight. In addition, acrid gasoline fumes often permeated the car. On short hops, these conditions might seem trivial, but given a blimp's glacial speed of sixty to seventy knots, pilots and their crews often had to endure them for twenty to thirty hours.

Training those with the right stuff remained a major LTA challenge throughout the war. Given their stepchild status, airship squadrons tended to be woefully understaffed. Qualified naval aviators were reluctant to abandon the carrier fleet and high-performance, fixed-wing aircraft for potentially career-killing duty in slumbering blimps.

At training facilities in Lakehurst and Moffett Field, California, aviation cadets had to master the usual subjects of any flight syllabus, plus aerostatics, the science of LTA flight built upon the properties and behavior of gases. As the war progressed, pilot training was shortened from a dozen to six, to four months; for enlisted men, from six to three months.

Upon graduation, airship pilots received the same Navy wings of gold as their HTA brethrens. As a carryover from earlier times, some LTA officers wore half-wings, a sign that they were checked out only in balloons. In 1941, the Navy had 100 pilots qualified for airships; by 1944, it had trained 1,500. By the end of World War II, most LTA pilots were also qualified in heavier-than-air planes, and were required to maintain their proficiency with a minimum of four flying hours a month.

Commanding these porky gasbags was clearly not *Top Gun* material. Several former LTA pilots told me of occasional sneers from hot-shot aviators in the carrier fleet. "We had to take a certain amount of joking," recalls Ross Woods, a longtime blimp skipper.

"But I never had any second thoughts or regrets, and truly loved flying them." As the war progressed, the heavier-than-air gang came to respect the remarkable endurance and enormous flying hours logged by their airship counterparts. Virtually every naval aviator marveled at the incredible dependability of these hidden heroes, whose average availability of 87.2 percent far exceeded that of every other military aircraft.

Thanks to their high availability and utilization rates, airships played a vital, if often unappreciated role, in winning the war. Prior to the use of significant blimp escorts in 1942, about sixty-three merchant ships were sunk by German U-boats off the East Coast of the United States. As the Navy acquired more blimps and convoy escorts increased, that number decreased to just three in 1943, none in 1944 and two in 1945. It is estimated that only one of approximately 88,000 ships in blimp-escorted convoys was lost to enemy action. Protective service was where naval airships especially shined. As guardians of vital sea lanes, they provided long-endurance air cover, which discouraged submarine fire on vulnerable merchant ships.

If there was any criticism of LTAs' contributions, it was their lack of speed, weaponry and inability to press home the attack on hostile submarines. "The aim of antisubmarine warfare is destruction," Althoff explains, and "offensively, LTA apparently achieved little." This is true. A slow-moving blimp rarely spotted a surfaced submarine, much less its periscope. By the time it reached a potential target, the U-boat had quickly disappeared out of range, far below the surface. Blimps hunting German subs "had a job often comparable to catching fish in the ocean with a hand crab net," lamented Admiral Rosendahl. "Our role was simply to keep submarines at bay," adds retired LTA skipper Mort Eckhouse, "to hold them in sight using radar-detection equipment until surface craft arrived to battle them."

There is no official record of a single U-boat sinking at the hands of a Navy airship. This, however, misses the point. There is considerable evidence from German naval logs that blimps caused their subs either to terminate their mission or deviate significantly from their assigned course. Moreover, at the end of the war, Grand Admiral Karl Donitz stated that "the American blimps were very disturbing to German U-boat activity." High praise from an enemy commander.

But within the Navy, carrier aircraft grabbed the headlines. "The airships' contributions were practically ignored," says historian Van Treuren. "Essentially, a defensive weapon, the non-rigid lacked the glamour of the more established naval hardware—surface ships and aircraft made famous by four years of global conflict."

To the American public, eager for glitzy news about the latest military conquest, airship sorties went unreported—with one minor exception. MGM's 1945 war movie *This Man's Navy* might surprise anyone expecting a high seas adventure. "Man's conquest of the air began with flight in a balloon," announces the opening card. "Today, in skies filled with American planes, our Navy remains loyal to the gallant blimp." With a blustery Wallace Beery in the lead, the film offered a respectful and serious portrait of the unsung heroes of naval aviation.

Beery starred as Chief Aviation Pilot Ned Trumpet, a rough-hewn, golden-hearted chief petty officer in the Navy's blimp service. Nicknamed "Old Gas Bag" for his long-winded, embellished war stories, the one-time silent screen villain and unlikely leading man transformed his bluster into a serious tribute to the men of the LTA. From opening images of a massive blimp descending into the fog for a tricky landing at Lakehurst to dramatic combat scenes of a submarine patrol, the film, directed by Oscar-winning William A. Wellman, created a sense of majesty and mystery of these unconventional airliners and their heroic crews. In so doing, *This Man's Navy* gave American audiences a rare glimpse into the wartime contributions of perhaps the nation's most obscure military unit.

Hollywood aside, skepticism of airships persisted within the naval hierarchy. Following severe demobilization at the end of the war, LTA fell out of fashion. For the next decade and a half, its needs continued to be subordinated to a variety of the latest weaponry, from nuclear submarines to jet aircraft and helicopters. Its standing low, the final blow came in August 1962 with the last flight of an airship at Lakehurst, ending forty-six years of the Navy's LTA involvement.

❖ ❖ ❖

"If the Boeings and Airbuses of the world had put all that money into airships, who knows what the future might be?" asks Joel Mokyr, an economic historian at Northwestern University. Yet, civilian and military organizations continue to demonstrate significant interest in the endurance and diverse capabilities of airships. In many respects, LTAs are getting a long-overdue makeover.

For more than ninety years, Goodyear has proven that blimps remain enormously successful marketing tools—precisely because of their unconventional appearance. Despite the cost—up to $21 million a pop, plus pilots, ground crews and expensive helium fill-ups—the Akron-based company remains committed to these flying billboards. In recent years, Goodyear, which made more than 300 airships— more than anyone else—began replacing its fleet of iconic blimps with three state-of-the-art dirigibles produced by the German firm Zeppelin. Although the new craft are semi-rigid, hence, technically not blimps, these recent acquisitions will still be called *blimp*.

"The term *Goodyear Blimp* is so universally recognized that the company is proud to have it continue, regardless of any technical difference," says Goodyear spokesman Doug Grassian. The first new airship, named *Wingfoot One*, made its initial flight on Saint Patrick's Day, 2014. So far it's been smooth sailing.

Elsewhere, others are convinced that airships can be much more than aerial advertisements in the sky. For "balloonatics," there has never been a shortage of futuristic designs for new military and civilian uses: nuclear blimps, stealth blimps, radar blimps, unmanaged blimps.

Defense contractors, in particular, have spent decades designing football-field-long, helium-filled blimps with sophisticated radar that can track planes, trains, automobiles—especially missiles. Yet one by one, the projects have floated away, victims of missed budgets and deadlines. Four years ago, for instance, the US Army shelved its $517 million program for a high-tech surveillance blimp that was supposed to provide troops in Afghanistan with everything from live video of militants to recordings of clandestine telephone conversations. Arizona Senator John McCain singled out the grant as a sign that the Pentagon was "still dominated by a culture of inefficiency." In October 2015, an unmanned military-surveillance blimp broke free from its mooring at an Army facility in Maryland to eventually collapse in central Pennsylvania—causing major power outages for thousands of residents.

Despite these setbacks, a small cadre of dirigible dreamers presses ahead with space-age versions of these lumbering contraptions. Inside a World War II-era blimp hangar in Tustin, California, sits a colossally ambitious attempt to revitalize the airship. Pilots are training for the next test flight of an Aeroscraft prototype, built by the Monterey, California-based Worldwide Aeros Corp. The project is the brainchild of Kazakhstan-born Igor Pasternak, who immigrated to the United States in 1994 and who hopes to produce a 770-foot-long, silver-skinned version. Kept aloft by helium, the ship could deliver fresh fruit to Alaska, drop triage units at disaster sites and deposit heavy machinery into remote locations. No ports, rail lines, roads or airstrips required.

Flying at speeds up to 140 miles per hour and able to travel 5,870 miles on a tank of fuel, the Aeroscraft will take off and land like a helicopter. As for financing, much of the ship's development costs have been covered by US government contracts and, to a lesser extent, private sources. The project has had its setbacks. Two years ago, part of the hangar roof collapsed, seriously damaging a smaller prototype. Yet, the patient Pasternak remains convinced that his airship could transform shipping the way the Internet changed communications.

Elsewhere, other starry-eyed inventors are designing sleek new airships that could float above layers of cloud and chart a course through the thin, icy air of the stratosphere, 65,000 feet above the ground—twice the usual altitude of a commercial jetliner. Unmanned, but steered by scientists on the ground, these ships could be equipped with onboard telescopes that peer into distant galaxies or gather oceanic data along a coastline.

"Stratospheric airships could give us space-like conditions from a space-like platform, but without the space-like costs," Sarah Miller, an astrophysicist at the University of California, Irvine, told *The New York Times*. An early version of the Hi-Sentinel blimp, based in San Antonio, first steered through the stratosphere successfully in 2005. Since then, other test ships have performed effectively. But funding for the unique craft remains tight. The Keck Institute for Space

Studies at Caltech is considering a prize for the first civilian team to build a better stratospheric airship.

One hundred fifty years ago, Victor Hugo romanticized that lighter-than-air flight had liberated mankind from the "tyranny of gravity." He further predicted that these glorious gasbags would lead to the abolition of frontiers and wars. Unfortunately, the résumé of airships has been littered with similar dreams that have crashed and burned. Perhaps we should heed the warning of the Chinese proverb: "The miracle is not to fly in the air, or to walk on the water, but to walk on the earth."

No doubt, skeptics abound, and no one wants to finance—or be on board—the next *Hindenburg*. Yet, airship proponents believe that futuristic technology could rescue these underdogs of the air from oblivion. Going forward, the obstacles are not technical; they are psychological and financial—and getting people to take them seriously.

❖ ❖ ❖

Former celebrity chef Iva Kinimaka traded in his popular brick-and-mortar restaurant for the Hawaiian Grinds food truck.

CHAPTER 9

MEALS ON WHEELS

"You can't beat our meat."

—Slogan on a Philadelphia food truck

T HE AROMA OF GARLIC CHICKEN from Iva Kinimaka's
kitchen in Honolulu's Sand Island industrial district is in
the air. Inside his Hawaiian Grinds food truck, the seventy-
five-year-old "Singing Chef" single-handedly turns out an
array of punchy, fresh and textured Hawaiian plate lunches selling
for a reasonable six to eight dollars. Besides his garlic chicken and
pork dishes, Kinimaka's most popular items are the Tutu Special
(smoked ham and kalua pig) and Tita Special (hamburger steak and
mushroom chicken). "On Fridays," he says, "I serve up my 'broke
da mouth' plate, complete with chicken long rice, squid luau, the
works." In addition to his culinary magic, Kinimaka will belt out
almost any tune at the drop of a hat. Small wonder that hundreds of
white- and blue-collar regulars line up at his battered white wagon,
parked on a nondescript side street.

Kinimaka was ten when he discovered cooking, an interest his
mother encouraged. It was later, while headlining as an entertainer
in Waikiki, that Iva opened his first lunch wagon at popular Sandy
Beach. Catering opportunities soon followed as the wiry part-
Hawaiian served up food and entertainment to the growing cruise

ship industry. Today, a throng of loyal fans and supporters continue to flock to Hawaiian Grinds.

Although Kinimaka also has had his share of bricks-and-mortar restaurants, he prefers the independence and simplicity of meals on wheels. "Operating a food truck is easy for me," he told *MidWeek*'s Mufi Hannemann. "I can do it all by myself. I love the creative aspect of cooking—to be able to come up with new recipes and more items—and to talk story with my customers."

But for all his sidewalk success, you won't find Iva Kinimaka in *Bon Appétit* or on the Food Network. Nor can he be found pitching skillets or cookbooks on QVC. The unassuming septuagenarian is the antithesis of the celebrity chef and Michelin-star restaurateurs. He is among the growing ranks of culinary trailblazers—men and women who labor daily in America's expanding food truck industry. Seventy-eight percent of these folks, like Kinimaka, employ four or fewer employees. On average, they work ten to twelve hours a day, and many hold other jobs.

Of course, mobile vendors have been around for years. In 1866, Texas cattle rancher Charles Goodnight modified a sturdy old US Army wagon with a kitchen and stocked it with easy-to-serve foodstuffs. Just six years later, Walter Scott cut windows into a small covered wagon, parked it in front of a Providence, Rhode Island, newspaper office and sold sandwiches, pies and coffee to journalists and pressmen working late.

"Lunch wagons," as food trucks were then known, soon spread. By the late 1880s, former lunch-counter boy Thomas Buckley was manufacturing them in Worcester, Massachusetts. Many were colorfully appointed and included sinks, refrigerators and cooking stoves. In just three decades, meals on wheels were becoming a fancy.

Fast forward to the 1950s, when numerous mobile canteens appeared on US military bases. They soon morphed into today's food trucks, initially serving construction sites, factories and other blue-collar locations. Typically they were concentrated in big cities, offering a quick bite at affordable prices to those on the go. However, as the suburbs grew in size and scope, others needed meals in places where restaurants were scarce. "'Roach coach' vending trucks, the kind with shiny aluminum sides, filled that market niche," writes

Daniel Engber of *The New York Times*

Over the years, food trucks continued to pop up, especially in response to a sputtering economy. Restaurants were extraordinarily expensive businesses to open and maintain; trucks were far cheaper and less risky. The barriers to entry were low, and rather than being confined to a single location, a mobile vendor could drive to a new venue if the business turned south. Customers, too, continued to seek inexpensive breakfasts and lunches. White- and blue-collar employees were pressed for time, with tougher workloads and shorter lunch breaks. These forces gave further impetus to the mobile-food movement.

The major hang-up was consumer confidence. Americans naturally had an aversion to "street meat," thinking of it as lower quality and lower standard than a traditional sit-down restaurant. But in recent years, those images have begun to change dramatically. The food truck industry has been experiencing a major upgrade in response to a combination of post-recessionary factors: changing consumer preferences for affordable, healthy food, new lifestyle choices and demographic shifts.

The trend toward healthier fare, coupled with an increasing preference for high-quality chow, has convinced more and more mobile entrepreneurs to introduce fresh, organic options from locally sourced produce. Add to this the rising popularity of ethnic cuisine, driven by the growing number of immigrants and a generally more adventurous American palate, which encourages many street vendors to offer an ever-growing assortment of ethnic and fusion cuisine. Today, food trucks are not your father's lowbrow, roach coaches serving up greasy burgers and bad dogs. These hidden heroes now represent "a respectable venue for aspiring chefs to launch careers," reports *New York Magazine*.

Although the goal of these gastronomic chariots is to be quick, convenient and cheap, they are decidedly anti-fast food. Gourmet food trucks, operated by ambitious chefs, peddle fresh sushi, Korean-barbecue tacos, red velvet cupcakes, specialty crepes and hundreds of other tasty dishes that combine different types of cuisine for anyone in search of affordable, eclectic, local eats. "They're about dispensing Alice Waters food in a McDonald's manner," says *TIME* magazine's Joel Stein, referring to the famed restaurateur at Chez Panisse in Berkeley, California.

New technology has been another big game changer, allowing trucks not only to move to where their customers are but enabling owners to cultivate the crucial element of community. By using devices such as Facebook, Twitter and YouTube, food trucks have created a sense of being locally connected. During this transition, savvy operators, says food expert Zachary Sniderman, "began talking to their customers, building what digital markets call 'brand loyalty.' That brand loyalty also played into the food truck ethos of 'community first.' Social outreach helped to grow these communities and make them feel more participatory."

Food blogging, of course, is the bane to many office bosses— the scourge of local workplace productivity. When a Twitter feed, for example, goes out for a trendy truck, legions of nine-to-fivers typically leave behind their privacy-challenged cubicles and dash into the fresh air for Shanghai-style soup dumplings, chicken marsala burritos or other tasty treats.

None of these changes have been lost on struggling restaurateurs. In view of the last financial crisis, experienced owners, along with unemployed chefs, have been hesitant to drop serious cash into a new or revamped sit-down establishment. Accordingly, more and more of them, even some of the most haughty, have felt the timing was right for a pivot, turning to moveable rigs as a cheap alternative to make up for their lost earnings.

Today, food trucks are the hallmark of hip. Some are even Zagat rated. They represent local, fresh, fusion and hip fare all in one convenient dining experience. Survey results conducted by Lafayette, California, consultants firm Emergent Research found that food truck customers like the fare and enjoy the experience. More than ninety percent of diners surveyed described street eats as excellent (forty-three percent) or good (forty-eight percent). They particularly appreciated the speed and convenience of mobile service, and almost every respondent said they planned to continue patronizing food trucks.

No surprise then that the mobile food industry is growing. According to another research firm, New York-based IBISWorld, in the past five years food truck sales nationwide grew at an annual rate of 9.3 percent, to $857 million, as the trend spread to cities from

Los Angeles to Boston. By contrast, traffic to conventional fast food outlets was flat, while traffic to mid-tier family restaurants declined over the same period.

In many respects, the food truck phenomenon represents what sociologists Todd Schifeling and Daphne Demetry call "the new authenticity economy"—a trend toward creating unique, eclectic and artisanal products. Think, too, craft breweries and farmers' markets.

Authenticity is definitely at the heart of another Honolulu-based mobile concept called Banán. Its brightly painted van specializes in a dessert made from one thing: frozen, locally grown bananas. The dairy-free, sugar-free, gluten-free dessert—similar in consistency to frozen yogurt—is creamy, sweet and smooth. If you aren't crazy about bananas, don't fret, they have other flavors on the menu. Fruits and herbs are added to the blended banana base to create options such as acai, pineapple, coconut, basil and ginger mint.

Banán is the brainchild of four graduates of Punahou School, whose more illustrious alums include Barack Obama, Steve Case and Michelle Wie. Matt Hong, Luke Untermann, Zak Barry and Galen McCleary reunited in the Islands after attending college on the US mainland. After discovering that Hawaii was one of the few states that commercially grows bananas, the four amigos moved home to launch the venture with the goal that they not only would make a buck, but also would help promote sustainability in the Aloha State. The company's stated mission: "To provide Hawaii a healthy, wholesome, and affordable meal made from fresh produce picked right from the Islands."

Setting up shop on Monsarrat Avenue on the secluded backside of Diamond Head, Banán opened for business in January 2015. Customers soon began to devour their deliciously cool treats on the run, or they would relax in lounge chairs or at picnic tables in the parking lot. They get their Banán three ways: a scoop in a cup for four dollars; a boat-a-mondo scoop in a half papaya for seven dollars; or a full bowl, a big serving of the stuff served with sliced bananas and puffed quinoa for nine dollars. My favorite: basil in a papaya boat topped with shaved coconut, puffed quinoa and more bananas. What's more, the creamy banana base doesn't melt into a drippy mess like ice cream or frozen yogurt, because bananas at room temperature are just...bananas.

Open daily from 9 a.m. to 5 p.m., Banán is attracting a growing following of health-conscious folks to its tiny stretch of asphalt. The *Honolulu Star-Advertiser* recently regaled the concept as one of "5 Things We Love"—a short list of newly discovered items to see, hear, wear or eat.

The homegrown entrepreneurs not only are satisfying a healthy craving, but caring for the *aina* (earth) and supporting local industry. Almost all of the fruit and ingredients used are sourced in Hawaii, with a freshness you can taste. As important, the founders are dedicated to giving back to the community. Their philosophy is farm-to-table, table-to-farm. Banán uses biodegradable utensils and bowls. In addition, all compostable materials, from banana peels to empty papayas, are donated to nearby farms to be reclaimed back into the soil.

It's safe to say that innovative street offerings like Banán's would probably not have existed without the pioneering efforts of forty-six-year-old Roy Choi, the acknowledged "King of the Streets." Most food critics credit the former Los Angeles street thug (who goes by "Papi") and law school dropout with demonstrating that good food can go trucking.

In late 2008, Choi's company, Kogi (Korean for "meat"), started selling two-dollar Korean tacos (a now popular combination of meat and Korean toppings wrapped in a tortilla) from a single food truck parked outside nightclubs on Sunset Boulevard. At the time, the only other food trucks on LA streets were classic "launcher" Mexican taco and catering clunkers that served day laborers and club kids desperate for anything at 2 a.m. But by sending out Twitter alerts to a growing number of converts to his adventurous, new cuisine, Choi revolutionized the food truck industry. He quickly proved that high-end street eats were no fluke and popularized meals on wheels.

Who knew at the time that the most influential LA restaurant would be a truck? But here we are now—eight years later—as hundreds of people still line up for Choi's mashup Korean and Mexican food. Roy has reached first-name-only celebrity chef status. His sprawling empire includes Kogi, with four trucks and outlets in an LA area nightclub and LAX's Terminal 4; restaurants (Chego, Sunny Spot, A-Frame, to name three); a new healthy fast food cafe (part soup kitchen, part hangout); a cookbook/memoir, *L.A. Son*; a hotel, the Line; and a new CNN.com series called *Street Food*, co-hosted with his mentor and pal Anthony Bourdain, who nominated him this year as one of the "100 Most Influential People" in *TIME* magazine.

Yet all roads lead back to Choi's Kogi trucks. "It's like my 'Sweet Caroline' and I'm Neil Diamond," the food truck guy turned culinary mogul told *The Los Angeles Times*, "I'll never be able to outlive Kogi. Kogi is a beast."

Roy Choi was born in South Korea and migrated to the United States before he was two years old. His parents ran a variety of businesses, from a liquor store and a dry cleaner to a Korean restaurant and a jewelry company. As their fortunes gradually improved, they moved a dozen times through various Southern California neighborhoods that ranged from sketchy to posh.

Early on, Choi attended a gifted-students program, but eventually dropped out and began to rebel. At age thirteen, he ran away from home several times and started hanging out with a crowd of gangbangers. In a last-ditch attempt to save their son, his parents sent him off to military school. That followed a brief teaching stint in Korea and, later, a bachelor's degree in philosophy from California State University, Fullerton. To appease Mom and Dad, he next attended Western State University Law School, but quit after only a semester.

Then in his early twenties, Choi was in freefall—turning to booze, crack and gambling "to heal my broken spirit," he says. That led to weeks of detox. Finally, at age twenty-four, the self-acknowledged misfit "decided it was time to face the world and become part of society again." Strangely, his epiphany came via the tube, when he became hooked on foodie Emeril Lagasse's culinary show. "Emeril saved my life," Choi says, inspiring him to seek formal food training.

In 1996, with his father's reluctant approval, Choi enrolled in the prestigious Culinary Institute of America in Hyde Park, New York, and found it "fit like a glove." Benefiting from the program's rigorous structure and platoon of talented chefs, he began to temper his rebellious streak. To his credit, the reinvigorated student secured an "externship" at the famed French restaurant Le Bernardin in the Big Apple. "I was becoming a cook in New York City," he recalls proudly.

"And it felt fucking great."

In 2001, Choi returned to Los Angeles, slowly working his way up the food chain at Hilton Hotels. It was at the Beverly Hilton, the conglomerate's flagship, that he met his future partner, Mark Manguera, then a hotel food and beverage director. Manguera brainstormed the idea of a Korean taco with him after a night out on the town, and asked Choi to come up with a recipe. In short order, Roy conceived Kogi's specialty: heavily marinated Korean barbecue slung over tacos and tossed in the kind of decadent, mouth-watering sauces you'd expect for someone with a background in five-star cuisine.

To transport their flavor bombs, Choi and partners Manguera and his wife, Caroline Shin-Manguera, turned to the food truck—a roving symbol of rebellion, independence and their belief that excellent grub could be delivered on the streets at low prices. "I got tired of running big kitchens where I never got to touch the food," Choi recalls. But the very nature of mobile service reinforced his earlier forays into street life and enabled him to get close—literally—to the customer. "Food trucks changed my life," he says, "as a person and a chef."

It was slow going at first. The Kogi truck was more of a curiosity than anything else. Then one night in December 2008, his van pulled up outside UCLA dorms during final exams. Using Twitter, Choi began to get the word out to students. "Tasty Korean barbecue for just $2!" What he got was a flash mob—but with much better food.

"There were thousands of kids out there," Choi says. "It kind of created this urban myth and groundswell. Then we started going out to Rosemead and Venice. But UCLA was the turning point."

The first year of operation, Choi kept the menu simple—Korean short ribs, spicy pork, spicy chicken or tofu tucked into griddled corn tortillas with shredded cabbage and a Korean relish of scallions, soy, sesame seeds and citrus. Regulars kept coming back, and Kogi grossed about $2 million, from orders averaging roughly thirteen dollars a person. Profit margins approached twenty percent, which enabled Choi and the Mangueras to invest in more trucks and, later, restaurants...and more.

Soon after Kogi's launch, Korean tacos began popping up everywhere. Competitors' trucks—Bool, Bull Kogi and Calbi (now owned by the Baja Fresh chain)—offered their own versions of Korean fare. In short order, Los Angeles became the heart of what restaurant critic and Pulitzer Prize winner Jonathan Gold called "the food truck nation." Then, it was the Flying Pig, with its tamarind duck tacos; the rich, pressed sandwiches of the Grilled Cheese Truck; Tamales Elena, serving up hearty handmade masa tamales; or authentic Philly cheese steak sandwiches from the South Philly Experience. The City of Angels emerged as the hotbed of the street food movement.

Many other cities are participating in the food truck craze. New York, Washington, Miami, Portland and Austin are among the most prominent. In addition, a growing number of mobile devotees are diversifying in and out of traditional restaurants. For example, Akash and Rana Kapoor started Curry Up Now with a mission to bring the Indian street foods from their childhood to the San Francisco area. With no formal training and a huge appetite, they were able to turn one food truck into three successful restaurants.

In New York City, David Schiller is attempting to transfer his food truck experience to a fledgling sit-down empire. In 2010, he quit his six-figure salary to start a new career selling a blend of Mexican and barbecue food out of a retrofitted van on the streets of Manhattan. Interestingly, the idea came to him from none other than Roy Choi, while visiting a college friend in Los Angeles a year earlier. He saw the hordes of customers lined up to buy food from Kogi-branded trucks. It was his aha moment, as he decided to bring the concept east.

With a partner, Schiller bought a food truck for $80,000 off eBay, drew up a Mexican-barbecue menu and launched Mexico. Their ride was bumpy at first, battling new competitors and chased off by angry restaurateurs and cops. So the twosome decided to diversify into sit-down eateries. To date, they have three in Manhattan, with plans to open at least two new units a year.

Most industry pundits are skeptical about the food truck to bricks-and-mortar transition. Julia Gallo-Torres of marketing research firm Mintel questions its viability. "A lot of food truck start-ups just remain food trucks," she says. "It's a cheap way to get into the restaurant business." But running a burgeoning series of restaurants brings with it its own set of serious challenges—financial and otherwise—that most mobile venders simply don't want to deal with.

For expansion-minded food-truckers, the preferable option remains organic growth, adding more rigs to the existing business. In 2008, for example, Natasha Case and Freya Estreller started baking cookies, making ice cream and combining them into architecturally inspired "cool houses." Their Coolhaus ice cream sandwiches made their debut a year later in a renovated postal van at California's famous Coachella Valley Music and Arts Festival. With inventive flavors such as "Whiskey Lucky Charms" and "Chocolate Chipotle BBQ with Jack Daniels," the Los Angeles-based gourmet ice cream maker has been on a roll—literally. Today, Coolhaus operates a national fleet of eleven trucks, two bricks-and-mortar storefronts and more than 2,500 retail partner stores in forty-plus states, as well as the Philippines and the Cayman Islands.

"Right now the US economy is all about small business and entrepreneurial start-ups," says food consultant Sonja Rasula, citing Coolhaus' expansion to include multiple trucks and concepts. "They're hiring people. They're growing at rapid speed and adding to the economy."

Besides adding vans, the more affluent mobile operators have also plunged into catering. Today, roughly twenty percent of their revenues come from special events, such as picnics, parties and fairs. Catering allows food truckers to reduce the risks of excessive inventories, since they only have to cook and deliver specifically ordered quantities. Because many catered functions are indoors, inclement weather isn't a problem.

In addition, food truck rallies are gaining popularity across the country. These are gatherings where foodies can find their favorite trucks in one convenient setting. In 2010, Shawna Dawson and Sonja Rasula created the first LA Street Food Fest, showcasing the city's best mobile operators. A whopping 20,000 fans waited for up to two hours for lamb roti roll-ups, Texas barbecue and Greek sausages. That led to a series of successful repeat performances. No doubt, Los Angeles' al fresco-friendly weather, the tradition of "launcher" trucks and the diverse blend of cultures contribute to the festival's huge crowds.

"The truck model is fantastic," Rasula says. "The mobility of it all, going to where people are and waiting for you to come to them." And, of course, the latest tweeting trucks are able to receive instantaneous feedback from their fans, and make the appropriate menu changes.

Based on the ever-increasing number of applications for future events, Dawson predicts that street food festivals are "just the tip of the iceberg." So, too, does Tampa Bay's Todd Stutz, a civil engineer by training and an enthusiastic supporter of his city's growing food truck scene.

In September 2011, he began organizing Tampa's first food fair. Compared to its Los Angeles cousin, the Florida event was on training wheels. Initially, Stutz capped the number of trucks at just ten to fit on the cramped grounds of a local church. Nevertheless, the festival drew more than 3,000 people, with some lined up more than an hour to buy food from vendors, who quickly sold out. The following year, Tasting Tampa attracted more than 4,000 customers from vans selling everything from gourmet popsicles to fresh sushi.

The rallies have been a godsend for truckers. "We've only been open six weeks, so this was a great way to get people out here," notes Heidi Nagle, owner of Fat Tortillas, a van selling Southwest cuisine. Consumers also gobbled up the upscale food at street food prices. "It's fun to look for something out of the ordinary," says Roberto Coccia, fifty-nine, who drove with his wife from Clearwater to attend. "These [mobile vendors] are creative, young and industrious. And we like to support young entrepreneurs."

Creating a positive environment for entrepreneurs is also the endgame of Poni and Brandon Askew. Half a world away, their Honolulu-based company, Street Grindz, is the premier resource for the mobile food community in the Islands. Whether it's staging major food events, providing full-service catering for private gatherings or offering vendor consulting for those thinking of starting a food truck operation, the company's track record is unmatched. Their monthly Eat The Street rallies, for instance, regularly attract more than 7,000 people eager to sample the best street eats in Hawaii. Every third Saturday of the month, the Honolulu Night Market blends a selected group of mobile vendors with some of the state's hottest fashion designers—all in a 5,000-square-foot warehouse. As for special events, Chevron,

Hawaiian Airlines, the City and County of Honolulu and the NFL Pro Bowl are just a few of the satisfied clients.

In its biggest initiative to date, Street Grindz was recently awarded the use of thirty acres of prime oceanfront property owned by the Office of Hawaiian Affairs. In this iconic location, the former site of Fisherman's Wharf, the company is committed to building "a community marketplace like no other." From its inventory of 250 mobile vendors, Street Grindz has begun to identify a mouth-watering mix of up to forty food trucks and pop-up concepts that will rotate periodically.

Makers and Tasters "will be run very much like a cooperative," forty-two-year-old Poni, a former Starbucks regional manager, tells me. "We believe that passionate local entrepreneurs are the key to creating a sustainable future, and we will do everything in our power to assist them." Mobile vendors, for their part, will receive an outstanding venue with eye-popping views, ample parking and a range of services, from signage design to security. They will also draw off of Street Grindz' social network of more than 30,000 followers.

Eventually, the Askews plan to develop five more mobile marketplaces on Oahu and eventually expand to the Neighbor Islands. To complement this effort, Street Grindz recently opened a food truck academy, complete with a formal certification process. "That's our future," Poni says, hoping to upgrade this underappreciated and, in Hawaii, often underperforming industry. Food trucks in the Aloha State average an anemic $600 to $700 a day. "That's totally unacceptable," she says. "By contrast, decently located vans in Los Angeles can crank out $5,000 to $6,000." Looking ahead, the Askews believe Makers and Tasters can double or triple vendor revenues.

In a parallel trend, street eats are going global. In virtually every major city in the world, entrepreneurs are taking to the road to try out their food ideas. Take Tokyo, where co-operative truck groups have banded together to feed Japan's hungry masses. One of the largest and best established is Neo-Stall Village. Its "villages" feature up to 300 food trucks in several registered locations in greater Tokyo. Every operator is registered, licensed and insured.

Unlike packaged bentos, Neo-sponsored food trucks cook and

sell hot meals on site. "You can see the kitchen," says one loyal customer, insisting that she has no inhibitions about the quality of the street food. Plus, the food is affordable, with most lunches priced at around six dollars. Great eats on the go have become the buzz in Japan. "Finally, lunch trucks are more socially recognized here," says a Neo spokesperson.

Down Under, Aussies are also warming up to street eats. In Melbourne, Rafael Rashid's Beatbox Kitchen and Taco Truck are satisfying a growing appetite for mobile service. Like many others, his biggest challenge was debunking the myth that street food was low quality. But after seven years on the road, Rashid has a devoted clientele.

So, too, for Stuart McGill, whose Eat Art Trucks roam Sydney's streets. Fan favorites include pulled pork in a bun with barbecue sauce, Japanese pepper-seasoned chicken wings and a Korean-style lettuce wrap with twice-cooked beef. A few miles away, a fleet of Cantina Mobiles serves up healthy Mexican fare. "Our high-quality offerings separate us from the questionable fast food chains that have long dominated Australia," says co-founder and former restaurateur Stephanie Raco. "People are excited on many levels."

Believe it or not, the artisanal food truck has even come to Paris, the birthplace of culinary haughtiness. Four years ago, American-style trucks selling restaurant-quality food began appearing on local streets for notoriously food-fussy Parisians. Among them: La Cantine California offering tacos stuffed with organic meat, and Le Camion Qui Fume (The Smoking Truck), a hugely popular burger van owned by French-trained Californian Kristin Frederick.

Street food itself isn't new to France. Traditional vendors hawking snacks ranging from pizzas to spicy Moroccan sausages have been around for some time. "But the notion of street food made by chefs, using restaurant-grade ingredients, technique and technology, is very new indeed," reports Julia Moskin of *The New York Times*.

But American—not French—chefs managed to get the first food trucks rolling. It wasn't easy. "I got every kind of push-back," says Frederick. "People said: 'The French will never eat on the street or with their hands. They will never pay money for food from a truck. And you will never get permission from the authorities.'"

Nonetheless, the feisty thirty-one-year-old Yank soldiered on. From day one, she has sold every last burger on every shift. At first, her clientele was primarily US expatriates. But, over time, she—and other American food truck operators—have been winning over French millennials. "Food trucks are a new culinary trend and most get real recognition as part of French gastronomy," Paris Mayor Anne Hidalgo says. Now one finds food trucks in half of the city's *arrondissements*.

Picking up on the globalization trend is highly respected Dorothy Cann Hamilton. In 1984, she started the French Culinary Institute (now the International Culinary Center) in New York, and began recruiting renowned chefs. She served as president of the Friends of the USA Pavilion at Expo Milano 2015. The theme was "Feeding the Planet, Energy for Life." The event attracted "the brightest-thinking people from over 140 countries," she told *The New York Times*. A main attraction of the 35,000-square-foot, Milan-based pavilion were six food trucks serving iconic, regional American foods, from lobster rolls to barbecue.

Whether at home or abroad, food trucks are roaring through their glory days. Does it sound simple? Before jumping on the bandwagon, experienced mobile vendors suggest potential operators ask themselves the following questions:

• How well have I researched the industry? Successful entrepreneurs spend hours reading guides and articles about mobile vending and contacting as many existing truckers as possible. Where will you operate your vans? In what cities or counties? Do they permit food trucks? What are the competitive dynamics in your particular food specialty?

Carefully consider your concept and brand. Try to soak up as much information as you can before making a decision.

• How much does it cost to start a truck? Typically, a mobile van outfitted with a fully loaded kitchen ranges in price from about $50,000 to $250,000, depending on whether the vehicle is new or used, as well as the type of cooking equipment installed. Add to that food supplies, fuel, parking, insurance and truck maintenance fees.

• Can you handle the heat? Operating food trucks takes a lot of hard work. A typical day starts three or four hours before hitting the road, after you've bought the necessary provisions and prepped them. "I try to get my trucks ready to go by 10:30 a.m.," says LA-based vendor Jonathan Salvatore. "Get there by 11:30 a.m. Then serve lunch, come back, restock and go out again—hitting the bars and the late-night scene."

The work is tiring, and the day is long. Most mobile operators labor at least ten to twelve hours daily. Then there are the lucrative, but labor-intensive, weekend events.

• Do you know the rules and regulations? Cities and state have myriad, often Byzantine laws regulating when and how long food trucks can park on public streets and even public property. New Orleans, for example, insists that mobile food vendors change locations after forty-five minutes in one spot, among other restrictions. Municipalities also require food truck operators to obtain annual permits and licenses before they can do business. Stringent health and food safety requirements with surprise inspections are commonplace. The list goes on.

• Are you prepared for bricks-and-mortar backlash? For some time, a street fight has been brewing between food truck vendors and restaurants. Retail operators complain vociferously that their profits are threatened by the presence of food trucks. As a result, politicians and bureaucrats across the country have put speed bumps—even walls—in the way of mobile vendors. Among these are tough laws that restrict where vans can serve customers in proximity to their sit-down rivals.

Despite the hurdles, the enormous size of the food industry—roughly $700 billion in revenue—allows room for savvy entrepreneurs to establish themselves, grab a bit of market share and, as Roy Choi and others demonstrate, stand up for what they believe in.

There used to be a time when food trucks were looked down upon. But, in the past few decades, they have slowly escaped from the gustatory underbrush and emerged as a go-to destination for healthy, affordable eats. Still, some suggest that their growing popularity could lead to oversaturation. "Like any other field, there will be a shakeout," predicts food expert Sonja Rasula. "But the truckers who have the best food and the best practices will continue to thrive and grow."

❖ ❖ ❖

Bestselling author Sally Collings also serves as an invisible wordsmith for would-be writers.

CHAPTER 10

GHOST STORIES

*"The height of cleverness is
to be able to conceal it."*

—François de La Rochefoucauld,
seventeenth-century French essayist

M*y Darling,*
A love letter, so they say, is a window on the soul. After
all these years the glass may have dimmed a little, but I
want you to know that the fire in my soul still burns as
brightly as the moment I first looked upon you.
With deep tenderness

❖ ❖ ❖

Love letters are the most intimate form of human
communication. Highly personal, they should reveal our inner soul
and inform our character. But in the above snapshot, an amoral
British publishing mogul created one of many audacious frauds—
commissioning Jennie Erdal to ghostwrite, among other things, his
letters of the heart. The extent of his deceit, unveiled in *Ghosting*,
the first book published under Erdal's own name, is truly jaw-
dropping.

In the early 1980s, the young Scottish translator was hired by
the flamboyant publisher, who she called Tiger because his office

"felt high-voltage and slightly dangerous." Lured to London, she began work editing Russian books. By degrees, Tiger co-opted her time and loyalty to the point where she ended up, twenty years later, producing a huge nonfiction book on women, two glossy novels, letters, speeches and hundreds of newspaper columns—all published under her patron's real name. All this for an enigmatic boss who wore crocodile shoes with purple and yellow socks, two gold watches on his right wrist and a platinum one on his left, timed each of his daily activities to the nearest five minutes, and ordered thousands of silver phallic key rings, believing they could save him from financial disaster.

In dealing with this "extraordinarily complex and charismatic character," Erdal tells us how she became seduced into becoming Tiger's "Minister of the Pen." She is equally candid in describing her motives for ghosting: money, a compulsion to please and a cloistered Scottish Presbyterian childhood that made the "irony and absurdity" of the job tolerable. Over the years, a number of people corresponded with the "author," unaware that the replies also came from a hired hand. "We made a great team," the egotistical Tiger often boasted. "And we did," Erdal admits.

As a willing partner in the fraud, the unacknowledged author— and, in some mysterious sense, his alter ego—says she "learned a great deal about vanity, the desire to belong, the lengths a man will go to be something other than himself. And the lengths a woman will go in colluding with the pretense."

After two decades of laboring in the shadows, Erdal ended her tryst with literary codependency. "I was finding it hard to keep everything afloat," she explains in her memoir, "the pretense, the masquerade, the constant magnifying of an ego." Lying to others and lying to herself had taken its toll. So Erdal decided to give up the ghost. She returned to Scotland, her reputation intact.

"No one respects a talent that is concealed," noted Dutch theologian Erasmus. In 2012, less than a decade after leaving London, Erdal brought those talents to bear with *The Missing Shade of Blue*, her first work of fiction under her own name. Moving, witty and wise, the book is a philosophical adventure of an inhibited translator, a bombastic academic and his enigmatic wife. "This is a writer of rare assurance and intelligence," *The Daily Telegraph* wrote in its glowing review. "Jennie Erdal is a name to watch for."

Nowadays, Erdal shuns the ghosting game. She is one of a group of authors who views the practice as shady, fraudulent, even repulsive—not unlike being a paid assassin. "Literary Lance Armstrongs," one critic calls ghosters, vilifying any wordsmith who permits someone else to take the credit for his or her work. Yet more and more writers, as well as their readers, have long abandoned any romanticized view of authorship.

"I think the idea of an isolated writer drinking whiskey in a garret and not coming out until he's finished a book is a notion that doesn't exist anymore," says Joel Hochman, co-founder of Arbor Books, which advertises itself as a "world-class ghostwriting company." Modern society has institutionalized ghostwriting as an established practice, and labeled its practitioners as hidden heroes. As a practical matter, not everyone can be a J.K. Rowling or a David McCullough. Short of being a perennial best seller, ghosting is one of the few ways to earn a very decent living writing full-time. Many authors for hire are thriving today.

"Money does not make you happy," Irish playwright Sean O'Casey reminded us, "but it quiets the nerves." Such is the lot of these skilled professionals.

❖ ❖ ❖

Ghostwriting, of course, is not new. "It might almost qualify as the oldest profession if prostitution had not laid prior claim," writes Erdal. "And there is more than a random connection between the two." There is an upfront fee for services rendered and both the client or the provider keep their activities under the covers.

Creative stand-ins have been around in a variety of fields. According to Harold Bloom, God had a ghostwriter. A number of papal encyclicals were written by invisible authors. Wolfgang Amadeus Mozart was paid to write music for wealthy patrons. Mark Twain, who edited and published the memoir of Ulysses S. Grant, is said to have ghostwritten much of it as well. And H.P. Lovecraft ghostwrote *Imprisoned with the Pharaohs* for Harry Houdini in the 1920s. But while hired hands have crafted all sorts of content for centuries, none perfected the production of "ghost stories" better than Edward L. Stratemeyer.

In the early to mid-1900s, Stratemeyer's writing syndicate emerged as, in the eyes of one critic, "the most important single influence in American juvenile literature." On the backs of crafty ghostwriters, he mass-produced more than 1,300 books, sold over 500 million copies and created many well-known characters such as the Hardy Boys, Nancy Drew, the Bobbsey Twins, the Rover Boys and others. Shortly after his death in 1930, *Fortune* magazine stated: "As oil had its Rockefeller, literature had its Stratemeyer."

The son of middle-class German immigrants, Edward Stratemeyer was born in 1862 in Elizabeth, New Jersey. As a youngster, he immersed himself in the popular books of the day, including those of Horatio Alger and William T. Adams, writers who penned beloved rags-to-riches tales of hardworking young Americans. After graduation from high school, Stratemeyer began writing juvenile fiction, often on wrapping paper in his family's tobacco shop. He was twenty-six when he sold his first story, "Victor Horton's Idea," to *Golden Days*, a popular boys magazine, for seventy-five dollars—roughly six times the standard weekly wage.

While working as a stationer, he began to churn out adventure stories under various pseudonyms at a prodigious rate to make ends meet. A few years later, he became editor of *Good News*, where his heroes Alger and Adams published their works.

Serendipity struck in 1898, when Alger wrote to Stratemeyer at *Good News* asking him to complete a story that he was too ill to finish. Stratemeyer completed the task and, at the request of the family, ghosted another ten of Alger's unfinished manuscripts for posthumous publication.

In 1899, the year of Alger's death, Stratemeyer also wrote *Under Dewey at Manila*, a novel on the Spanish-American War. The book was an immediate success, selling 6,000 copies. It transformed Stratemeyer "from an 'unknown author' to a writer of some renown," wrote biographer Trudi Johanna Abel.

On the heels of his success, the ambitious author now sought financial rewards. Impressed by the sales of his earlier Frank Merriwell short stories, he dashed off *The Rover Boys*, the schoolboy exploits of three prankster brothers who attend a military academy. The dime novels were a smash hit, selling more than six million copies by 1920. But Stratemeyer wanted more, sensing that America's boys—ten to sixteen, in particular—lusted for his brand of exciting adventure stories, not moralistic tomes disguised as mysteries.

"A wide awake lad has no patience [for the] namby-pamby," he wrote in a 1901 letter to one publisher. "He demands real flesh and blood heroes who do something." Stratemeyer's timing was superb. Literacy rates were rising, as advances in printing technologies and declining paper prices were creating a "culture of print." In addition, "the spread of primary education spawned a host of independent young readers, and juvenile fiction was on the verge of becoming hugely popular," explains Meghan O'Rourke in *The New Yorker*. To catch this wave, Stratemeyer began building an empire in the children's book industry. But this meant scaling up—and quickly.

In 1905, the clever businessman established the Stratemeyer Syndicate as a way to produce more literary material at a faster rate than he could achieve alone. Under an uncompromising formula, Stratemeyer insisted that publishers sell his titles for fifty cents, appearing only in hardback, with snappy illustrations and eye-catching covers. Breakeven was roughly 6,250 copies per book, based on a two-cents per copy royalty. To minimize the downside, the Syndicate released each series in a set of three books. That way, young readers didn't have to wait for a sequel if they liked the first book; the second and third volumes were already in print and waiting to be read. This strategy allowed the company to gauge the potential success of a particular series, with slow sellers easily pulled after the first three books.

Typically, Stratemeyer would offer a series to a potential publisher with several sample titles and brief summaries. If selected, he then would expand them into outlines, which were next turned over to a ghostwriter. From his earlier days at *Good News*, Stratemeyer had amassed a long list of subalterns, mostly journalists and freelancers, to flesh out the serial proposals he had started. These writers, in return, would churn out a 220-page, roughly 30,000-word manuscript in four to six weeks. He then checked their work for irregularities and made the appropriate tweaks.

Perhaps more important, Stratemeyer insisted on total ownership of the merchandise. Abolish all that royalty nonsense.

Writers, he reckoned, were always broke. So pay them a flat rate at the lowest possible figure, typically fifty to $250 a pop. And never, under any circumstance, permit a writer to sign his own name to a book. Give the authors a pseudonym that would remain anonymous, have it copyrighted and insist on the release of all rights to the company.

All the Syndicate's Hardy Boys books, for example, list Franklin W. Dixon as the author. There's only one problem: Franklin W. Dixon never existed. How about Leslie McFarlane? Maybe you never heard of him, but over the years he penned nineteen—including the first eleven—titles in the Hardy Boys series.

In 1926, Stratemeyer approached the young Canadian newspaperman to ghost *The Tower Treasure*, highlighting Frank and Joe Hardy, two innocent, suburban, fresh-faced, would-be sleuths. He provided an information sheet for guidance and the plot outline for the initial volume. In return, McFarlane hammered out the first Hardy Boys' escapade on his secondhand Underwood typewriter in a cabin in northern Ontario. For his twenty-five-chapter manuscript, the author got $125.

Although McFarlane's efforts would eventually sell millions of copies and be translated into fifty languages, he received no royalties. But as an underpaid reporter for *The* [Springfield, Massachusetts] *Republican*, he needed the dough. "His major focus was money," explains Carl Spadoni, the retired manager of the McFarlane archives at McMaster University in Canada.

Stratemeyer would give her father an outline, recalls daughter Norah McFarlane Perez. "But to make it palatable, he'd inject his wonderful sense of humor. And then he'd finish and say, 'I will never write another juvenile book.' But then the bills would pile up and he'd start another."

Over the years, McFarlane received an estimated $5,000 from the Syndicate. But even a small percentage of the royalties would have made him wealthy. "It's kind of sad," his son, Brian, reflects. "We never owned a car. The house was rented and a little chilly. But we never thought we were poor."

Leslie McFarlane, for his part, showed no rancor. "I was not swindled," he later said. "I accepted the terms of Edward Stratemeyer, and the importance of the money was related to my needs. I was free to reject any of the assignments. Writing is not a profession in which one embarks under duress. No one forces anyone to become a writer." While the quality of many of Stratemeyer's hired guns varied, the self-effacing McFarlane was generally considered the best of the lot.

But, eventually, he got "pretty bored" with the Hardy Boys and regarded the assignments as "a nuisance." So McFarlane moved on to other projects—from novels and novellas to film scripts and television documentaries. His work ethic was prodigious. One year, he produced six novels—300,000 words—sometimes turning out a complete book in three or four weeks. Yet, it was Frank and Joe Hardy that largely defined the hyper-productive Canadian. "He left a wonderful legacy," says son Brian. "He got millions of kids hooked on reading."

A year before his death, the anonymous author went public. In his 1976 autobiography *The Ghost of the Hardy Boys*, he threw caution to the wind, informing the world of his role in their creation.

Besides McFarlane, sixteen others ghosted the fifty-eight titles in the original Hardy Boys mysteries, published between 1927 and 1979. Stratemeyer always had a block-long lineup of eager candidates waiting to join his literary bandwagon. By 1929, the entrepreneur's creativity and assembly-line techniques were producing thousands of books in multiple volumes that dominated the juvenile market. Thirty-one series were in full swing. Then came his next big idea: an adventure series for young women, the counterpart to the Hardy Boys books. He would call his strong-headed detective Nancy Drew, and the fictitious author Carolyn Keene.

The series' first ghostwriter was a young college graduate named Mildred Wirt (later, Mildred Wirt Benson). The product of small-town Iowa, young Millie read everything she could get her hands on and soon began to pen her own stories. At age thirteen, her first article was published in *St. Nicholas,* a children's magazine. After high school and college, she went on to become the first woman to graduate from the University of Iowa's master's program in journalism. It was there that she began ghosting for Stratemeyer.

He sent Benson the outline for *The Secret of the Old Clock*, but at first found her manuscript to be "flip" and "too aggressive" for a female audience. Nonetheless, the Syndicate went on to publish the book in 1930. Unfortunately, Stratemeyer never got to see it, dying of a heart attack at sixty-seven.

From the start, the set sold better than any of the other Stratemeyer titles, overturning the then-conventional publishing notion that boys' books outsold girls'. Over the years, Benson wrote twenty-three of the first thirty Nancy Drew books under the Carolyn Keene pseudonym. Despite the series' success, ghosting for the Syndicate—still a mere $125 a book—remained a part-time job for Benson. Like many others, she was forced to turn to other writing projects to survive.

"I wrote from early morning to late night for a good many years," she later recalled. "One year, I wrote 13 full-length books and held down a job besides. That takes a good deal of work."

In 1953, Benson submitted her last Nancy Drew title, *The Clue of the Velvet Mask*. Whether it was bickering over fees or making unwanted revisions, her relationship with the Syndicate had soured. Nonetheless, she was proud of her time with the series. "I think Nancy Drew was the character girls were waiting for," she explained. "They were just waiting for someone to verbalize it."

Mildred Benson went on to write numerous children's books and short stories, often using various pseudonyms. She worked as a journalist in Ohio from 1944 to 2002, when she passed away at ninety-six. Though her identity remained shrouded for many years, a 1980 court case involving the Syndicate revealed the real Carolyn Keene. Fourteen years later, the University of Iowa hosted a Nancy Drew Conference in Benson's honor.

Edward Stratemeyer clearly understood the power of joint effort. "When it came to refining a catchy story," says Meghan O'Rourke, "two heads often proved to be better than one." Relying on hidden heroes like McFarlane and Benson, the father of the fiction factory saw the merits of "outsourcing," long before the term became popular. Now entering their ninth decade, the Hardy Boys and Nancy Drew have gone on to inspire children around the world to dream big and achieve success in life.

After Stratemeyer's death, his daughter, Harriet Stratemeyer Adams, took over the Syndicate. Although the business was scaled back, she continued to employ her father's assembly-line format and authored a number of titles in the Nancy Drew series. She died in

1982. Three years later, publishers Simon & Schuster acquired the Syndicate and, to this day, continue to produce the Hardy Boys and Nancy Drew.

Today, Stratemeyer's high-velocity methods are still popular in children's series. But as big-book dependency grows more intense each season, a number of successful adult authors have also followed suit. Former advertising executive turned author James Patterson, for example, employs a dozen "co-authors," who take his detailed outline, flesh it out, then turn it back to him for edits. Using this collaborative approach, Team Patterson cranks out a best seller every two or three months. Last year, nine of his novels hit *The New York Times* best-seller list. Over the years, his titles have sold more than 355 million copies, and he was the first person to crack one million e-books. According to *Forbes*, Patterson earned $95 million in 2015, making him the world's richest wordsmith.

Unlike the Stratemeyer model, however, Patterson's partners receive full attribution, with their names on the book jacket. In addition, they participate in the receipt of royalties and ancillary income. No shortchanging here.

Similarly, even in death, Tom Clancy's thrillers survive—thanks to a supporting cast of ersatz authors. His latest, *Tom Clancy Under Fire*, released two years after his passing, cites the author—in small print—as Grant Blackwood. Three more Clancy titles are soon expected. "It's anyone's guess who will write them," says Joe Queenan in *The Wall Street Journal*. "When you're publishing books beyond the grave, anything is possible."

Returning dead authors to life—with the help of a visible or invisible wordsmith—was the accepted tradition of V.C. Andrews' publisher, who produced an assortment of gothic family horror novels written by Andrew Neiderman since Andrews' death in 1986. So, too, for Robert Ludlum, whose thrillers continue to flow from the pen of Eric Van Lustbader, even though Ludlum passed in 2001.

In today's publishing world, the brand is everything. The actual writing is secondary. Fame sells books, and publishers value the importance of name recognition. From a corporate perspective, securing the rights to produce a book by a celebrity author "is the closest thing to a sure thing in book publishing," claims Alex Mayyasi in his blog *The Ghostwriting Business*. "Like television executives and venture capitalists, publishers are in the hits business. Each Harry Potter pays for many other books that don't sell well and register a loss."

Hilary Liftin knows the allure of celebrity power. The publishing industry veteran has been ghostwriting for ten years for A-listers such as Miley Cyrus, Tori Spelling, Tatum O'Neal, MacKenzie Phillips and three others who didn't give her official credit. "No one grows up thinking they are going to be a ghostwriter," she admits. But Liftin was always fascinated by the "plight" of celebrities, adding that "I feel a level of sympathy for the complexity of a life that is in the public eye."

As a ghostwriter, the talented forty-five-year-old brings to her craft the frequently forgotten notion that no one is born a celebrity. "It's something that comes upon them externally and that they want but also can't imagine," she explains. "So I try to make these celebrities very human, [and] make their problems accessible to readers."

Liftin worked in publishing in New York during her twenties ("I was working on e-books before e-books were viable," she told *The Daily Beast*). After penning two memoirs of her own, she moved to Los Angeles, and "just by sheer drive," landed a ghosting gig. That, in turn, led to more assignments. In short order, she realized "I was totally meant to do this," adding that she doesn't demand her name on book covers—opting instead for a credit on the title page. And she is discreet.

She recalls one of her clients joking with her after returning from a wildly successful book tour: "Guess how many people asked about you? Zero!" Liftin responded: "That's exactly as it should be. Nobody should buy a celebrity's book because my name is on it."

No tattletales here. Liftin remains tight-lipped about her clients. As a result, she says, "we develop a bond that never goes away," describing the ghostwriter's role as "equal parts therapist, editor, and close friend."

In 2015, she put her ghosting pen aside to write her first novel, *Movie Star by Lizzie Pepper*, the story of a young actress who finds herself in a failed marriage with a Hollywood megastar and cult member. For someone who had never written fiction before, Liftin received rave reviews. "I thought it was just compelling and entertaining and fascinating," ex-client Phillips said about the book. "I really enjoyed it. And I love that it's 'By Hilary Liftin.'"

But unlike Jennie Erdal, the multifaceted writer hasn't given up the ghost. She has a list of stars whose lives she hopes to capture. At the top: Caitlyn Jenner.

"There's certainly a high correlation between fame or infamy and commercial success," adds William Novak, another hidden hero, the scribe behind Lee Iacocca, Oliver North, Magic Johnson, Nancy Reagan and Tim Russert. "And I've made a living off that correlation." The publisher of George Stephanopoulos' memoir touted hiring Novak as if having an elite ghostwriter were a mark of prestige. In fact, many agreed that if Stephanopoulos had decided to write his own book, it would have been widely perceived as self-serving, a desperate grab at fame.

Which is why calling Liftin, Novak and others "ghostwriters" may just be a lingering habit. "The word is now a pure anachronism," journalist and author Jack Hitt argues in *The New York Times*. "Most ghosts are out of the attic and prefer names like 'collaborator' or 'co-author.'" The top performers get their names on the book jacket (albeit sometimes in tiny print) and routinely command big bucks (in Novak's case, anywhere from ten percent to fifty percent of the book advance, which can run into the millions). Industry experts estimates that, on any given week, somewhere between fifty percent and eighty percent of any nonfiction best-seller list was ghosted; fiction, perhaps half that amount.

Again, name recognition counts. Consumers buy the same authors again and again. When mega-selling author J.K. Rowling released her mystery novel *The Cuckoo's Calling* under a pseudonym, it failed to sell despite good reviews. But when word eventually got out that Rowling was the author, sales exploded.

No surprise then that *Time*'s Joe Klein (then at *Newsweek*) understood that his book, *Primary Colors*, stood a better chance of success with a celebrity name on the jacket. So he ghosted his own novel and created the most mysterious author of the time, Anonymous. After months of emphatic denials, the invisible wordsmith of this best-selling tale of political intrigue and deceit fessed up and admitted his true colors. Many readers were furious with Klein for hoodwinking them. They were beside themselves that the book's creator was not a famous person at all. He was just a writer.

"Authorship cannot be confirmed," wrote Penn Medical School professor and journalist John Edward Huth. Eventually, Joe Klein reached the same conclusion. But he may be the exception.

In today's world, it is an open secret in publishing books or even shorter pieces like articles and blog posts that the true "author" is a ghostwriter, a hired hand who receives little or no credit for the work produced. Time-constrained chief executives have a romanticized view of seeing their name in print. Politicians on the prowl lust for the opportunity to build their brand. Academics, imprisoned in a publish-or-perish world, seek help in becoming more productive. Celebrities see big dollar signs in potential best sellers. Consultants, too, view authorship as a way to boost their profile. Even hesitant public speakers contemplate engaging their own private Cyranos to ghostwrite toasts.

Does this mean that the art of writing has slipped so low that the craft must be outsourced to hired guns? Perhaps, but clearly the demand for gifted ghostwriters has never been higher. "There is plenty of work to go around," says ghosting star Kelly James-Enger. Moreover, nearly every book authored by a celebrity or politician is ghostwritten by a professional writer.

Using ghosts to produce self-serving political books, for instance, is so common that the HBO sitcom *Veep* satirized it. The vice president, played by Julia Louis-Dreyfus, can barely recognize anything mentioned in her book, which was written by a campaign aide and which she hasn't read.

"Ideally, you want a book to be authored by a true author," says editorial consultant Wendy Walker, "but today, with a lot of people [who write] celebrity books, you don't get the writing. You get the person." And nine times out of ten, that person doesn't know how to write a book or doesn't have the time to do so.

Writing a book is difficult, time consuming and, as George Orwell once put it, "a horrible, exhausting struggle." "Books are a huge amount of work," says Mark Sullivan, owner and director of Manhattan Literacy, a New York-area ghostwriting firm. "It takes a lot of experience. Some very capable people want books written but don't have the time or the expertise to do it."

For his firm's services, fees start at $15,000 per book, but the price can quickly escalate depending on its length and complexity. At 2M Communications Ltd., a ghostwriting matchmaker, Madeleine Morel says the average ghosting fees for a nonfiction book range from $40,000 to $70,000 per title. "But," she told me, "we've been able to secure a lot of six-figure fees for our writers." The New York-based firm represents more than 100 professionals, each one specializing in a nonfiction area, from business to parenting and history to multicultural topics. All have had multiple books published, including eighty *New York Times* best sellers.

"No kid ever grows up believing he wants to be a ghostwriter," says William Novak, agreeing with Hilary Liftin. "And as a writer, there are obviously things I want to do on my own. But this work can be seductive, very seductive indeed."

Typically, ghostwriters get a flat fee or a percentage of the advance with a guaranteed minimum. At 2M Communications, the house gets a fifteen percent commission of the writer's take. Net, the average ghostwriter's advance, is between $30,000 and $100,000, which is "a hell of a lot more than they can make on their own," says Morel.

However, elite ghostwriters—those contracted by publishing houses to produce a potential best seller—can score as much as $500,000 for their work. Do the math: Bill Clinton inked a $15 million advance for his memoir; Hillary, $8 million. That leaves mucho dinero for their literary helpers. Putting words in somebody's mouth definitely pays.

No tears then for the muse. "If the only true happiness comes from squandering ourselves for a purpose," as journalist John Mason Brown once suggested, it is likely more and more frustrated writers will turn to ghosting for a living.

Once stigmatized, ghosting is no longer a sub-craft of publishing. "It is a metaphor for all of publishing," says Jack Hitt. Today, it's widely accepted that the writing of a book is no longer the important part of authoring one. Despite its ubiquity, it's impossible to gauge ghosting's size, but Joel Hochman of Arbor Books says: "From what I've seen, I'd imagine [it's] a billion-dollar industry."

With so much camouflage, you can no longer tell who wrote a book by its cover. In what appears to be a Faustian bargain, most ghostwriters sign nondisclosure agreements that prohibit them from revealing the extent of their involvement or their remuneration. Forget transparency. Most literary surrogates must remain in the shadows; few receive a byline or the more dignified title of "contributor." They get no respect.

As a result, ghostwriters must deal with an identity problem. They may pen a million-dollar memoir, but they are unknown to most Americans. Hence, "they must have no ego," Morel says. They can't expect to be a fixture on talk shows or score front row tickets to Lakers games. All the kudos accrue to the credited author. Tough medicine for some writers.

Demian Farnworth, for example, was making a decent living ghosting five articles a week. "But there was one problem," he says. "Someone else got all the credit. See, I traded cash for credit. During this time, I discovered something about myself. I missed the attention, the recognition, the authority of having my name on the writing. In fact, after about three months, I was utterly depressed. Like, near suicidal."

Obviously, some writers are more adept at staying under the radar than others. Palo Alto, California-based Sally Collings, for example, has ghosted dozens of books with great aplomb. A former nonfiction publisher and editor, she told me that those earlier roles required her to remain anonymous. "You discover early on to be totally invisible," she says. "It's the author's book that gets the attention. So, for me, the transition to writing on demand came easily."

In addition, Collings claims ghosting allows her to focus on writing and editing, which she loves, and not having to deal with the less appealing marketing and promotional aspects of authorship. "I'm just not always comfortable in the limelight," she admits.

An accomplished author in her own right (her first book, *Sophie's Journey*, was an immediate best seller), Collings is frequently asked when she'll write another of her own books. "I feel I do that all the time," she says. "In ghosting, I have a secret sense of ownership."

Similarly, another hidden hero, David Jacoby, claims that some of his best and most rewarding work is when he's ghosting. "Because," he explains, "the lack of a byline allows my normally rather obnoxious ego to take a nap."

Another benefit in ghosting is the opportunity to get up close and personal with some interesting personalities. William Novak admits being "spoiled" by all the "wonderful people he's worked with." There have been White House meetings with the Reagans, visits to former House Speaker Tip O'Neill's home on Cape Cod, clandestine interviews with Oliver North and trips to Hawaii with Magic Johnson. Not a dull life.

Nevertheless, the work can be brutally demanding and often driven by tight deadlines. A top ghostwriter must write quickly, often under enormous pressure. "Fast, faster, fastest, is the norm," says super agent Morel. "And the required turnaround times seem to get accelerated every year."

"I had a book come together in a series of just 10 interviews— one per chapter," says the speedy Collings. "Each interview took an hour. The entire project still took four laborious months." Yet it's not unusual for a writer to ghost two or three books a year, plus their own creative projects.

Part of the ghostwriter's professionalism is understanding and accepting that he or she is writing someone else's story. "It took a while to understand that I am writing a book about how [the client] sees him or herself," Novak explains. "I represent what they remember, their views." Ghostwriters must learn to acquire the client's real persona or "voice." In his highly acclaimed novel, *The Ghost Writer*, Philip Roth described "voice" as "something that begins at around the back of the knees and reaches well above the head." Not an easy task to capture. "The more you work with someone, the easier it is to get their voice," claims ghostwriter Leslie Lang. Still, it may take months to nail a client's voice, but it is a vital element in becoming a credible conduit for any "author."

Peter Osnos, founder of PublicAffairs books and former editor of several Novak titles, gives his colleague high marks for these skills: "[He] is the equivalent of a great character actor—someone who has the ability to subsume his own character, no matter how interesting the part that he's playing."

Yet mimicking the author appears dishonest when it comes to ghostwriting fiction. "Can one write from another person's heart?" asks Jennie Erdal, the infamous Tiger's scribe. "I'm not sure it can be done. Without a doubt there is something intrinsically contradictory about ghosting a novel. It's like trying to fake sincerity." Most publishing pros agree. Madeleine Morel told me that ghosting fiction "just doesn't work." Nonetheless, it still represents almost one-third of industry revenues, most of it generated from the entertainment world.

❖ ❖ ❖

"The noblest service comes from nameless hands," observed Oliver Wendell Holmes Sr. "And the best servant does his work unseen." Some might quibble with describing ghostwriting in such noble terms, particularly the practice of permitting someone to take credit for another's work. But ghostwriting firms have no ethical problem with it.

"A client who hires a ghostwriter is still the author of their book," says Kevin Anderson, who runs a self-named ghostwriting firm in New York. "With the exception of some research-based projects, the content, ideas and concepts for a book come directly from the client."

Seasoned ghostwriters, for their part, view their efforts as "just a job," and a book as "just a product." Yet, these hidden heroes speak proudly of their ability to bring a client's story to life and allow tales to be told that would not otherwise. Perhaps true nobility then is like ghosts, which everyone talks about but few have seen.

❖ ❖ ❖

Climbing in the footsteps of the legendary Tenzing Norgay, courageous Sherpas put their crampons on every day to ensure the safety of foreign climbers.

CHAPTER 11

INTO THIN AIR

"To climb Everest is an intrinsically irrational act—a triumph of desire over sensibility. Any person who would seriously consider it is almost by definition beyond the sway of reasoned argument."

—Jon Krakauer, author and mountaineer

"**A**PRIL IS THE CRUELEST MONTH,**"** T.S. Eliot observed. On April 18, 2014, the death of thirteen Sherpa guides and three other Nepalese workers made it, at the time, the deadliest day in the cruelest month in the history of the world's highest mountain. The disaster was twice as costly as the infamous May 1996 storm that killed eight people and became the subject of the best seller *Into Thin Air*. For more than a century, Western climbers have hired Nepal's elite Sherpas to do the most dangerous work on Mount Everest. For them, mountaineering has been a lucrative way of life in an extremely poor region. Unfortunately, no service industry kills and maims its workers as frequently as does high-altitude climbing.

Dying on Everest, or *Sagarmatha*—"mother goddess of the world"—has been an occupational hazard for Sherpas ever since George Mallory and his team became the first alpinists to ascend above the lower flanks of the mountain. On a bright afternoon in June 1922, Mallory and his rope mates heard an ominous sound, called *kan runu*, or crying ear, by the Sherpas, and turned to see an avalanche fracturing the steep slope above them. Seven Sherpas from Darjeeling, India, were swept to their death. Mallory was racked by guilt over the tragedy and vowed never again to put his native guides in harm's way.

Yet, since then, Sherpas have accounted for an estimated forty percent of climbing deaths on Everest. Today, these fearless heroes continue to bear a disproportionate amount of the risk in Himalayan climbing. "The odds may be worse for them than they were in the days of those grand British expeditions," contends professional climber and guide Freddie Wilkinson. In fact, *Outside* magazine, calling them "disposable," calculated that the death rate for Sherpas on Everest over the past decade was more than ten times higher than for US military personnel in Iraq from 2003 to 2007.

Renowned for their toughness and grit, Sherpas have been doing the heavy lifting on jagged Himalayan peaks for years. Their legendary strength, endurance at high altitudes and cheerful smiles have been an integral part of Everest climbing since the very beginning. Few significant successes have been achieved without them. The most famous Sherpa was Tenzing Norgay, one of the first two men—New Zealander Edmund Hillary, the other—to summit the great mountain in 1953. Since then, Everest has always loomed large in the minds of climbers—but never more so than on that fateful April day.

In the early morning hours, members of thirty-two international expeditions were asleep in their tents at Everest Base Camp in the thin air at 17,290 feet. While most of the foreign climbers slept, Kaji Sherpa began his day with a traditional *puja* ceremony, leaving offerings and praying to the gods of the mountain. A veteran of six Everest expeditions, Kaji and the other Sherpas were embarking on the most hazardous segment of the day's journey—working through a splintering section of the ever-shifting expanse of glaciers known as the Khumbu Icefall, a treacherous passage likened to an outsized glass full of frozen waterfalls. The steep, twelve-mile series of crevasses and contorted ice extends from just above base camp and rises to 19,500 feet. Crossing it can take twelve frightful hours.

In the frigid darkness, Kaji and his colleagues carried backbreaking loads up to eighty pounds each as they moved up and down the mountain to establish a series of higher camps necessary for the summit assault. Some hauled ropes, snow shovels, ice anchors and other gear to set a handrail of fixed lines all the way to Everest's summit at 29,035 feet. Others lugged equipment for four intermediate camps higher on the mountain: sleeping bags, dining tents, tables, chairs, cooking pots, and heaters, rugs and plastic flowers to spruce up mealtime for their foreign clients.

Earlier, a number of Sherpa specialists known as Icefall Doctors had fixed ropes through what they believed to be the safest paths, and used aluminum ladders to bridge the deep crevasses. But because the Khumbu can shift six feet in just a day, the Sherpas needed to go out every morning to repair sections that had broken overnight and, if necessary, alter the climbing route. This often meant making up to thirty exhausting trips through the deadly maze. "Every time I go through the Icefall, in my heart, I always fear the worst," said Pemba Chhoti Sherpa, a member of Kaji's team.

Shortly after 6:45 a.m., the Sherpas heard a thunderous crash. "I thought, this is what death sounds like," recalled Pemba Chhoti. Before anyone could look up, a massive section of ice shaped like an enormous canine tooth, 113 feet tall and weighing sixteen million to thirty million pounds, came hurtling down the mountain, fracturing into large lethal pieces and creating a wall of wind. "It was like the whole mountain was falling," recalls Kaji, who escaped with just two broken ribs and a lung contusion.

About two dozen climbers were directly in the path of the avalanche. There was no chance of running. "I saw the ice coming, and I thought we were gone. I'm going to die," said Sherpa Pasang Dorje. Survivors saw their comrades buried in the snow and ice and scrambled to dig them out. Most of those caught in the avalanche's wake—all Nepalis working for guided climbing teams—were dead.

"They died in harness," wrote Chip Brown in *National Geographic*, "laboring to put their children through school, or to build a new house, or to buy medication for elderly parents." Twenty-eight children were orphaned. The death of a productive dad took a particularly onerous toll, since many Nepalese families often rely on only one person to support eight or nine dependents. Yet the impact of the cruelties of that April day were only beginning to unfold.

Removing bodies was an especially grisly task for the deeply superstitious Sherpas, who believe that until the souls of the deceased are properly guided to the afterlife, they can negatively affect the living in many ways. "For Sherpa, if we can help someone in life, it is very, very good for our religion," according to Pemba Tashi, a lead climber and trusted expedition lieutenant. "But to move body is always hard, very hardest thing I have to do."

In the ensuing days, Sherpas were engaged in a sorrowful series of pujas and funerals, followed by several emotional and contentious meetings. The Nepalese government's underwhelming response to the tragedy—offering the victims' families just $400 each in compensation—sparked a heated debate on pay and working conditions and prompted Sherpas to consider ending the climbing season. Among their demands to the government: increase compensation to $1,000 per family; provide $10,000 to those who were seriously disabled; establish a permanent relief fund for injured climbers; double insurance benefits to $21,000 per climber; and erect a monument in the capital city of Kathmandu to memorialize the deceased Sherpas.

For cash-starved Nepalis, anything that jeopardized the centerpiece of the country's $360 million trekking and tourist industry would be disastrous. The Mount Everest cash machine brings the impoverished country more than $3 million to $4 million annually in permit fees, with ancillary economic benefits estimated by foreign expedition operators at more than $15 million. Consequently, the Nepalese government—keen not to endanger the golden goose—quickly gave in to many of the Sherpas' demands. It raised by fifty percent the insurance paid out to families of those killed working at high altitude to $15,000; established a modest relief fund to help those injured in mountaineering accidents, as well as the families of those killed; agreed to pay for any rescue efforts on the mountain; and erected a memorial to lost guides.

Nevertheless, the shock to the tight-knit Sherpa community, which accounts for less than one percent of Nepal's population of twenty-eight million, led many to seriously question the risks of high-altitude climbing. This had a "huge impact on us all," recalls Nima Namgyal Sherpa, a physician and guide for the Nepal-based Asian Trekking. "The Sherpas were freaked out and scared." But they also knew their overseas clients had invested a lot of time and money to come to Everest. If the season ended, many of them would have to forfeit most or all of the money they had spent to go up the mountain—at a cost of $75,000 or more.

After several days of tense wrangling, nearly the entire staff of 400 Sherpas decided to leave Everest. "It's just impossible for us to continue," said Ang Dorje Sherpa, an experienced mountain guide. Sensing the somber mood, leaders of most of the thirty-two expeditions also abandoned their climb, and the season was effectively canceled. "We're in support of the Sherpa people," said Tim and Becky Rippel, owners of a guiding company called Peak Freaks. "They are our family, our brothers and sisters and the muscle on Everest. We follow their lead. We are guests here."

Yet many wondered whether these high-altitude heroes would ever put their crampons on again. Would they return to the mountain, or had the events of April 18 changed their lives forever?

❖ ❖ ❖

Sherpas—*Sharwa* in their own language, meaning "people of the East"—are of Tibetan stock, having immigrated from the high plateaus into the Himalayas about 500 years ago to escape the rampaging Mongols. They found their *beyul*, or sanctuary, in Khumbu, Nepal's gateway to Everest, where they began to live in relative peace and practiced an ancient form of Buddhism. Poor and isolated from the rest of the world, they eked out a difficult living at 13,000 feet on meager rations of a barley-loaded porridge named *tsamba*, potatoes, yak milk and *chang*, a rice-brewed beer.

Ironically, it was the Sherpas' remarkable ability to withstand the harsh high-altitude and bitter cold over countless generations that provided them with an unexplained aptitude for mountaineering. Some studies show that they may have a higher hemoglobin level, allowing their bloodstreams to carry and absorb oxygen more efficiently. This facilitates better metabolic function at higher altitude.

At 28,000 feet, air contains only one-third as much oxygen as at sea level. On the ground, even when exercising strenuously, our lungs need fifty liters of air per minute. Near Everest's upper reaches, most climbers suck in as much as 200 liters. "Run in place for a few minutes, then try to breathe through a straw," Gary Guller, the first one-armed man to summit the great mountain, told me. "That's how it feels at Everest's base camp. Now, run in place and do the same thing with a skinny coffee stirrer. That's what it's like on the summit."

Sherpas, though, are uniquely able to function at very low oxygen density levels. Some reach the summit of Everest without using supplemental oxygen; others can stay in thin air for incredibly long periods without it. Babu Chiri Sherpa, for instance, held the record of staying on the peak for twenty-one hours without supplemental oxygen in 1999. In 2001, he fell to his death, aged thirty-five, on what would have been his eleventh summit.

In addition, Sherpas can produce twice as much nitric oxide as almost anyone else. This chemical acts as a vasodilator, opening up constricted vessels in the lungs—perhaps explaining why Sherpas are nearly immune to acute mountain sickness, which can lead to pulmonary or cerebral edema with fatal consequences. Furthermore, they produce less lactic acid than the rest of us, which may explain their ability to maintain high fuel-burning efficiency even in low oxygen environments, using enzymes we still haven't identified.

One final advantage: Sherpas are especially able to tolerate the bone-chilling cold, which can plunge to minus fifty degrees in the Himalayas. Somehow, they benefit from a carefully modulated limb-salvage reflex, called the "hunter reflex," present in warm-blooded animals. This enables many of them to walk nearly barefoot over fresh snow and ice because their bodies have an innate potential to withstand subzero temperatures.

Taken together, these unusual attributes place the hearty Sherpas in high demand for Everest expeditions. Originally, however, they had no interest in mountaineering. "Sherpas didn't climb for recreation," says Jamling Tenzing Norgay, son of Tenzing Norgay. "They climbed because it was a job for them, a way of living."

Depending on their talent, experience, foreign language skills, how many loads they carry up and down the mountain and how generously they're tipped by their clients, climbing Sherpas generally take home between $2,000 and $8,000 at the conclusion of an Everest season, which commences for them in late March and typically ends around the first of June. By any reasonable measure, this is a pittance for the risk involved. "But in Nepal, where the medium annual income is less than $700, most of the Sherpas' countrymen would eagerly take similar risks for the opportunity to receive that kind of pay," says famed author and mountaineer Jon Krakauer. (By contrast, Western guides can make as much as $50,000 during the season.)

Kaji Sherpa, for example, never planned to be an Everest climber. He had spent years growing potatoes and barley on his small farm. But he kept hearing about the big paychecks his friends were scoring from the expeditions. "I got a lot of pressure from my wife not to climb," he said. "But we needed the money."

Perhaps no one better understands the plight of his people better than Apa Sherpa, nicknamed Super Sherpa, who owns the world's record of twenty-one successful Everest ascents. Since 1990, he had climbed the mountain every year, except 1996 and 2001, scaling the summit twice in 1992. He knows well the draw of the mountain for the Sherpa.

Apa was raised in the remote village of Thame in Khuma. Life was hard, and his family, like most in the region, was extremely poor. At the age of twelve, his father, a yak herder, died, and Apa took over responsibility of providing for the family, carrying supplies for various trekking parties. In 1985, he joined his first serious expedition to 26,545-foot Annapurna, where he worked as a cook and, later, a porter. Three years later, he was hired to carry loads on Everest, participating in several unsuccessful summit attempts.

However, in May 1990, the five-foot-four, 120-pound dynamo ultimately reached the pinnacle for the first time with Peter Hillary, son of Sir Edmund, and Rob Hall, who led several expeditions on Everest, including an ill-fated trip in 1996. For the next two-plus decades, he embarked on an almost unbroken string of annual ascents up the Great Mountain, often serving as *sidar*, or chief Sherpa.

In a strange twist of fate, he declined his good friend Rob Hall's repeated requests to join his team during the tragic season of 1996. Apa's wife, Yangjin Sherpa, told him he had tested the mountain enough, and it was time to let it rest. So he stayed home with his family, while Hall and seven others perished in a rogue storm that blew in without warning while they were still high on the peak.

No doubt shaken by Hall's death, the then-veteran of sixteen summits took his children to America "for their education." But he also wanted to do something for his people. In 2009, he founded the Apa Sherpa Foundation, dedicated to the improvement of education and economic development in Nepal. From his home in Draper, Utah, he still manages to visit his native land every year to raise awareness of the region's special needs.

In the interim, the Super Sherpa rails against the plight of his countrymen. "It is the Sherpas who do all the hard work," he told *The Washington Post*. "And Westerners take the credit to have reached the summit successfully. While we make them climb, we take entire responsibility for their safety—just like parents take care of their children."

Money isn't the sole driving force for navigating the mountain. Sherpas have a much deeper and more spiritual connection with Everest than their pampered clients. True to their Buddhist upbringing, they believe that to attain enlightenment, they must live in service of others. Hence, these hidden heroes ascend the lofty peaks not for themselves, but to support the other climbers—to ensure their safety upward and their safe return. Such is the Sherpa way.

Tenzing Norgay, in fact, described Mount Everest as "warm, friendly and loving," terms others might use to depict a good friend. It's clearly not a portrayal Westerners would use to describe a place requiring such demanding physical exertion—and one fraught with danger every step of the way. At the higher altitudes, trekkers begin to see the numerous tombs of courageous Sherpas who have fallen prey to the mountain.

More than 4,440 climbers have reached the peak since Sherpa Norgay and Edmund Hillary first ascended it in 1953—most of them very recently. In 2013 alone, 658 people climbed the mountain; the previous year, 234 climbers reached the peak on a single day. As a result, the top of the world has a serious overcrowding problem. Climbing Everest, says mountaineer and author Graham Hoyland, "isn't a wilderness experience. It's a McDonald's experience."

Gone are the days when scant numbers of tweedy gentlemen pioneered their way up a virgin alpine landscape. Today, Everest has become "a high-altitude playground where conga lines of novice clients clog the route," writes climber Nick Heil in *Dark Summit*. By and large, climbers nowadays are tourists, not mountaineers. Anyone with a bit of training and in moderately decent shape can climb Everest—provided, of course, they pay a bare bones $30,000 to a whopping $100,000 per person for the privilege.

During their historic ascent, Hillary and Norgay survived on sardines, dates and tinned apricots. Today's deep-pocketed dilettantes can pay to enjoy a much higher degree of luxury while conquering nature. At Base Camp, high-end expeditions offer yoga classes, sushi and bars fully stocked with wine, beer and liquor in heated tents. On the peak, there is even enough cell reception to send a celebratory tweet.

Before his death in 2008, Sir Edmund lamented the commercialization of Everest. "Having people pay $65,000 and then be led up the mountain by a couple of experienced guides," he said in 2003, "isn't really mountaineering at all." Son Peter Hillary, at sixty-one, sympathizes with his late father and the times when great alpinists were celebrated for their ability to climb and scale the world's most forbidding mountains. Now, he told *The Japan Times*, "it's a [different] game—mountaineers climb with laptops and they feed their experience directly into the Internet. Everything has changed."

To be sure, advances in technology—equipment, medicine and weather forecasting—have significantly improved climbers' abilities to reach the peak. In 1990, only eighteen percent made it to the top; today, it's about fifty-six percent. But for the dutiful Sherpas, the risks have been increasing.

For starters, the expensive medicines and equipment that their Western *sahibs* enjoy aren't available to them. Sherpas, for instance, almost never receive dexamethasone, a powerful stimulus used to ward off the lethal effects of high-altitude pulmonary and cerebral edema, because, among other things, they don't have personal physicians in their villages who will prescribe the drug on request. They also aren't provided nearly as much bottled oxygen, because it is so expensive to buy and to stock on the upper mountain—and expedition leaders assume that Sherpas tend to be much better acclimated than their foreign clients.

But most important, these high-altitude heroes do the heavy

lifting. "Westerners climb Everest for adventure only once or twice," says Apa Sherpa. "We have to do it all over again and again. While Westerners cross an icefall four or five times at most, Sherpas have to do it over fifteen to twenty times, fixing the ropes, making camps and transporting luggage."

"Most Western climbers feel more than a little guilty about this," Krakauer admits. "But I know of none who has ever offered to take an extra lap through the Icefall with a heavy load in order to reduce a Sherpa's exposure."

Then, there's the impact of climate change. As the planet continues to warm, Everest is seeing a gradual loss of its glaciers. In recent years, this has made areas like the Khumba Icefall even more unstable. Less snow on the ice rocks means likelier chances of falling. And since Sherpas spend considerably more time in these unstable regions than their foreign employers, they put themselves in greater danger.

Finally, the swelling tide of climbers, including the relatively unprepared, means more Sherpas working on the mountain— and more people exposed to risk. "There are fewer hardcore mountaineers" on Everest today, laments Susmita Maskey, a thirty-five-year-old Nepali veteran of life on the edge. "It's a circus."

Despite the hazards, there is stiff competition among Sherpas for the twelve to eighteen positions on a typical Everest expedition. They remain dependent on mountaineering because, says *Outside* magazine senior editor Grayson Schaffer, "the industry has taken a lot of poor men and turned them into relatively rich men." High-altitude climbing has allowed them to open businesses and educate their children. When the only real alternative is subsistence farming, most Sherpas prefer to head for the hills, literally.

❖ ❖ ❖

After the April 2014 avalanche, Super Sherpa Apa argued that the mountain needed a rest, and that too many people were climbing. "Leave Everest alone," he said. "It will always be there. [People] can try next year."

Kaji Sherpa, for his part, not only supported the shutdown, but vowed to never climb Everest again. "I think it's better not to climb again because so many people are dying," he said. The injured father of four returned to a less dangerous vocation: farming potatoes, maize and wheat. About seventy other Sherpas announced that they, too, would find a new profession, because they thought mountaineering was just too risky. But over the course of the following months, many changed their minds. "Sherpas need to eat," explained Kami Noru Sherpa, who organizes foreign expeditions. "And they need to earn."

The following year, Nepali officials geared up for twenty-five expeditions, a drop from the usual thirty-plus. Pasang Tenzing Sherpa, who had climbed Everest nine times, said he was returning "not because of the money, but out of respect for my profession. Every profession has its risks. The focus should not be on whether to quit, but on how to minimize the risks."

An official at the Nepal National Mountain Guides Association, Pasang reported that trekkers would continue to use the southeast ridge route to Everest, where the deadly avalanche had occurred. "I think everyone has realized by now that what happened last year was an act of nature," he said, a month before the new season started. "An unfortunate natural disaster will not make Mount Everest less attractive."

Pasang's prognostications could not have been more wrong. Just three weeks later, once again in the cruel month of April, a powerful 7.8 magnitude earthquake hit Nepal near Kathmandu, flattening sections of the city's historic center and trapping dozens of sightseers in a 200-foot watchtower that came crashing down into a pile of bricks.

In quieter times, the colorful capital, at 4,200 feet, served as the gateway to the Alps. Navigating the city's busy streets, arriving climbers experienced the ancient appeal of this poor, but vital jumping-off point. From trekking agencies to curry houses, they met sari-clad women and Hindu holy men and were greeted by a cacophony of motorcycle engines, truck horns, rooster calls, police whistles and fruit hawkers. While Kathmandu could not be compared to the mythical Shangri-la—crumbling buildings, rusted-out vehicles, emaciated dogs and impoverished families filled the poorly drained streets—the proximity to the snowcapped Himalayas made it one of the planet's most powerful magnets for adventure seekers.

But now things had changed dramatically. In the aftermath of the disaster, the fear of aftershocks was all consuming—and warranted. Within days, there would be sixty more quakes of magnitude 4.1 or greater, and scientists warned that the residual shaking could continue for years.

A week after the quake, at least sixteen tent cities had sprouted up around Kathmandu. Many of the people living in them were technically not homeless. Their houses were still intact. But they chose to sleep outside in fear that more structures would collapse as aftershocks continued. "Camped in parks, open spaces and golf course, they cuddled children or pets against chilly Himalayan nighttime temperatures," the Associated Press reported.

About 100 miles east of the capital, the tremors rattled Everest to the core. The earthquake triggered avalanches on the great mountain. A record nineteen people perished, some of them Sherpas—another reminder of the unpredictable dangers of high-altitude mountaineering in the Himalayas. The quake knocked house-sized blocks of ice from the mountain, sending an explosion of ice and snow hurtling toward the brightly colored tents at base camp, where most of the fatalities occurred. Helicopters evacuated the most critically injured climbers, mostly Sherpas.

Across the country, emergency workers struggled to cope with the devastation, which left almost 9,000 Nepalis dead. In the midst of this unprecedented humanitarian crisis, hospitals were overwhelmed; the limited capacity at Kathmandu's airport, plus the damaged roads and difficult mountain terrain, made aid distribution almost impossible. The quakes also threatened to undo the country's fragile economy, which was poorer, per capita, than even destitute Haiti before the quakes. Losses were expected to exceed Nepal's $20 billion annual gross domestic product, and push an additional 700,000 citizens below the poverty line—a pitiful $200 a year.

While the Himalayan nation was still mourning its dead and just beginning to recover from the April tremors, another 7.3 magnitude quake hit a mountainous area east of Kathmandu three weeks later. Large aftershocks continued for weeks. "We are in a state of shock," reported Ang Tenzing Sherpa, who was in the nation's capital when the latest quakes struck. The city seemed to be returning to normal, but now, residents again began setting up tents.

As Nepalis coped with "earthquake hangover," international aid poured into the shell-shocked country. The new price tag for short-term and immediate rebuilding ran as high as $6.7 billion. "But long-term needs could be much higher," predicted Kenichi Yokoyama of the Asian Development Bank. However, the major concern was whether Nepal could deploy these funds quickly and efficiently. "If [the government] can't address this issue—the rehabilitation work—properly," said Dr. Min Bahadur Shrestha, executive director of the Central Bank of Nepal, "then we see a looming political and social crisis." That assessment came as no great surprise.

Well before the recent earthquakes, Nepal was in disarray, a political and economic basket case. A ten-year Maoist insurgency ended in 2006, but an astonishingly ineffective and corrupt government had difficulty producing a proper constitution. Manufacturing has declined for years and now represents a paltry six percent of the country's economy. Poverty is endemic, air pollution is stultifying and health statistics are deplorable.

For years, the impoverished nation has shipped its men and women abroad to find work as construction laborers, security guards, housekeepers and nannies in India, the Persian Golf and elsewhere. With few jobs at home, young Nepalis regularly line up in Kathmandu to apply for passports, a long and expensive process. On average, 1,500 people manage to escape every day in search of a better life—up thirty-seven percent in just the past two years. "The country is bleeding its best people," warns Maurizio Busatti, chief of the International Organization for Migration mission in Nepal.

One perverse "benefit" is that no other country receives a greater share of its wealth from emigrant workers—a whopping twenty-nine percent of gross domestic product, or roughly $5.9 billion a year. What's more, Nepal's diaspora, including the 88,000 expats in the United States, has financed a big chunk of post-quake rebuilding and recovery—more that $700 million, according to one estimate.

For Sherpas, these natural disasters have been catastrophic. There were no successful climbs in 2015. "No mountaineering means no tourists," said Nima Doma Sherpa, whose husband died in the first avalanche. "No tourists means no jobs, and no jobs means no income."

These humble mountain men have carved out a livelihood in the Himalayas that is hard to walk away from. But this is exactly the path Apa Sherpa took when, at the urging of his wife and children, he retired from climbing at forty-six. If he could have planned his life differently, he says he would have given up his high-altitude records for a good education and a career as a medical doctor. That is why educating his own kids and other Nepalis is his top priority— one that brought him to the United States.

Regardless of all the risks in climbing the majestic mountain, "there were no other options for us to meet our basic needs," he says, reflecting on his previous vocation. For future generations, Apa believes the answer is education. "If young Sherpas have access to education," he says, "they can take on new professions. That is exactly why I started the foundation: To help Sherpas find new avenues in life."

"Mountains are the means, man is the end," Italian alpinist Walter Bonatti once observed. "The goal is not to reach the top of the mountains, but to improve man." Use the mountain in a positive way, and new opportunities will open up, goes a longstanding Buddhist belief. With full-time climbing behind him, Apa Sherpa shifted his focus away from the world's highest peaks to educating future generations of his people to accomplish new dreams. Now, at fifty-one, the accomplished motivational speaker is on a mission to impart those lessons to others. For his contributions, he received an honorary doctorate from the University of Utah in 2013.

But for others, "life is either a daring adventure or nothing at all," wrote legendary Helen Keller, who knew something about risk. It is clear that Everest has become a deadly folly—"a preposterously dangerous undertaking," says Krakauer. Ultimately, climbing the world's highest peak, with its deep crevasses, fragile ice towers and deadly avalanches, will always be daunting. But despite back-to-back disasters—the 2015 earthquake and the massive avalanche the year before—hundreds of mountaineers came back for the 2016 season, although forty percent fewer than previous years.

Many had hoped the new climbing season would bring success and restore confidence in climbing the great mountain. But within a matter of days, four foreigners died on Everest, with another thirty suffering from serious frostbite or altitude sickness.

"The mountain still holds the master card," wrote Eric Shipton in 1938. "It will grant success only in its own good time." Yet summit-seekers still pit their frail resources against this cold, capricious citadel in ever-increasing numbers. Defying danger alongside them, dutiful, though less subservient, Sherpas continue to practice their perilous profession.

"We often hear our Western outfitter friends acknowledge that the skilled Sherpa climbers deserve more," says Sumit Joshi, a climbing Sherpa and partner in a Nepalese-owned guide service. "But what are they actually willing to give more of? More money? More benefits? More fame?"

In the final analysis, a better life will only come from the Sherpas themselves. "You cannot prevent the birds of sorrow from flying over your head," says a Chinese proverb. "But you can prevent them from building nests in your hair."

❖ ❖ ❖

CHAPTER 12

TOP BILLING FOR HEROES

*"The world can do without its masters better
than it can do without its servants."*

—Samuel Gridley Howe, physician and
founder of the Perkins School for the Blind

"A H, BUT A MAN'S REACH SHOULD EXCEED HIS GRASP. Or what is heaven for?" wrote poet Robert Browning. The temptation—indeed, the obligation—to strive for the brass ring is so deeply ingrained in our DNA that many people feel compelled to climb slippery, often treacherous, mountains. Hidden heroes, on the other hand, understand that you don't have to put on crampons to ascend to happiness. Exercising one's energy to serve a worthy cause is far more satisfying than basking in the limelight. These invisible but invaluable acolytes have discovered the rare ability to distinguish between celebrity and success. As the late Erma Bombeck advised, "Don't confuse fame with success. Madonna is one, Helen Keller is the other."

"To believe in the heroic makes heroes," Benjamin Disraeli wrote. Exceptional subordinates, while understanding the frustrations of the workforce, gain that respect largely by deflecting credit to others—an all-too-rare commodity in today's workplace. Hidden heroes' attention is on the task at hand, not on themselves. But they aren't masochists. They don't choose to work for and with others because it hurts. They do so because they understand the merits of doing something important with others they respect.

What, then, have we learned about incorporating service through subordination into our daily lives? The following sections explore how talented men and women and their superiors can help level the playing field.

Turning first to those operating in the shadows, here are some tips for achieving success:

1. Get Personal.

An old Chinese proverb says happiness depends on something to work on, something to hope for and someone to love. To serve in support of others, your heart must be in it. As we have seen, subordination—often unrecognized and unappreciated—demands dedication and energy, nothing less.

"All truths are easy to understand once they are discovered," observed astronomer Galileo. "The point is to discover them." What matters most to you? Fame? Fortune? Self-expression? Helping others? Look inside. Listen to your gut, your heart. Examine yourself objectively and pinpoint what turns you on.

Highly accomplished backup singer Lisa Fischer loves supporting other artists—a role she describes as "sacred." For her, "stardom was war. It scared me too much," she says.

Therefore, get personal. Analyze your hidden dreams. The starting point, in philosopher Joseph Campbell's words, is to "follow your bliss." Then, beat the drum—call attention to your needs.

2. Chemistry Lessons.

After searching your soul, you have decided, like Ms. Fischer, that supporting others is for you. When everything's clicking, subordinating oneself comes easily. But situations change, and the chemistry between you and your superiors can fizzle. Therefore, ask yourself the following hot-button questions:

- Are your goals really in sync with the organization and/or your boss?
- In tough times, will the top dog have your back? Or are you dealing with an autocratic control freak?
- What loyalty demands will the enterprise and/or the boss

place on you? Are they unreasonable?
- What level of trust and respect do they typically extend to you and others?
- How generous are the rewards and incentives, monetary and otherwise, offered to those in supporting roles?
- Are you willing to spend the bulk of your career in the shadows?
- Finally, what, if any, are the prospects for upward advancement?

If you're satisfied with the answers to these questions, you're probably in a good place. If, on the other hand, the responses were less than satisfactory, act accordingly. Don't squander your future. Move on.

Unwilling to become a "disposable don," adjunct professor Ingrid Steffensen embarked on literally a high-speed exit from academia. Shedding substandard pay and working conditions, she began a second life as a professional racecar driver. Much better chemistry.

3. Take Risks.

Not everyone can be a Danica Patrick. But every hidden hero should push his or her comfort zone, just for the thrill of it. Don't confine yourself to the narrow corridors of a single career. You may discover that you are more in demand than you think.

"Don't shrink from risk," advises Apple CEO Tim Cook. "The world needs your energy. Your passion. The sidelines are not where you want to live your life." Stay in front. Be prepared to shine—slowly. This, of course, takes courage—the courage to search for new mountains to climb, or to avoid.

Record-setting Super Sherpa Apa abandoned a successful high-altitude climbing practice at age forty-six. In 2009, he established a foundation to provide young Sherpas with career options beyond the dangerous world of mountaineering. "I started it," he says, "to help others find new avenues of life." True to his Buddhist upbringing, Apa believes that to attain enlightenment, one must live in service to others. That's the Sherpa way.

4. Dare to Dream.

> *"What happens to a dream deferred?*
> *Does it dry up like a raisin in the sun?"*

In these lines, the poet Langston Hughes wonders what happens to dreams that don't come true. Accept that nothing is perfect. Nobody gets everything they yearn for, but clever cohorts who dream boldly shouldn't wait forever to find their bliss.

"Not failure, but low aim, is a crime," claimed poet, critic and diplomat James Russell Lowell. Resist the temptation to rationalize what others view as success instead of what you feel in your gut is the right choice. "That's your North Star," Vice President Joseph Biden told recent Yale graduates. "Trust it. Follow it."

For more than six decades, Washington Generals owner Red Klotz created a dream where coming down on the wrong side of the win-loss column had its own rewards. In a lifetime of losing to the Harlem Globetrotters, Klotz's Generals offered fans around the world not only a better understanding of sports but also an appreciation of African-American culture. In Red's dream, everyone won.

5. Don't Beat Yourself Up.

"In the long run, we are all dead," observed John Maynard Keynes. There is no happy ending earning a trip to a cold grave. Look inside: Embrace your inner David. Don't undervalue your principles or compromise your dreams. It's easy to look at the world in terms of winners and losers. But in reality, life is more complicated than that, and laboring in the trenches isn't easy.

Top guns, for instance, can subvert their subordinates in dozens of ways, from undermining their authority to discrediting their achievements. Crap happens. Expect some dry spells along the way. It's rare to achieve traction right away. Overcoming disappointments requires "a delicate balance of remembering and forgetting," says self-help author Rabbi Harold S. Kushner.

Resilient folks don't stumble in the mire. They accept adversity and move on. Recall the ups and downs of America's sprint football teams. Besides playing second fiddle to gigantic, heavyweight players, these scrappy athletes and their coaches toil away in relative obscurity. On campus, they remain virtually anonymous—scavenging for crumbs from the athletic department. But inwardly, these hyperkinetic dynamos don't beat themselves up. They celebrate their victories and proudly demonstrate college football as it ought to be, taking the field for the right reason—for the love of the game.

6. Focus on the End Game.

Don't let yourself get distracted. Hidden heroes remain intensely focused on the work itself. "That all-important task acts as a social lubricant," Warren Bennis and Patricia Ward Biederman reported in their best seller, *Organizing Genius*. "Sharing information and advancing the work are the only real social obligations."

Nobody has to instruct Nepal's elite Sherpas to concentrate on the task at hand. No profession kills or maims its workers as frequently as does high-altitude climbing. One missed step carrying backbreaking loads up and down the world's highest peaks means early death. Consequently, Sherpas focus in the face of adversity. But they pace themselves. They think incrementally. As William Faulkner advised: "The man who moves a mountain begins by carrying away small stones."

In less perilous situations, other high performers remove the clutter. They do the simple things well. They refuse to get sidetracked—and focus, focus, focus.

7. Build Alliances.

Going it alone can make for a solitary existence. Huddle up. Connect with colleagues. Identify with them. Human interaction is vital.

"We can do as partners what we cannot as singles," Daniel Webster once said. Trust is the coin of the realm in any partnership. It is as important as hard work and common sense.

Again, trust tends to flourish in organizations that stay tightly focused on the mission. In the lighter-than-air community, blimp pilots were famous for their special brand of esprit. Staunchly dedicated to winning the war, there was little time for the constant intrigue that undermines collaboration in many other enterprises.

Connections, therefore, are invaluable. Resourceful men and

women keep good company. They revel in the talent of others and celebrate their accomplishments. The best ones smell out knowledgeable people—mentors, peers and friends—to consult in advancing their dreams.

"Lean on someone you can trust," advises management expert Stephen Covey. "Good colleagues and mentors give you honest feedback. They will shake you out of your comfort zone." If you don't see the big picture, they "can help you frame it."

Cast a wide net. Connect offline and online. Assemble a team inside and outside your field of interest. Go to professional meetings, attend workshops, accept speaking engagements, publish articles. These activities afford you valuable exposure. And stay wired. The Internet and various forms of social media can be tremendous tools to help you serve more effectively.

8. Don't Sell Your Soul (or Ruin Your Body).

One of the intrinsic challenges of being a hidden hero is the pressure—both internal and external—to satisfy one's superiors. In the process, overly ambitious types often make a Faustian bargain, which can cost them soul and substance.

"Don't let making a living prevent you from having a life," warned Hall of Fame basketball coach John Wooden. Entertainer Carole Kai understood this. Early in her career, the bright lights of Las Vegas beckoned, where she worked as an opener and slowly began to build her brand. However, she soon discovered that the sexual advances of both headliners and Vegas heavyweights clashed with her born-again Christian values. So she packed it in and "headed home with my reputation intact."

Don't befriend the wrong cause or an abusive or toxic boss. And don't bend the rules to play the game. Character counts. Hidden heroes don't wimp out. They know when to walk away.

9. Don't Quit Your Day Job...Yet

Not everyone has to pack it in. It would be foolish, as well as self-defeating, to abandon your vocation prematurely.

No doubt, there are nightmarish situations out there where talented men and women, quite often for reasons beyond their control, seem destined to walk the plank. But they are the exception.

Gritty staffers allow for some stops and starts, some difficult moments, along the way. They grin and bear it. As former secretary of state Colin Powell often says, "Perpetual optimism is a force multiplier."

In the interim, hang in there. Look to unleash your passions. Now might be the time to "repurpose your life," as University of Michigan professor Victor Strecher suggests, to engage in issues bigger than yourself: poverty, race relations, youth unemployment. On a more modest level, set yourself up for a second act or a side gig to fill the voids in your life.

In doing so, don't draw lines that limit what you are and are not. "Become who you are," Nietzsche told us. Learn something new. This may lead to novel invitations, interesting opportunities and a renewed sense of purpose. You might even attain remarkable new heights. Recall how talented Scottish writer Jennie Erdal jettisoned a lucrative career ghosting to pen highly acclaimed books under her own name. Rebels with a cause like Erdal are willing to let new ideas take root. They maintain a maverick mindset, refusing to become pigeonholed.

10. Don't Dillydally.

Don't just dream—do something. Start now: you may not have a chance later. Set in motion a chain of activities that will channel your feelings of restlessness, normal for all of us.

"Don't wait forever to follow your bliss," says TV news anchor Katie Couric. "Get your rear in gear and take a job, even a less perfect one. It could lead to a better job, open your eyes to something else or, just as importantly, tell you what you don't want to be doing."

Recall the amazing career transition of Hollywood Walk of Fame actor and singer Jim Nabors. From working as a film cutter to moonlighting at a Santa Monica comedy club to supporting stints on *The Andy Griffith Show*, the Alabama native skyrocketed to fame as the lovable country bumpkin Gomer Pyle. Ambitious personalities like Nabors understand that you need to learn the ropes and pay your dues if you aspire to stardom. As comedian Phil Silvers put it: "If you want to be top banana, you gotta start at the bottom of the bunch."

Nonetheless, top billing is not for everyone. As stardom becomes less associated with genuine achievement, more and more people are beginning to reflect more clearly on what is best for themselves, their families and their organizations. They remind us once again that you don't need to be captain to play on the team. It is only in fruitful alliances with others that we can do great things and put down, if only for a time, the burden of self.

❖ ❖ ❖

Because hidden heroes tend not to toot their own horns, those in command "need to figure out who they are and what makes them tick," says *Invisibles* author David Zweig. Here are some tips for helping your talented subordinates succeed:

1. Provide Protection.

Even in these most well-intentioned enterprises, too many underlings feel diminished and victimized. Oftentimes their invisibility functions as a metaphor for powerlessness, a common cause of employee dissatisfaction. It doesn't have to be that way.

Good stewards understand the potential susceptibility of misunderstandings, resentment, even fear. They offer protection. They find ways to insulate their people from bureaucratic meddling and belittling bosses. "They keep the 'suits' and other conventional thinkers at a distance," note Bennis and Biederman, allowing subordinates to work undistracted.

Recall, for instance, the life-ending beating that adjunct Margaret Mary Vojtko took at Duquesne University. By contrast, a string of supercharged Navy admirals, most notably William Moffett and Charles Rosendahl, provided cover and deflected ridicule for the brave souls flying America's tortoise-like blimps. They vigorously championed the case for lighter-than-air aviation within the military establishment that allowed it, and their pilots, to see the light of day.

2. Unleash the High Performers.

Power down. Relinquish control. It's a paradox: There is great freedom in surrender. "Strange as it sounds, great leaders gain authority by giving it away," said former Vietnam POW and Vice Admiral James B. Stockdale. Hence, there is real clout in being generous.

First-rate leaders recognize the value of removing the handcuffs on their exemplary performers. At the University of Hawaii Community College system, chief executive John F. Morton regularly unleashes his top faculty on a wide range of award-winning initiatives in vocational education, job training and community-based projects. By leveraging their talents, he has created a healthy environment for others to emulate. Morton understands that you get power by ceding it to others.

Recognize, too, that no one is a lost cause. Effective leaders treat every subordinate as an opportunity to achieve top results. "You owe it to your people to get them to a better spot," says Victor Prince, co-author of *Lead Inside the Box*.

3. Share the Spotlight.

Though most hidden heroes are content to toil away with a minimum of fanfare, every American craves what French nobleman Alexis de Tocqueville termed "the longing to rise." If the most self-effacing staffers were to confess their most secret desires, the ones that inspire their plans, their actions, they would say: "We want to be praised." No one should be relegated to the obscurity of a witness protection program.

"I praise loudly; I blame softly," said Catherine the Great. Don't applaud your best folks with one hand. And don't shoot down those who begin to shine too brightly. "We are all in this alone," comic Lily Tomlin once quipped. Farsighted leaders get the importance of extending kudos to those key people impatient for recognition. They make them feel appreciated and trumpet their accomplishments. Colleagues, whatever their level, are not competitors. "I fight against myself, not others," says opera singer Luciano Pavarotti.

4. Tweak the Rewards.

Simple solutions can make the workplace more humane and desirable. Ask yourself: What would make your unsung heroes feel more engaged and more inspired? "If you want to retain invisible stars and to embolden others to emulate them, intrinsic rewards are critical," David Zweig recommends.

Consultant Tony Schwartz and Georgetown professor Christine

Porath of the Energy Project have studied how to create a culture that effectively engages people. Successful enterprises address employees' physical needs first, through wellness and well-being programs—everything from fitness facilities and nap rooms to giving them more downtime or the option to telecommute one or two days a week. Far less common, the researchers found, is a broader shift from trying to get more out of employees to investing more in meeting their needs, so that they're both motivated and capable of performing better.

In the world of ghostwriting, crafty businessman Edward Stratemeyer mass-produced a mountain of novels on the backs of woefully undercompensated freelancers. But more recently, James Patterson, one of the world's richest wordsmiths, dramatically scrapped this approach—creating a bevy of lucrative and visible partnerships with some of the nation's most gifted writers. In this case, more traditional perks, money and recognition, paid off.

5. Create a Partnership Culture.

In healthy organizations, caste distinctions are kept to a minimum. Top-flight leaders understand that elitism is an expensive slave that doesn't work. They avoid creating "Downton Abbey" environments where a tiny privileged class thrives while being served by underlings struggling to make ends meet. Such divisions are most evident when things go wrong.

Unlike the Sherpa situation that pits the haves with the have-nots, effective executives know that real success is characterized by camaraderie grounded in shared accomplishment. It is powered by teams of people working toward a common goal, doing important work and doing it collaboratively. They welcome diversity and recognize that one size doesn't fit all when it comes to managing people. Those who fail to do so risk losing any organization's most important resource—its talent.

"None of us is as good as all of us" should be the mantra. Top dogs must be crystal clear about the importance of this message: creating powerful alliances of their own. Subordinates, in turn, take cues from their superiors. They give weight to everything a chief says or does. Therefore, a leader's own example, passionately presented, sets the strongest statement for dedicated followers.

"Never doubt the power of a small group of people to change the world," anthropologist Margaret Mead pointed out. "Indeed, it is the only thing that ever has." Airman Spencer Stone's courageous action in Chapter 1 and the others profiled in this book demonstrate the invaluable contributions of America's hidden heroes.

Mitch Albom, author of the best-selling *Tuesdays with Morrie*, learned these same lessons from a dying man. "So many people walk around with a meaningless life," his former college professor, Morrie Schwartz, told him. "The way to get meaning in your life is to devote yourself to loving others, devote yourself to the community around you, and devote yourself to creating something that gives you purpose and meaning." I hope my stories have galvanized you to create greater purpose and meaning in your life.

❖ ❖ ❖

NOTES

Unless otherwise indicated, quotations are from interviews with the author. The following references, in chapter sequence, complement those interviews.

Chapter 1. In Praise of Hidden Heroes

1   The Thomas Carlyle quote is from Stefan Stern, "Behind every great leader you will find a great team," *Financial Times*, January 13, 2009, p. 12.

2   The Spencer Stone incident is discussed in Helene Cooper, "A Vacation That Ended With the Legion of Honor," *The New York Times*, September 3, 2015, p. A4; and her "A Hero's Welcome at the White House," *The New York Times*, September 18, 2015, p. A17. For his later exploits, see Dan Lamothe, "Paris train hero stabbed in Calif.," *The Washington Post*, October 9, 2015, p. A3.

2   President Hollande is quoted in Cooper, "A Vacation that Ended with the Legion of Honor," *The New York Times*, September 3, 2015, p. A4.

2   Will Rogers' quote is from www.brainyquote.com.

3   President Kennedy's well-remembered axiom on success was uttered in the immediate aftermath of the 1962 Bay of Pigs invasion in Cuba.

3   See David Brooks, "The Leaderless Doctrine," *The New York Times*, March 11, 2014, p. A19; and his *The Road to Character* (New York: Random House, 2015), p. 8. Also Rich Karlgaard, "Fading Emperor Bosses," *Forbes*, April 19, 2015, p. 36.

4   Henry Ford's quote is from www.brainyquote.com.

6   The Cicero quotation is from www.famousquotesindex.com.

6   See Del Jones, "It's lonely—and thin-skinned—at the top," *USA Today*, January 16, 2007, p. 2B. Also Andrew Hill, "The perils of appointing a high-profile chief executive," *Financial Times*, March 15, 2016, p. 10. For a contrary opinion, see Joe Queenan, "The Case of the Missing Celebrities," *The Wall Street Journal*, January 16–17, 2016, p. C11.

6   See Annie Murphy Paul, "Second place is worth emulating," www.time.com cited in *The Week*, July 20, 2012, p. 39. Also Jodi Kantor, "Finding Satisfaction in Second Best," *The New York Times*, September 15, 2013, p. 12; Joshua Ferris, "Let Us Now Praise Infamous Men," *The Wall Street Journal Weekly Magazine*, November 13, 2014, pp. 51–52; Adam K. Raymond, "In Praise of the Nobodies," United Hemispheres, March 2014, p. 55; and L. Jon Wertheim and Sam Sommers, "The Eternal Appeal of the Underdog," *The New York Times*, March 15, 2016, p. A25.

7   Lisa Fischer is quoted in Brook Barnes, "The Voice Behind the Mick (and Others)," *The New York Times*, June 7, 2013, p. D4.

8   Judy Greer's quote is from Alexandra Wolfe, "Behind the Scenes with Judy Greer," *The Wall Street Journal*, May 17–18, 2014, p. C11.

8   Steve Jobs' famous "ship" remarks are from "The magician," *The Economist*, October 8, 2011, p. 15; and Jon Swartz and Scott Martin, "Apple's Steve Jobs abruptly resigns as CEO," *USA Today*, August 25, 2011, p. B20.

9   See David Brooks, *The Road to Character* (New York: Random House, 2015), pp. xvi, 20.

9   Aristotle's "sharing salt" is from www.famousquotesindex.com. See Mark Vernon, "Is true friendship dying away?" *USA Today*, July 27, 2010.

10   Tom Hanks' quote is from his "I Owe It All To Community Colleges," *The New York Times*, January 14, 2015, p. A23.

10   The Fischer quote is found in Brook Barnes, "The Voice Behind the Mick (and Others)," *The New York Times*, June 7, 2013, p. D4.

11   Nicole Beth Wallenbrock is quoted in Paul Solman's "Is academia suffering from 'adjunctivitis'?" *PBS NewsHour*, February 6, 2004.

11   C.S. Lewis' "shadowlands" is from https://www.goodreads.com/author/quotes/1069006.C_S_Lewis.

11   The Euripides quote on happiness is from www.famousquotesindex.com.

11   See Howard Schultz, "Howard Schultz: America Deserves a Servant Leader," *The New York Times*, August 6, 2015, p. A27. Also Joann S. Lublin, "The Case for Humble Executives," *The Wall Street Journal*, October 21, 2015, p. B7; Alan Murray, "Should leaders be modest?" www.fortune.com, September 15, 2015; Andrew Hill, "End of the imperial corporate leader," *Financial Times*, November 19, 2013, p. 12; and Kent M. Keith, *The Case For Servant Leadership* (Westfield, IN: The Greenleaf Center for Servant Leadership, 2008).

12   The Einstein quote is from Alice Calaprice, ed., *The Quotable Einstein* (Princeton, NJ: Princeton University Press, 1966).

12   Chad Griffin is quoted in Patrick Healy, "Bernie Sanders Can Take Heart From a Broadway Champ," *The New York Times*, June 14, 2015, p. 3.

12   For more on David and Goliath, see Malcolm Gladwell, "How David Beats Goliath," *The New Yorker*, May 11, 2009; and his *David and Goliath: Underdogs, Misfits, and the Art of Battling Giants* (New York: Little, Brown and Company, 2013).

12   See James M. Danko, "2016 teaches graduates the wrong lessons," *USA Today*, May 9, 2016, p. 10A.

Chapter 2. Hoop Dreams

15   Vince Lombardi on "winning" is from www.famousquotesindex.com.

15   John R. Tunis' "heroes" are cited in Steve Rushin, "Celebrating the Noncelebrators," *Sports Illustrated*, January 14, 2013, p. 78.

15   The definitive story of Red Klotz and the Washington Generals was penned by Tim Kelly. See his *The Legend of Red Klotz: How Basketball's Loss Leader Won Over the World—14,000 Times* (Margate, NJ: ComteQ Publishing, 2013). Also Sam Dolnick, "Red Klotz: 14,000-plus losses, 1 win," *The New York Times Magazine*, December 28, 2014, p. 28; Richard Goldstein, "Red Klotz, Beloved Foil for Globetrotters, Dies at 93," *The New York Times*, July 16, 2014, p. A21; "Louis 'Red' Klotz dies at age 93," www.espn.com, July 14, 2014; Tim Crothers, "The General Whose Army Never Wins," *Sports Illustrated*, February 20, 1995; and Tim Kelly, "Red Hot," *New Jersey Monthly*, February 4, 2008, p. 1.

16   Red Klotz's "losing is part of life" is from Kelly, *The Legend of Red Klotz*, (Margate, NJ: ComteQ Publishing, 2013), p. 7. Also Ethan Rouen, "Louis 'Red' Klotz," March 15, 2004, *Sports Junkie*, www.sportsjunkie.info/Red%20Klotz.htm.

16   The Harlem Globetrotters' story has many sources. See Ben Green, *Spinning the Globe: The Rise, Fall, and Return to Greatness of the Harlem Globetrotters* (New York: Harper Collins, 2005); Fredrick McKissack Jr., *Black Hoops: The History of African-Americans in Basketball* (New York: Scholastic Press, 1999); Chuck Melville, *The Harlem Globetrotters: Fifty Years of Fun and Games* (New York: D. McKay Co., 1978). Also "Harlem Globetrotters," *New World Encyclopedia*, www.newworldencyclopedia.org/entry/Harlem_Globetrotters; and Scott Cacciola, "Globetrotters always find a way to win," *The New York Times* (International Edition), February 10, 2015, p. 13.

17   Chuck Melville's discussion of discrimination is from his *The Harlem Globetrotters: Fifty Years of Fun and Games* (New York: D. McKay Co., 1978), p. 40. Also Fredrick McKissack Jr., *Black Hoops: The History of African-Americans in Basketball* (New York: Scholastic Press, 1999), pp. 69–72; and Ben Green, *Spinning the Globe: The Rise, Fall, and Return to Greatness of the Harlem Globetrotters* (New York: Harper Collins, 2005), pp. 10–11, 268–9.

18   See Ben Green, *Spinning the Globe: The Rise, Fall, and Return to Greatness of the Harlem Globetrotters* (New York: Harper Collins, 2005), pp. 4, 11, 223.

18-19   Wilt Chamberlain is quoted in Tim Crothers, "The General Whose Army Never Wins," *Sports Illustrated*, February 20, 1995, p. 4.

19   For "seeds of discontent," see Ben Green, *Spinning the Globe: The Rise, Fall, and Return to Greatness of the Harlem Globetrotters* (New York: Harper Collins, 2005), p. 228.

20   Klotz's "Thrill to be a champion..." is from Tim Crothers, "The General Whose Army Never Wins," *Sports Illustrated*, February 20, 1995, p. 2; and Tim Kelly, *The Legend of Red Klotz: How Basketball's Loss Leader Won Over the World—14,000 Times* (Margate, NJ: ComteQ Publishing, 2013), p. 124.

20   The Klotz-Tatum exchange and quotes are from Ben Green, *Spinning the Globe: The Rise, Fall, and Return to Greatness of the Harlem Globetrotters* (New York: Harper Collins, 2005), pp. 334–335.

20   The Saperstein-Klotz kibitz is from Tim Crothers, "The General Whose Army Never Wins," *Sports Illustrated*, February 20, 1995, p. 3; and Tim Kelly, *The Legend of Red Klotz* (Margate, NJ: ComteQ Publishing, 2013), pp. 192, 168.

20   Klotz's naming his team the Generals is from Tim Kelly, *The Legend of Red Klotz: How Basketball's Loss Leader Won Over the World—14,000 Times* (Margate, NJ: ComteQ Publishing, 2013), p. 176.

21   Klotz's "We never try to lose..." is from Franz Lidz, "Biggest loser," SI.com, http://www.sportsillustrated.cnn.com/2006/writers/franz-lidzloz/16/klotz/i.html.

21   See John Branch, "When the Generals Lose to the Globetrotters, Everyone Wins," *The New York Times*, February 13, 2009.

21   "Dancing backwards" is from Michael Zitz, "World's Biggest Losers: Globetrotters Foil Red Klotz," *Fredericksburg News*, March 15, 2007, p.2.

21   See Jonathan Mahler, "The Coach Who Exploded," *The New York Times Magazine*, November 6, 2013, p. 34.

21   Phil Jackson's goal of success is from Joe Saraceno, "A Conversation With Phil Jackson," *AARP Bulletin*, January/February 2014, p. 10.

21   See Vincent Jackson, "Celebrating Margate's Red Klotz and his unusual life in sports," *Press of Atlantic City*, January 15, 2014.

22   Klotz's "straight men" is from Richard Goldstein, "Red Klotz, Beloved Foil for Globetrotters, Dies at 93," *The New York Times*, July 16, 2014, p. A21. Also "Red Klotz, 81," *Sports Illustrated*, December 29, 2014, p. 93.

22   The Gene Hudgins quote may be found in Tim Kelly, "Red Hot," *New Jersey Monthly*, February 4, 2008, p. 2.

23 Klotz's need for players with a sense of humor is discussed in Ethan Rouen, "Louis 'Red' Klotz," March 15, 2004, *Sports Junkie*, www. sportsjunkie.info/Red%20Klotz.html; and Tim Crothers, "The General Whose Army Never Wins," *Sports Illustrated*, February 20, 1995, p. 2.

23-24 The Lebanese incident is presented in Tim Crothers, "The General Whose Army Never Wins," *Sports Illustrated*, February 20, 1995, pp. 1–2.

24 Meadowlark Lemon's little midget description is from Tim Crothers, "The General Whose Army Never Wins," *Sports Illustrated*, February 20, 1995, p. 4. Also Tim Kelly, *The Legend of Red Klotz: How Basketball's Loss Leader Won Over the World—14,000 Times* (Margate, NJ: ComteQ Publishing, 2013), p. 225.

24 Klotz's terrific ball game and discussion of the Generals' last victory over the Globetrotters are from Tim Crothers, "The General Whose Army Never Wins," *Sports Illustrated*, February 20, 1995, p. 4; Ben Green, *Spinning the Globe: The Rise, Fall, and Return to Greatness of the Harlem Globetrotters* (New York: Harper Collins, 2005), pp. 334–335; John Branch, "When the Generals Lose to the Globetrotters, Everyone Wins," *The New York Times*, February 13, 2009, p. 3; and Tim Kelly, *The Legend of Red Klotz: How Basketball's Loss Leader Won Over the World—14,000 Times* (Margate, NJ: ComteQ Publishing, 2013), pp. 265–275.

24 Joe Anzivina's "blanket of doom" remarks are offered in Ben Green, *Spinning the Globe: The Rise, Fall, and Return to Greatness of the Harlem Globetrotters* (New York: Harper Collins, 2005), pp. 352–353, 355.

25 For Klotz's "We're still here," see Ben Green, *Spinning the Globe: The Rise, Fall, and Return to Greatness of the Harlem Globetrotters* (New York: Harper Collins, 2005), p. 373.

25 Kurt Schneider's remarks are reported in John Branch, "When the Generals Lose to the Globetrotters, Everyone Wins," *The New York Times*, February 13, 2009, pp. B1–B2; and Richard Goldstein, "Red Klotz, Beloved Foil for Globetrotters, Dies at 93," *The New York Times*, July 16, 2014, p. A21.

25 For more on Herschend Family Entertainment, see Abram Brown, "The Wild Ride Of The Herschends: When Amusement Parks Are The Family Business," *Forbes*, May 26, 2014, p. 133. Also Curt Yeomans, "Peachtree Corners company moving Harlem Globetrotters to Gwinnett," *Gwinnett Daily Post*, July 21, 2015, p. 1.

27 Klotz's passing was reported in "Red Klotz, 81," *Sports Illustrated*, December 29, 2014, p. 93; and Richard Goldstein, "Red Klotz, Beloved Foil for Globetrotters, Dies at 93," *The New York Times*, July 16, 2014, p. A21.

27 Schneider's tribute to Klotz is from "Louis 'Red' Klotz dies at age 93," www.espn.com, July 14, 2014; and Richard Goldstein, "Red Klotz, Beloved Foil for Globetrotters, Dies at 93," *The New York Times*, July 16, 2014, p. 21.

27 Tim Kelly, *The Legend of Red Klotz: How Basketball's Loss Leader Won Over the World—14,000 Times* (Margate, NJ: ComteQ Publishing, 2013), p. 5.

28 Klotz's "helped pioneer basketball..." is from Tim Kelly, *The Legend of Red Klotz: How Basketball's Loss Leader Won Over the World—14,000 Times* (Margate, NJ: ComteQ Publishing, 2013), p. 5.

28 His "worshipping winners," is from Tim Crothers, "The General Whose Army Never Wins," *Sports Illustrated*, February 20, 1995, p. 5.

28 Coach McGuire is quoted in Steve Rushin, "Celebrating the Noncelebrators," *Sports Illustrated*, January 14, 2013, p. 78.

28 For more on Meadowlark Lemon's appreciation of Klotz, see Richard Goldstein, "Red Klotz, Beloved Foil for Globetrotters, Dies at 93," *The New York Times*, July 16, 2014, p. A21; and Tim Crothers, "The General Whose Army Never Wins," *Sports Illustrated*, February 20, 1995, p. 4.

28 The Barnum quote is from "Wit & Wisdom," *The Week*, May 6, 2016, p. 10A.

29 The Generals' GM John Ferrari's "It's over..." is from Darren Rovell, "After 63 years, Globetrotters drop rival Generals as primary opponent," www.espn.com, August 13, 2015. Also Chuck Schilken, "Harlem Globetrotters won't play longtime opponents Washington Generals anymore," *Los Angeles Times*, August 14, 2015; and Paul Newberry, "Column: Generals take final defeat, and it's a loss for us all," *Star Tribune*, August 14, 2015, p. 1.

29 The Ferrari comments and lament are reported in Darren Rovell, "After 63 years, Globetrotters drop rival Generals as primary opponent," www.espn.com, August 13, 2015.

Chapter 3. Football-Lite

31 For more on the University of Pennsylvania football, see Dan Rottenberg, *Fight On, Pennsylvania: A Century of Red and Blue Football* (Philadelphia: University of Pennsylvania, 1985). The Fabulous Forties are discussed on pp. 68–72.

32 F. Scott Fitzgerald's pony teams description is from Kevin Helliker, "The Football Genius of F. Scott Fitzgerald," *The Wall Street Journal*, October 25–26, 2014, p. C5.

32 The Izenberg "too small, too slow..." quote is from www.youtube.com/watch?.

33   President Gates' quotes are from Dan Rottenberg, *Fight On, Pennsylvania: A Century of Red and Blue Football* (Philadelphia: University of Pennsylvania, 1985), p. 46.

34   *The Daily Pennsylvania* citation and evolution of lightweight football at Penn are discussed in University of Pennsylvania 75th Anniversary of 150 lbs., Lightweight, Sprint Football (Philadelphia: University of Pennsylvania, 2008), p. 5.

35   The current rules of Collegiate Sprint Football League (CSFL) may be found at www.sprintfootball.com.

36   Coach Wagner's career is variously examined in the *University of Pennsylvania 75th Anniversary of 150 lbs., Lightweight, Sprint Football* (Philadelphia: University of Pennsylvania, 2008); and www.pennathletics.com.

37   Grace Calhoun's quote and Wagner's response are from "Sprint Football Announces Coaching Endowment," September 9, 2014, www.pennathletics.com.

38   Dave Zeitlin, "Varsity Rules," *The Pennsylvania Gazette*, Nov/Dec 2013, pp. 23–24.

38   The Wolfe quote is from Dave Zeitlin, "Varsity Rules," *The Pennsylvania Gazette*, Nov/Dec 2013, p. 23.

39   George Allen's famous quote is variously reported. See Sam Borden, "The Spill of Victory," *The New York Times*, January 21, 2012, p. D1.

40   Wagner's comments on Army are from Steven Jacobson, "Penn sprint football suffers tough loss on senior night," *The Daily Pennsylvanian*, October 26, 2014, p. 3.

41   The VanderZwaag quote is from *University of Pennsylvania 75th Anniversary of 150 lbs., Lightweight, Sprint Football* (Philadelphia: University of Pennsylvania, 2008), p. 35.

41   Izenberg's description of the Pride Bowl is from the ESPN YouTube video referred to above.

41   Cadet Burrell is quoted in the ESPN YouTube video.

42   Carl Hiaasen's thoughts on money are from "Carl Hiaasen Picks Martin Amis' 'Money' for WSJ Book Club," *The Wall Street Journal*, November 21, 2014, p. D5.

42   Mike Lopresti, "Meyer Saga reminds us coaches are people first," *USA Today*, December 28, 2009, p. 2C.

42   Andy Staples, "Coaching Lesson," *Sports Illustrated*, July 26, 2010, p. 26

42   Bobby Johnson's comments are from Andy Staples, "Coaching Lesson," *Sports Illustrated*, July 26, 2010, p. 26.

43   Nick Saban's salary and the relevant survey information are from Erik Brady, Steve Berkowitz and Christopher Schnaars, "Wisconsin bucks coaching salary trend," *USA Today*, October 9, 2015, p. C1, C6–C7. Also Gilbert M. Gaul, *Billion-Dollar Ball: A Journey Through the Big-Money Culture of College Football* (New York: Viking, 2005); Brad Wolverton, "10 Revealing Tidbits We Found in Football Coaches' Contracts," *The Chronicle of Higher Education*, January 8, 2016, p. A12; and John A. Fry, "We're Glad to Say No to College Football," *The Wall Street Journal*, January 4, 2016, p. A15.

43   Coach Snyder's criticism is reported in Jason Gay, "When Colleges Tell the Truth," *The Wall Street Journal*, November 13, 2014, p. D.6.

43   Knute Rockne's famous quote is from Karl Shmavonian, "Thoughts On Football, 2014," *Forbes*, September 8, 2014, p. 152.

44   Adam Thompson, "A Small League for Little Dudes Is the New Hope at Mansfield U," *The Wall Street Journal*, September 26, 2008, pp. D1–D3.

45   Izenberg's "what it should be" comment is from the above referenced ESPN YouTube video.

45   Wagner's optimism is cited in *University of Pennsylvania 75th Anniversary of 150 lbs., Lightweight, Sprint Football* (Philadelphia: University of Pennsylvania, 2008), p. 48.

Chapter 4. Supporting Acts

47   George Jessel's human brain quote is found at www.brainyquote.com.

47-50   Harry Maurer's career is examined in "Meet Guest Entertainer Harry Maurer," *Passages*, April 5, 2015, p. 3; and www.hmmagic.com.

50   The Daniel Webster quote was offered at the signing of the Declaration of Independence, Philadelphia, July 4, 1776.

51   Judy Greer's "not a movie star" is from her *I Don't Know What You Know From Me: Confessions of a Co-Star* (New York: Doubleday, 2014), p. xiiii. See Patrick Ryan, "Judy Greer is summer's best supporting star," *USA Today*, July 21, 2015, p. 10B; Alexandra Wolfe, "Behind the Scenes with Judy Greer," *The Wall Street Journal*, May 17–18, 2014, p. C11.

52   Jimmy Stewart's advice may be found in Eric Felten, "In Hollywood, New Rage Against Age," *The Wall Street Journal*, June 25, 2010, p. W11.

52   Greer's "I'm diversified..." is from her *I Don't Know What You Know From Me: Confessions of a Co-Star* (New York: Doubleday, 2014), p. 155.

52   Her "normal person" is from Alexandra Wolfe, "Behind the Scenes with Judy Greer," *The Wall Street Journal*, May 17–18, 2014, p. C11.

52   The "celebrity pee" is discussed in *I Don't Know What You Know From Me: Confessions of a Co-Star* (New York: Doubleday, 2014), pp. 104, 108–109.

53   Her "direct and honest" remarks are from *I Don't Know What You Know From Me: Confessions of a Co-Star* (New York: Doubleday, 2014), p. 113.

53   "Small roles..." is from *I Don't Know What You Know From Me: Confessions of a Co-Star* (New York: Doubleday, 2014), p. xiv.

53   For "The fear of it all ending..." see her *I Don't Know What You Know From Me: Confessions of a Co-Star* (New York: Doubleday, 2014), p. 156.

53   Her "peaks and valleys" comment are from her *I Don't Know What You Know From Me: Confessions of a Co-Star* (New York: Doubleday, 2014), p. 231. Also Patrick Ryan, "Judy Greer is summer's best supporting star," *USA Today*, July 21, 2015, p. 10B.

54   See Roger Rosenblatt, "The Straight Man," *Modern Maturity*, July–August 1996, p. 20.

54   Van Morrison's quote is from www.quoteshut.com.

54-55 Jim Nabor's career is variously reported. See "Comedies: Success Is a Warm Puppy," *Time*, November 10, 1967, p. 1; Susan King, "Just like Gomer, Jim Nabors Remains the Optimist," *Los Angeles Times*, December 6, 2008, pp. F14–F15; Vernon Scott, "Jim Nabors Follows His Instinct to fame," *The Bryan Times*, November 22, 2008, p. 16; Paulette Cohn, "Jim Nabors Lives Happily in Hawaii," *American Profile*, January 13, 2008; "Jim Nabors Honored in Home State," *The Washington Post*, April 24, 2006; "A night for heroes," *Honolulu Star-Bulletin*, December 12, 2006; Keoki Kerr, "Exclusive: Actor Jim Nabors marries his longtime male partner," Hawaii News Now: KGMB/KHNL, January 29, 2013; Peter Carlisle, "Jim Nabors Shares Life Lessons in Hawaii," *Honolulu Civil Beat*, March 23, 2015; and "Jim Nabors 'Impossible Dream,'" Hawaii News Now: KGMB/KHNL, November 22, 2015.

55   His relocation to Hawaii is discussed in Peter Carlisle, "Jim Nabors Shares Life Lessons in Hawaii," *Honolulu Civil Beat*, March 23, 2015; and Keoki Kerr, "Exclusive: Actor Jim Nabors marries his longtime male partner," Hawaii News Now: KGMB/KHNL, January 29, 2013.

56   For more on Carole Kai, see Kaysen Jones, "True Grit," *Generations Hawaii*, February/March 2007; Jo McGarry, "Carole Kai," *MidWeek*, September 7, 2007; and John Berger, "Loyal Divas," *Honolulu Star-Bulletin*, July 28, 2010.

56   "Always had food..." is from Kaysen Jones, "True Grit," *Generations Hawaii*, February/March 2007, p. 2.

56   "Hawaii's golden years..." is from Kaysen Jones, "True Grit," *Generations Hawaii*, February/March 2007, p. 2.

56   The Las Vegas/Reno/Lake Tahoe days are discussed in Kaysen Jones, "True Grit," *Generations Hawaii*, February/March 2007, pp. 3–4.

57   Her depression is from Kaysen Jones, "True Grit," *Generations Hawaii*, February/March 2007, p. 3.

57   The advice to return home is found in Kaysen Jones, "True Grit," *Generations Hawaii*, February/March 2007, p. 4.

58   Her pride in the Great Aloha Run is from "God's Great Aloha—Carole Kai," *Danny Yamashiro Ministries*, April 16, 2013, p. 2. Also www. greataloharun.com.

58   Johann Sebastian Bach is cited in Arthur C. Brooks, "How to Avoid Commencement Clichés," *The New York Times*, May 12, 2015, p. A23.

58   For Kai's "thank God," see Kaysen Jones, "True Grit," *Generations Hawaii*, February/March 2007, p. 4.

58   The Ethel Merman quote is cited in Elysa Gardner, "Ready to take a chance again, here's Barry Manilow," *USA Today*, June 13, 2011.

58   For more of Lisa Fischer, see Christian John Wikane, "The Women of '20 Feet from Stardom': Lisa Fischer," *PopMatters*, June 17, 2013; Mandalit Del Barco, "Spotlighting Background Singers In 'Twenty Feet From Stardom,'" *NPR Morning Edition*, June 11, 2013; Jon Bream, "Superstar backup singer Lisa Fischer is a stone-cold knockout at Dakota," [Minneapolis] *Star Tribune*, September 12, 2014. Also Sheena Metal, "Opening Acts..." www.musicbizacademy.com, October 2006.

58   Brook Barnes, "The Voice Behind the Mick (and Others)," *The New York Times*, June 7, 2013.

58   Fischer's preference for backup is from Mandalit Del Barco, "Spotlighting Background Singers In 'Twenty Feet From Stardom,'" *NPR Morning Edition*, June 11, 2013, p. 4; and Brook Barnes, "The Voice Behind the Mick (and Others)," *The New York Times*, June 7, 2013, D.4.

59   Robin Clark's comments are from Christian John Wikane, "The Women of '20 Feet from Stardom': Lisa Fischer," *PopMatters*, June 17, 2013, p. 2.

59   Fischer's "safe zone" is from Mandalit Del Barco, "Spotlighting Background Singers In 'Twenty Feet From Stardom,'" *NPR Morning Edition*, June 11, 2013, p. 3; and Marilou Regan, "Backup Diva: Lisa Fischer is 20 Feet From Stardom," *Love You Live, Rolling Stones, Fanzine from the Common Fan*, March 5, 2014, p. 5.

59   Her early struggles are discussed in Brook Barnes, "The Voice Behind the Mick (and Others)," *The New York Times*, June 7, 2013, p. 4.

59   The Rolling Stones engagement is from Bream, p. 1; and Marilou Regan, "Backup Diva: Lisa Fischer is 20 Feet From Stardom," *Love You Live, Rolling Stones, Fanzine from the Common Fan*, March 5, 2014, p. 9.

59   "Abandoning solo..." is from Mandalit Del Barco, "Spotlighting Background Singers In 'Twenty Feet From Stardom,'" *NPR Morning Edition*, June 11, 2013, p. 3, and Regan, p. 6.

59-60   Marilou Regan, "Backup Diva: Lisa Fischer is 20 Feet From Stardom," *Love You Live, Rolling Stones, Fanzine from the Common Fan*, March 5, 2014.

60   See *20 Feet From Stardom*, Tremolo Productions and Gil Friesen Productions, 2013.

60   Fischer's "my happy..." is from Brook Barnes, "The Voice Behind the Mick (and Others)," *The New York Times*, June 7, 2013, p. D4.

Chapter 5. Perfect Gentlemen

63-64   "Mama Lee" Wachstetter's quotes are from Lynn Cook, "Retiree is at home on dance floor and at sea," *Honolulu Star-Advertiser*, February 2, 2015, pp. F1, 10. Also Susanna Kim, "What It's Like for 86-year Old Woman Living Aboard Luxury Cruise Ship," ABC News, January 20, 2015; and Si Liberman, "Woman pays $164k per year to live on luxury cruise ship," *USA Today*, January 20, 2015, p. B1.

64   The Chaneys, "We thought," are quoted in "Cruise Line Hires Gentlemen 'Hosts,'" ABC News, http://abcnews.go.com/2020/story?id=124042.

64   Mama Lee's "most wives" is from Lynn Cook, "Retiree is at home on dance floor and at sea," *Honolulu Star-Advertiser*, February 2, 2015, pp. F1, 10.

65   For more on the Cunard Line, see Andrea Sachs, "One Dignified Deck," *The Washington Post*, September 13, 2015, pp. F1–F6; and Ian Thomson, "Cunard celebrates 175 years of crossing the Atlantic," *Financial Times Weekend*, August 1–2, 2015, p. 5.

65   CLIA's Richard Sasso is quoted in Kelani Best, "Cruise group celebrates growth of 'floating cities,'" *Florida Today*, March 17, 2010, p. C6.

65   The changing demographics of the cruise industry are presented in Paul Lasley and Elizabeth Harryman, "Good Fellowship," *Westways*, June 2015, p. 30; Brekke Fletcher, "Rocking the Boat," *The Wall Street Journal Magazine*, July/August 2015, p. 28; and "Cruise Market Watch Announces 2015 Cruise Trends Forecast," *Cruise Market Watch*, December 20, 2014, pp. 1–2.

66	For more on the prospects for Chinese cruisers, see Leo Lewis and Malcolm Moore, "Cruise lines set sail for China as holiday boom gathers steam," *Financial Times*, October 19, 2015, p. 15; and Laurie Burkitt, "Carnival Cruises Expansion in Asia," *The Wall Street Journal*, October 15, 2015, p. B2; Christopher Beam, "The cruise industry is coming to China," *Bloomberg Business Week*; Christopher Beam, "The People's Republic of Cruiseland," *Bloomberg Business Week,* April 22, 2015, pp. 50–57; and "Eastward ho!" *The Economist,* January 2, 2016, p. 51.
66	The British survey on satisfaction levels is found in "Top 5 Annoyances of Cruisers Revealed," *Cruise Market Watch*, April 13, 2014, p. 2. Also Lucy Kellaway, "On board but never bored," *Financial Times Weekend*, May 2–3, 2015, p. 7.
68	The Disraeli quote on delight is from www.freepaperz.com.
68	Doug Jones' quote on dancing is from Bob Morris "Male Cruise Ship Dancers," *Travel + Leisure*, May 2009, p. 2. Also Linda Coffman, "Let the Little Girl Dance," www.cruisediva.com; and Brian David Bruns, *Cruise Confidential: A Hit Below The Waterline* (Palo Alto, CA: Travelers' Tales, 2008).
68	For more on the Compass Speakers Website, see www.compassspeakers. com.
69	Bob Morris' remarks are from his "Male Cruise Ship Dancers," *Travel + Leisure*, May 2009, p. 2.
69	Alan Benedict is quoted in Ann Brenoff, "To Lovely Ladies: Gentlemen Hosts," *Huffpost 50*, March 3, 2014, pp. 1–2.
70	Diane Zammel's comments on "favoritism" are from Julie Lavanchy Laviolette, "It's strictly ballroom for these gents," *Orlando Sentinel*, March 11, 2007, p. 3.
70	Omar Ales' quote is from "Cruise Line Hires Gentlemen 'Hosts,'" ABC News, http://abcnews.go.com/2020/story?id=124042.
70	See Bob Morris "Male Cruise Ship Dancers," *Travel + Leisure*, May 2009, p. 3.
70	See *Out to Sea*, Twentieth Century Fox, July 2, 1997. Also Bob Morris "Male Cruise Ship Dancers," *Travel + Leisure*, May 2009, p. 3.
70	Escort Peter Drew's quote is from "Cruise Line Hires Gentlemen 'Hosts,'" ABC News, http://abcnews.go.com/2020/story?id=124042.
70	Bill Rolfing is quoted in "Cruise Line Hires Gentlemen 'Hosts,'" ABC News, http://abcnews.go.com/2020/story?id=124042.
71	Jack Ross' remarks is from "Cruise Line Hires Gentlemen 'Hosts,'" ABC News, http://abcnews.go.com/2020/story?id=124042.

71	Ken Hickey's "endless fun" is from Julie Lavanchy Laviolette, "It's strictly ballroom for these gents," *Orlando Sentinel*, March 11, 2007, pp. 2–3.
71	Ronne Infeld is quoted in Julie Lavanchy Laviolette, "It's strictly ballroom for these gents," *Orlando Sentinel*, March 11, 2007, p. 2.
71	The *Crystal Serenity* team is introduced in "Meet Our Ambassador Hosts," *Crystal Serenity*, May 15, 2013, p. 4.
71-72	Harry Norton's quotes are from John and Sandra Nowlan, "Hamilton's Harry dances the seas," *Hamilton Spectator*, August 8, 2011, pp. 1–2.
72	His "great time" quote is from Jeff Mahoney, "Nice work if you can get it (and if you dance)," *Hamilton Spectator*, August 12, 2012, pp. 1–2.
73	vanLee Hughey, *You Could Be at Sea Dance Hosting* (Atlanta; 1st Books, 2003), p. 11.
73	Tom Goodale's comments on jealousy are from Bob Morris "Male Cruise Ship Dancers," *Travel + Leisure*, May 2009, p. 3.
73	"It's a shame…" was posted on Brenoff on February 17, 2012.
73	Jaime Hayes' blog is also from Brenoff, February 17, 2012.
73-74	Rosemary Hirsch's comments are from Brenoff, February 17, 2012.
74	Ms. Platt is quoted in Brenoff, February 17, 2012.
75	James Russell Lowell's quote is from his 1864 *Fireside Travels*. See www.izquotes.com.

Chapter 6. Disposable Dons

77	"The job can kill you" is from Philip Nel. See on his blog: "This Job Can Kill You. Literally," September 9, 2013,
77-78	Ms. Vojtko's story is variously told. See Lindsay Ellis, "An Adjunct's Death Becomes a Rallying Cry for Many in Academe," *The Chronicle of Higher Education*, September 19, 2013, p. 1; L.V. Anderson, "Death of a Professor," *Slate*, November 17, 2013; Daniel Kovalik, "Death of an adjunct," *Pittsburg Post-Gazette*, September 18, 2013; and Francis X. Caiazza, "Margaret Mary the adjunct professor," *Pittsburgh Post-Gazette*, September 25, 2013, p. 1.
78	Professor Sowards' quote is from Lindsay Ellis, "An Adjunct's Death Becomes a Rallying Cry for Many in Academe," *The Chronicle of Higher Education*, September 19, 2013, p. 2.
78	Professor John Hess' remarks are from Don Eron, "The Case for Instructor Tenure," in Keith Hoeller, ed., *Equality for Contingent Faculty* (Nashville: Vanderbilt University Press, 2014), p. 31.

78   See L.V. Anderson, "Death of a Professor," *Slate*, November 17, 2013, pp. 10–11.

79   Vojtko's "teaching is not..." is from L.V. Anderson, "Death of a Professor," *Slate*, November 17, 2013, p. 5; and Francis X. Caiazza, "Margaret Mary the adjunct professor," *Pittsburgh Post-Gazette*, September 25, 2013, p. 2.

79   Her remarks on unionization are from L.V. Anderson, "Death of a Professor," *Slate*, November 17, 2013, pp. 7-8.

80   Her EEOC complaint is examined in L.V. Anderson, "Death of a Professor," *Slate*, November 17, 2013, p. 8.

80   For criticism of her classroom effectiveness, see L.V. Anderson, "Death of a Professor," *Slate*, November 17, 2013, p. 7.

80   Daniel Kovalik's comments are from his "Death of an adjunct," *Pittsburgh Post-Gazette*, September 18, 2013, p.1; Lindsay Ellis, "An Adjunct's Death Becomes a Rallying Cry for Many in Academe," *The Chronicle of Higher Education*, September 19, 2013, pp. 3–4; and Julian Routh, "Priest details late adjunct's stay on campus," *The Duquesne Duke*, September 20, 2013, pp. 1–2.

80   "For a proud professor..." is from Daniel Kovalik, "Death of an adjunct," *Pittsburgh Post-Gazette*, September 18, 2013, p. 1; and L.V. Anderson, "Death of a Professor," *Slate*, November 17, 2013, p. 9.

81   "A sad sight..." is reported in Nel above; and Julian Routh, "Vojtko remembered for pride, eloquence," *Duquesne Student Media*, September 19, 2013; and Francis X. Caiazza, "Margaret Mary the adjunct professor," *Pittsburgh Post-Gazette*, September 25, 2013, p. 2.

81   The Henry James quote is from www.whatquote.com.

81   Philip Nel's quote is from his above cited blog.

81   Professor Cerasoli's remarks on "bridge to nowhere" are from Simone Pathe, "Homeless professor protests conditions of adjuncts," PBS NewsHour, http://www.pbs.org/newshour/making-sense/homeless-professor-protests-conditions-adjuncts.

81-82   For more on the changing demographics of American faculty, see Keith Hoeller, "The Future of the Contingent Faculty Movement," *Inside Higher Ed*, http://insidehighered.com/views/2007/11/13/hoeller.

82   Adriana Kezar's comments are from Colleen Flaherty, "Imperative For Change," *Inside Higher Ed*, February 22, 2003, p. 1.

82   The flex or gig economy is variously considered. See Simone
      Baribeau, "Part-Time Nation," *The Christian Science Monitor
      Weekly*, June 9, 2014, pp. 27–34; Damian Paletta, "Temp Jobs
      Surge as Firms Contain Expenses," *The Wall Street Journal*, April
      7, 2014, p. A2; "The Freelance Economy," *Money*, October 2015,
      p. 21; Emma Jacobs, "The silent anxiety of the sharing economy,"
      Financial Times, June 26, 2015, p. 10; Mortimer Zuckerman,
      "The Full-Time Scandal of Part-Time America," *The Wall Street
      Journal*, July 14, 2014, p. A15; and Neil Irwin, "Job Growth in Past
      Decade was in Temp and Contract," *The New York Times*, March
      31, 2016, p. A3.

83   The Ardent Partners' findings and predictions are from Simone
      Baribeau, "Part-Time Nation," *The Christian Science Monitor
      Weekly*, June 9, 2014, pp. 28–29.

83   See Eric Morath, "Temp-Worker Freeze Bodes Ill for Economy,"
      The Wall Street Journal, May 23, 2016, p. A7.

83   President Carlos Migoya's remarks on "rightsizing" are reported
      in Simone Baribeau, "Part-Time Nation," *The Christian Science
      Monitor Weekly*, June 9, 2014, p. 29.

83   The happiness with freelancing is from Simone Baribeau, "Part-
      Time Nation," *The Christian Science Monitor Weekly*, June 9,
      2014, p. 31.

83   Nate Ginsberg's remarks are from Simone Baribeau, "Part-Time
      Nation," *The Christian Science Monitor Weekly*, June 9, 2014, p.
      31.

83   "It was great at the time..." is from Rob Walker, "The Frustrations
      of a Part-Timer," *The New York Times*, April 6, 2014, p. D7.

84   Sara Sutton Fell's "pivot point" thoughts are from Simone
      Baribeau, "Part-Time Nation," *The Christian Science Monitor
      Weekly*, June 9, 2014, p. 28.

84   Professor Christian Pyle's obscene remarks are from his
      "Adjuncts: the invisible majority," *North of Center*, April 27, 2011,
      p. 1. Also "The College Faculty Crisis," *The New York Times*, April
      14, 2014, p. A20; Katie Rose Guest Pryal, "The University Is Just
      Another Client," *The Chronicle of Higher Education*, Winter/
      Spring 2016, p. D14.

84   Terry Hartle is quoted in Paul Solman's "Is academia suffering
      from 'adjunctivitis'?" *PBS NewsHour*, February 6, 2014.

84   See Jeffrey J. Williams, "The Great Stratification," *The Chronicle
      of Higher Education*, December 6, 2013, p. B1. Also Marlana Eck,
      "How to Be an Adjunct (and Also a Cliché)," *The Chronicle of
      Higher Education*, Winter/Spring 2016, p. D14.

85   "The working poor" description is from Scott Jaschik, "Call to Arms for Adjuncts...From an Administrator," *Inside Higher Ed*, October 14, 2008, p. B1.

85   Professor Nicole Beth Wallenbrock's remarks are from Paul Solman's "Is academia suffering from 'adjunctivitis'?" *PBS NewsHour*, February 6, 2004.

85   Professor Joseph Fruscione is quoted in Rebecca Schuman's "Hanging Up on a Calling," *The Chronicle Review*, January 31, 2014, p. B16; and Rebecca Schuman, "Getting a literature Ph.D. will turn you into an emotional trainwreck, not a professor," *Slate*, April 5, 2013, www.slate.com.

85-86 For more on the dreadful hygiene factors, see "25 Telling Facts About Adjunct Faculty Today," *Best Colleges Online*, September 17, 2012, pp. 1–7.

86   Professor Betsy Smith is cited in Stacey Patton, "The Adjunct Is In. But Is She Getting Paid?" *The Chronicle of Higher Education*, March 28, 2014, p. A48.

86   Sacha Flanders' comments are from her "I'm an Adjunct, Not a Volunteer," *The Chronicle of Higher Education*, Winter/Spring, 2014, p. D18. Also Sharon Ullman, "How I Became Invisible," *The Chronicle Review*, October 2, 2015, p. B20.

86   See Christian Pyle, "Adjuncts: the invisible majority," *North of Center*, April 27, 2011, p. 2.

86   The Shimers' situation and quotes are from Tamar Lewin, "More College Adjuncts See Strength in Union Numbers," *The New York Times*, December 4, 2013, p. A13.

86   See Michael Dubson, ed., *Ghosts in the Classroom: Stories of College Adjunct Faculty—and the Price We All Pay* (Boston: Camel's Back, 2001); and Brian Croxall, "The Absent Presence: Today's Faculty," *The Chronicle of Higher Education*, December 27, 2009, p. 1.

87   Professor Fruscione's quote is from Paul Solman's "Is academia suffering from 'adjunctivitis'?" *PBS NewsHour*, February 6, 2004. Also Joe Fruscione, "Adjunct, Help Thyself," *Vitae*, October 14, 2013.

87   The National Bureau of Economic Research report is cited in Dan Berrett, "Adjuncts Are Better Teachers Than Tenured Professors, Study Finds," *The Chronicle of Higher Education*, September 9, 2013, p. 1.

87   For more on the Northwestern study, see Dan Berrett, "Adjuncts Are Better Teachers Than Tenured Professors, Study Finds," *The Chronicle of Higher Education*, September 9, 2013, pp. 1–3.

87   Confucius' remarks on respect are found at www. famousquotesindex.com.

87   Professor Báthory-Kitsz is quoted in Phil Nel's blog cited above.

88   John Carroll's David Wilder is cited in Peter Schmidt, "Advocates for Adjuncts Think Broadly in Search for Allies," *The Chronicle of Higher Education*, November 29, 2013, p. A10.

88   Claire Potter's remarks are from her "The Associate Professor Blues," *The Chronicle of Higher Education*, September 28, 2013, p. 3.

88   The American Federation of Teachers' initiative is cited on "25 Telling Facts About Adjunct Faculty Today," *Best Colleges Online*, September 17, 2012, p. 4.

88   Akron professor A.G. Monaco is quoted in Scott Jaschik, "Call to Adjuncts...From an Administrator," *Inside Higher Ed*, October 14, 2008, pp. 1–2.

88   See Douglas Belkin, "Job-Seeking Ph.D. Holders Look to Life Outside School," *The Wall Street Journal*, June 15, 2016, p. A3.

88   Professor Nel's remarks are from his above cited blog.

89   The Fidelity survey is cited in Melanie Hicken, "Professors teach into their golden years," *CNN Money*, June 17, 2013, p. 12.

89   Professor Christian Pyle's "dead-end job" is from his "Adjuncts: the invisible majority," *North of Center*, April 27, 2011, p. 4. See also Paula Krebs, "Trapped?" *The Chronicle of Higher Education*, Winter/Spring 2015, p. D18; and Debra Erickson, "Why It's So Hard to Leave Academe," *The Chronicle of Higher Education*, Winter/Spring 2016, p. D21.

89   "The Adjunctivitis Epidemic" was reported by Paul Solman, "Is academia suffering from 'adjunctivitis'?" *PBS NewsHour*, February 6, 2014.

89   Terry Hartle is quoted in Paul Solman's "Is academia suffering from 'adjunctivitis'?" *PBS NewsHour*, February 6, 2004.

89   William Pannapacker's thoughts are offered under the pen name, Thomas H. Benton, "Just Don't Go, Part 2," *The Chronicle of Higher Education*, March 13, 2009.

89   Maha Muslimah's "stop training" is from her blog, www. mahamuslimah.wordpress.com, posted September 24, 2013. Also Stacey Patton, "The Adjunct Is In. But Is She Getting Paid?" *The Chronicle of Higher Education*, March 28, 2014, p. A48.

89   The Pannapacker quote is from Thomas H. Benton, "Just Don't Go, Part 2," *The Chronicle of Higher Education*, March 13, 2009.

89   President Trachtenberg's thoughts on PhDs are from Paul Solman, "Is academia suffering from 'adjunctivitis'?" *PBS NewsHour*, February 6, 2004.

89   SooJin Pate is quoted in her, "What's Next for You?" *The Chronicle of Higher Education*, April 11, 2014, p.41.

89   The Deepak Chopra advice on wisdom is from SooJin Pate, "What's Next for You?" *The Chronicle of Higher Education*, April 11, 2014, p. A41.

89   Ingrid Steffensen's transition and quotes are from her "Two loves: An adjunct's journey from the classroom to the racetrack," *Director*, April 8, 2014, http://www.pbs.org/newshour/making-sense/two-lovers-adjuncts-journey-classroom-racetrack/.

90   RPI President Jackson's pithy remarks are from my *Bright Triumphs From Dark Hours: Turning Adversity into Success* (Honolulu: University of Hawaii Press, 2010), p.41.

90-91   The Henry Ford quote may be found in *Bottom Line*, January 1, 1998, p. 2.

91   The adjunct feeling stuck is from Arik Greenberg, "How one professor's American dream teaching turned into the American nightmare," *PBS NewHour*, February 14, 2005.

91   Professor Wallenbrock's "dreams" are from Paul Solman, "Is academia suffering from 'adjunctivitis'?" *PBS NewsHour*, February 6, 2014.

91   Richard Moser, "Overuse and Abuse of Adjunct Faculty Members Threaten Core Academic Values," *The Chronicle of Higher Education*, January 17, 2014, p. A20.

91-92   Robin Soward's remarks are from Mark Oppenheimer, "For Duquesne Professors, a Union Fight Transcends Religion," *The New York Times*, June 22, 2012, p. B2. Also Lindsay Ellis, "An Adjunct's Death Becomes a Rallying Cry for Many in Academe," *The Chronicle of Higher Education*, September 19, 2013, pp.2–3.

92   David Rodich is quoted in "Adjunct Professors Seek Union Representation," *America Magazine*, September 9–16, 2013, p. 2. Also Paul Davidson, "Temporary, part-time workers not taking it anymore," *USA Today*, May 4, 2016, p. 8A

92   The Georgetown official is quoted in Peter Schmidt, "Adjuncts Appeal to Higher Power in Debate Over Working Conditions at Religious Colleges," *The Chronicle of Higher Education*, December 13, 3013, p. A2, A4. Also Nick DeSantis, "Georgetown Backs Academic Freedom of Adjunct Who Alluded to Assassinating Obama," *The Chronicle of Higher Education*, January 24, 2014, p. A22.

92   USC Professor Kezár's comments on unionization are from Tamar Lewin, "More College Adjuncts See Strength in Union Numbers," *The New York Times*, December 4, 2013, p. A18. Also Douglas Belkin, "Professors Raise Hands for Unions," *The Wall Street Journal*, January 20, 2016, p. A2; and Douglas Belkin, "Adjuncts' Moves To Join Unions Sharpen Debate," *The Wall Street Journal*, March 27, 2016, p. A2.

92   The Coalition on the Academic Workforce may be found in Stacey Patton, "The Adjunct Is In. But Is She Getting Paid?" *The Chronicle of Higher Education*, March 28, 2014, p. A48.

92   Gary Rhoades' comments on unionization are from L.V. Anderson, "Death of a Professor," *Slate*, November 17, 2013, p.19.

93   Professor Joseph Fahey's gutless remarks are from Peter Schmidt, "Advocates for Adjuncts Think Broadly in Search for Allies," *The Chronicle of Higher Education*, December 29, 2013, p. A10.

93   Fruscione's quote is from Schuman, p. B16; and Solman cited above.

93   Professor Ann Kottner's "most natural allies" is from Schmidt, "Advocates for Adjuncts Think Broadly in Search for Allies," *The Chronicle of Higher Education*, December 29, 2013, p. A10.

93   K.B. Brower is quoted in Jeffrey J. Williams, "The Great Stratification," *The Chronicle of Higher Education*, December 6, 2013, p. B7.

93   See Debra Leigh Scott's forthcoming film, *Junct: The Trashing of Higher Ed in America*; and her remarks are from Lindsay Ellis, "An Adjunct's Death Becomes a Rallying Cry for Many in Academe," *The Chronicle of Higher Education*, September 19, 2013, p. 4.

93-94   Representative Miller's remarks are from Ronald Roach, "Report: Part-time Professors Represented Among the Working Poor," *Diverse Education*, February 6, 2014, p. A1.

94   Professor Kezar's "invisible problem" is found in Audrey Williams June, "Adjuncts Gain Traction with Congressional Attention," *The Chronicle of Higher Education*, February 9, 2014, p. A3. See George Miller's "Presidents, Do Right by Athletes and Adjuncts," *The Chronicle of Higher Education*, June 20, 2014, p. A29.

94   Maria Maisto's remarks are from Lindsay Ellis, "An Adjunct's Death Becomes a Rallying Cry for Many in Academe," *The Chronicle of Higher Education*, September 19, 2013, p. 3; and Ronald Roach, "Report: Part-time Professors Represented Among the Working Poor," *Diverse Education*, February 6, 2014, p. 2.

94   Robert Frost on universities is from www.write-out-loud.com.

94   President Michael Crow is cited in Douglas Belkin, "Design For a New College," *The Wall Street Journal*, March 10, 2014, p. R5.

95   The Gandhi quote is from www.motivatingquotes.com.

Chapter 7. Halls of Ivy

98   Helen Keller's "happy life..." is from www.quotationspage.com.

99   Plato's comments on the value of education is from www.quotationspage.com.

99   Professor Toma's comments on prestige are referenced in Jeffrey Selingo, "From Tennessee: A Solution for Mission Creep," *The Chronicle of Higher Education*, February 21, 2014, p. A56.

99   See Cornell professor Suzanne Mettler, "College, the Great Unleveler," *The New York Times*, March 2, 2014, p. B5.

100   Frank Bruni, "Class, Cost and College," *The New York Times*, May 18, 2014, p. A30. Also Frank Bruni, *Where You Go Is Not Who You'll Be: An Antidote to the College Admissions Mania* (New York: Grand Central Publishing, 2015).

100   John Quiggin, "Campus Reflection," *The Chronicle Review*, May 16, 2014, p. B5.

100   For more on the problems and challenges confronting US universities, see Kate Bachelder's interview with Mitch Daniels, "How to Save American Colleges," *The Wall Street Journal*, April 25–26, 2015, p. A9; William Deresiewicz, "The Miseducation of America," *The Chronicle Review,* July 4, 2014, p. B6; Kevin Carey "'Too Big to Fail' Can Also Happen in Higher Education," *The New York Times,* July 15, 2014, p. A3; "Making college cost less," *The Economist*, April 5, 2014, p. 11; Mary Beth Marklein, "Colleges flunk happiness survey," *USA Today*, May 7, 2014, p. 3A; Frank Mussano and Robert V. Iosue, "Colleges Need a Business Productivity Audit," *The Wall Street Journal*, December 29, 2014, p. A15; Douglas Belkin, "Test Finds College Graduates Lack Skills for White-Collar Jobs," *The Wall Street Journal*, January 17–18, 2015, p. A5; Michael Roth, "What Is a University For?" *The Wall Street Journal*, March 5–6, 2016, p. C7; and Tim Harford, "Are universities really worth it?" *Financial Times*, August 28, 2016, p.27.

101 "Creative destruction," *The Economist*, June 28, 2014, p. 12.

101 See Suzanne Mettler, "College, the Great Unleveler," *The New York Times*, March 2, 2014, p. 5; and Suzanne Mettler, *Degrees of Inequality: How the Politics of Higher Education Sabotaged the American Dream* (New York: Basic, 2014).

101 The Gallup study is found in Douglas Belkin, "Recent Grads Doubt College's Worth," *The Wall Street Journal*, September 29, 2015, p. A3.

101 For more on student debt levels, see David Collins, "More student borrowers face private lenders' suits," *Honolulu Star-Advertiser*, November 22, 2015, p. A21.

102 The Pew Research Center is from Shaila Dewan, "Wage Premium From College Is Said to Be Up," *The New York Times*, February 12, 2014, p. B3. Also Mary Beth Marklein, "College degree still worth the investment, data suggest," *USA Today*, June 25, 2014, p. A1.

102 Tom Hanks' quote is from his "I Owe It All To Community Colleges," *The New York Times*, January 14, 2015, p. A23.

103 The rise of MOOCs are discussed in "Massive open online forces," *The Economist*, February 8, 2014, p. 74; Della Bradshaw, "Teaching revolution gathers pace," *Financial Times Special Report*, March 10, 2014, p. 1; Douglas Belkin, "Can MOOCs and Universities Co-Exist?" *The Wall Street Journal*, May 12, 2014, p. R3; and Alexandra Wolfe, "Daphne Kelley," *The Wall Street Journal*, June 6–7, 2015, p. C11.

103 For professor David Deming's comments on for-profit education, see Eduardo Porter, "The Bane and the Boon of For-Profit Colleges," *The New York Times*, February 26, 2014, p. 8. Also Patricia Cohen, "For-Profit Colleges Fail Standards, But Get Billions," *The New York Times*, October 13, 2015, p. A1.

104 Rob Jenkins' remarks on bias are from his "The 'Middle of the End' for Community Colleges?" *The Chronicle of Higher Education*, February 25, 2015, p. A28; and Rob Jenkins', "How the Job Search Differs at Community Colleges," *The Chronicle of Higher Education*, November 22, 2013, p. A31.

104 The "pernicious message" description is from Katherine Mangan, "Educators Who Serve Low-Income Students: Been there, Done That," *The Chronicle of Higher Education*, January 24, 2014, p. A4.

104 Mao Zedong's famous quote is from the *Encyclopedia Britannica*, vol. 4, p. 465.

104   Arthur M. Cohen and Florence B. Brawer, *The American Community College, 5th ed.*, (San Francisco: Jossey Bass, 2008), p. 91.

104-105   Professor Matthew Tuthill's quote on loss of equity is from his "Campus Considerations," *The Scientist*, March 1, 2014, p. 1.

105   SooJin Pate, also referenced in the previous chapter, is quoted in her "What's Next for You?" *The Chronicle of Higher Education*, April 11, 2014, p. A41.

105   For more on dual enrollment programs, see Henry T. Kasper, "The changing role of community college," *Occupational Outlook Quarterly*, Winter 2002–2003, pp. 16–17; Lisa Ward, "A Low-Cost Strategy for a College Degree," *The Wall Street Journal*, February 10, 2014, p. R9; Mark Keienleber, "4-Year Colleges' View of Transfer Credits May Hinder Graduation," *The Chronicle of Higher Education*, April 11, 2014, p. A8; and Nanea Kalani, "A Matter of Degrees," *Honolulu Star-Advertiser*, January 12, 2016, p. A1.

105   The AAUP information on teaching loads and salaries is found in Arthur M. Cohen and Florence B. Brawer, *The American Community College, 5th ed.*, (San Francisco: Jossey Bass, 2008), pp. 91–99. Also Audrey Williams June, "Raises for Public-College Faculty Edge Past Those at Private Colleges," *The Chronicle of Higher Education*, March 21, 2014, p. A8.

106   Ann Hubert, "How to Escape the Community-College Trap," *The Atlantic*, January/February 2014, p. 70.

106   Peter S. Bryant is quoted in Sara Lipka, "2-Year Colleges Get Strategic About Enrollment," *The New York Times*, November 15, 2013, p. A2.

106   The Association of Community Colleges opinion is also explored in Sara Lipka, "2-Year Colleges Get Strategic About Enrollment," *The New York Times*, November 15, 2013, p. A2.

106-107   The Obama grants are examined in "Federal aid for community college," *The Week*, August 1, 2014, p. 32.

107   John Ladd's thoughts on apprenticeships are found in Patricia Cohen, "The New Shop Class," *The New York Times*, March 11, 2015, p. B4. Also Kelly Field, "Apprenticeships Can Do What Colleges Can't, Advocates Say," *The Chronicle of Higher Education*, January 8, 2016, p. A14.

107-108   The Obama "college scorecard" is examined in Douglas Belkin, "Obama Spells Out College-Ranking Framework," *The Wall Street Journal,* December 19, 2014, p. A24; and Katherine Mangan and Beckie Supiano, "Proposed College Ratings: What the Metrics Mean," *The Chronicle of Higher Education*, January 9, 2015, p. A8.

108   The College Board statistics on tuition and fees are from Jillian Berman, "Questions Families Need to Ask About Paying for College," *The Wall Street Journal*, September 21, 2015, p. R1.

108   Kevin Fudge's "shift the goalposts" remarks are also discussed in Jillian Berman, "Questions Families Need to Ask About Paying for College," *The Wall Street Journal*, September 21, 2015, p. R2.

109   For more on the Tennessee Promise, see Katherine Mangan, "In Tennessee, Free Community College Jolts Enrollments as Questions Persist for 4-year Campuses," *The Chronicle of Higher Education*, September 20, 2015, p. A8.

109   The Obama proposal to make community college free is examined in Douglas Belkin, Byron Tau and Caroline Porter, "Obama Makes Case for Free Community College," *The Wall Street Journal*, January 10–11, 2015, p. A3; Michelle R. Weise, "Obama's Dead-End Community College Plan," *The Wall Street Journal*, January 13, 2015, p. A11; and Catherine Hill, "Free Tuition Is Not the Answer," *The New York Times*, November 30, 2015, p. A23.

109   Richard Kahlenberg's shedding community remarks are from Matthew Dolan and Caroline Porter, "Community-College Quiz: What's in a Name?" *The Wall Street Journal*, April 21, 2015, p. A4.

110   Chancellor Carroll's advocacy is discussed in Andy Thomason, "California's 2-year Colleges Consider Offering 4-year Degrees," *The Chronicle of Higher Education*, December 6, 2013, p. A8.

110   Professors Arthur M. Cohen and Florence B. Brawer's contrary view is from *The American Community College, 5th ed.*, (San Francisco: Jossey Bass, 2008), p. 430.

110   George Boggs' thoughts are from Matthew Dolan and Caroline Porter, "Community-College Quiz: What's in a Name?" *The Wall Street Journal*, April 21, 2015, p. A4. Also John Merrow, "The Smart Transfer," *The New York Times*, April 22, 2007, p. A14.

111   Arizona State's Jeffrey Selingo's "one-size-fits-all" remarks are from his "From Tennessee, a Solution for Mission Creep," *The Chronicle of Higher Education*, February 21, 2014, p. A56.

111   Robert Agrella's "all things" sentiment is from Jim Carlton and Caroline Porter, "One Man's Mission to Save City College of San Francisco," *The Wall Street Journal*, November 12, 2013, p. A3.

111   Professor Tuthill's quote is from his "Campus Considerations,"
        The Scientist, March 1, 2014, p. 2 and his "Community college
        benefits extend beyond economics," *Honolulu Star-Advertiser*,
        August 17, 2016, p.A15.

111   The AACCS report on doctorates is cited in Arthur M. Cohen
        and Florence B. Brawer, *The American Community College, 5th ed.*,
        (San Francisco: Jossey Bass, 2008), p. 86.

111-112 Chancellor Lacro's remarks and contributions are from "Erika
        Lacro," *Hawaii Business*, March 2014, p. 84.

112   Professor Robert Chaney's quotes may be found in Lindsey Ellis,
        "Professors of the Year Reflect on How Failures Helped Them
        Improve," *The Chronicle of Higher Education*, November 22, 2013,
        p. A14.

112   See Arthur M. Cohen and Florence B. Brawer, *The American
        Community College, 5th ed.*, (San Francisco: Jossey Bass, 2008), p. 430.

113   Terry O'Banion's "Andy Warhol moment" may be found in
        Katherine Mangan, "2-Year Colleges Are Urged to Capitalize on
        Their Time in the Spotlight," *The Chronicle of Higher Education*,
        March 14, 2014, p. A24. Also Alina Tugend, "A Case for Change,"
        The New York Times, June 23, 2016, p. F8.

113   For Chaney's "dream come true..." see Ellis, "Professors of the
        Year Reflect on How Failures Helped Them Improve," *The
        Chronicle of Higher Education*, November 22, 2013, p. A14.

Chapter 8. Underdogs of the Air

115   The "giggle factor" is from Steven Lee Myers, "A Busted Blimp
        Releases a Large Giggle Factor," *The New York Times*, July 11, 1993.

115-116 For more on the history of dirigibles, see Arthur Frederick Daube
        Ventry and Eugene M. Kolesnik, *Airship Saga: The History of Airships
        Seen Through the Eyes of the Men Who Designed, Built, and Flew
        Them* (Poole, UK: Blandford Press, 1982); Douglas Hill Robinson and
        Charles I. Keller, *Up Ship!: A History of the U.S. Navy's Rigid Airships
        1919–1935* (Annapolis, MD: US Naval Institute Press, 1982); Douglas
        Hill Robinson, *Giants in the Sky: A History of the Rigid Airship* (Seattle:
        University of Washington Press, 1975); John Toland, *Ships in the Sky:
        The Story of the Great Dirigibles* (New York: Henry Holt, 1957); C.
        Michael Hiam, *Dirigible Dreams: The Age of the Airship* (Lebanon,
        NH: ForeEdge, 2014); and Richard Holmes, *Falling Upwards: How We
        Took to the Air* (New York: Pantheon Books, 2013).

116   "All work...stopped" is from Douglas Hill Robinson, *Giants in the Sky:
        A History of the Rigid Airship* (Seattle: University of Washington Press,
        1975), p. xv. Also John Toland, *Ships in the Sky: The Story of the Great
        Dirigibles* (New York: Henry Holt, 1957), p. 9.

116-117   The impact of World War II on US blimp activity is examined in Richard G. Van Treuren, *Airships vs. Submarines* (Edgewater, FL: Atlantis Publications, 2009); J. Gordon Vaeth, *Blimps & U-Boats: U.S. Navy Airships in the Battle of the Atlantic* (Annapolis, MD: US Naval Institute Press, 1992); William F. Althoff, *Sky Ships: A History of Airships in the United States Navy* (New York: Orion Books, 1990); William F. Althoff, *Forgotten Weapon: U.S. Navy Airships and the U-Boat War* (Annapolis, MD: Naval Institute Press, 2009); Charles E. Rosendahl, *United States Navy Airships in World War II* (Edgewater, FL: Atlantis Publications, 2007); Herman G. Spahr, *Aweigh And Up: Personal Memories of Lighter-Than-Air* (Lafayette, IN: unpublished manuscript, undated); Don Kaiser, "K-Ships Across The Atlantic," *Naval Aviation News*, Spring 2011, pp. 20–23; and John A. Fahey, *Wasn't I the Lucky One* (Virginia Beach, VA: B&J Books, 2000). Also www.naval-airships.org and www.airships.net.

117   William F. Althoff, *Forgotten Weapon: U.S. Navy Airships and the U-Boat War* (Annapolis, MD: Naval Institute Press, 2009), p. 2.

117   A discussion of the last flight of a military airship is presented in William F. Althoff, *Sky Ships: A History of Airships in the United States Navy* (New York: Orion Books, 1990), ch. 9, especially pp. 256–263; and Richard G. Van Treuren, *Airships vs. Submarines* (Edgewater, FL: Atlantis Publications, 2009), p. 406.

118   Alexander Charles' quotes are from Jonathan Rosen, "'Our Place Is In the Sky,'" *The Atlantic*, December 13, 2014, p. 44; and Paul Elie, "Upper Atmospherics," *The New York Times Book Review*, November 17, 2013, p. 19.

118-119   Ms. Blanchard is described in Jonathan Rosen, "'Our Place Is In the Sky,'" *The Atlantic*, December 13, 2014, p. 44; and Paul Elie, "Upper Atmospherics," *The New York Times Book Review*, November 17, 2013, p. 19.

119   Andrée's North Pole disaster is considered in Jonathan Rosen, "'Our Place Is In the Sky,'" *The Atlantic*, December 13, 2014, pp. 45–46. Also C. Michael Hiam, *Dirigible Dreams: The Age of the Airship* (Lebanon, NH: ForeEdge, 2014), pp. 28–44.

119   Santos-Dumont's view of Paris is from C. Michael Hiam, *Dirigible Dreams: The Age of the Airship* (Lebanon, NH: ForeEdge, 2014), pp. 15–25.

119   Zeppelin mania is examined in Manfred Griehl and Joachin Dressel, *Zeppelin!: The German Airship Story* (Colchester, UK: Arms & Armour 1991); Douglas H. Robinson, *The Zeppelin in Combat: A History of the German Naval Airship Division* (Atglen, PA: Shiffen Publications, 1994); Peter W. Brooks, *Zeppelin Rigid Airships 1893–1940* (Washington: Smithsonian Institution Press, 1992); and C. Michael Hiam, *Dirigible Dreams: The Age of the Airship* (Lebanon, NH: ForeEdge, 2014), ch. 3.

120   The dangers of hydrogen are presented in C. Michael Hiam, *Dirigible Dreams: The Age of the Airship* (Lebanon, NH: ForeEdge, 2014), pp. 12–15, 120; and Ash Carter, "Gasbag," *Town and Country Magazine*, April 2014, p. 46.

120   For more on the *Shenandoah* disaster, see C. Michael Hiam, *Dirigible Dreams: The Age of the Airship* (Lebanon, NH: ForeEdge, 2014), p. 129–132; and William F. Althoff, *Sky Ships: A History of Airships in the United States Navy* (New York: Orion Books, 1990), ch. 2.

120   The *Akron* plunge is from C. Michael Hiam, *Dirigible Dreams: The Age of the Airship* (Lebanon, NH: ForeEdge, 2014), pp. 136–139; John Toland, *Ships in the Sky: The Story of the Great Dirigibles* (New York: Henry Holt, 1957), pp.50–51; Althoff, *Sky Ships: A History of Airships in the United States Navy*, Ch. 4; Richard K. Smith, *The Airships Akron & Macon: Flying Aircraft Carriers of the United States Navy* (Annapolis, MD: Naval Institute Press, 1965); and "Ceremony will mark 80 years since Naval dirigible crash killed 73 of 76 aboard," *Honolulu Star-Advertiser*, April 1, 2013, p. A5.

120-121   See J. Gordon Vaeth, *Blimps & U-Boats: U.S. Navy Airships in the Battle of the Atlantic* (Annapolis, MD: US Naval Institute Press, 1992), p. 54.

121   Henry Cord Meyer's sentiments are from his *Airshipmen Businessmen & Politics 1890–1940 (Smithsonian History of Aviation and Spaceflight Series)* (Washington: Smithsonian Institution Press, 1991), p. 242.

121   For more on the *Hindenburg*, see C. Michael Hiam, *Dirigible Dreams: The Age of the Airship* (Lebanon, NH: ForeEdge, 2014), pp. 216–228; William F. Althoff, *Sky Ships: A History of Airships in the United States Navy* (New York: Orion Books, 1990), pp. 129–141; and Robinson, *Giants in the Sky: A History of the Rigid Airship,* pp. 282–293.

121   Dan Grossman's quotes are from Matt Schudel, "Werner Franz, one of the last survivors of the 1937 Hindenburg crash, dies at 92," *The Washington Post*, August 21, 2014, p. C8.

121-122   The *Hindenburg* crash and Morrison quotes may be found in Matt Schudel, "Werner Franz, one of the last survivors of the 1937 Hindenburg crash, dies at 92," *The Washington Post*, August 21, 2014, p. C8; C. Michael Hiam, *Dirigible Dreams: The Age of the Airship* (Lebanon, NH: ForeEdge, 2014), pp. 228–229; and John Toland, *Ships in the Sky: The Story of the Great Dirigibles* (New York: Henry Holt, 1957), p. 322.

122   William F. Althoff, *Sky Ships: A History of Airships in the United States Navy* (New York: Orion Books, 1990), p. 141. Also C. Michael Hiam, *Dirigible Dreams: The Age of the Airship* (Lebanon, NH: ForeEdge, 2014), pp.229–231; and John Toland, *Ships in the Sky: The Story of the Great Dirigibles* (New York: Henry Holt, 1957), p. 339.

122   See C. Michael Hiam, *Dirigible Dreams: The Age of the Airship* (Lebanon, NH: ForeEdge, 2014), p. 7.

122   President Roosevelt's skepticism about the role of LTA is from William F. Althoff, *Forgotten Weapon: U.S. Navy Airships and the U-Boat War* (Annapolis, MD: Naval Institute Press, 2009), pp. 5, 54; Henry Cord Meyer, *Airshipmen Businessmen & Politics 1890–1940 (Smithsonian History of Aviation and Spaceflight Series)* (Washington: Smithsonian Institution Press, 1991), pp. 73, 241; Robinson, *Giants in the Sky: A History of the Rigid Airship*, p. 288; and Richard G. Van Treuren, *Airships vs. Submarines* (Edgewater, FL: Atlantis Publications, 2009), p. 410.

123   Adm. Charles E. Rosendahl's query is from his, *What About the Airship?: The Challenge to the United States* (New York: Charles Scribner's Sons, 1939), p. 123.

123   See Richard G. Van Treuren, *Airships vs. Submarines* (Edgewater, FL: Atlantis Publications, 2009), p. 53.

124   William F. Althoff, *Forgotten Weapon: U.S. Navy Airships and the U-Boat War* (Annapolis, MD: Naval Institute Press, 2009), p. 49.

124   "Unmitigated hell" is from J. Gordon Vaeth, *Blimps & U-Boats: U.S. Navy Airships in the Battle of the Atlantic* (Annapolis, MD: US Naval Institute Press, 1992), p. 42.

125   LTA's exceptional availability is examined in Richard G. Van Treuren, *Airships vs. Submarines* (Edgewater, FL: Atlantis Publications, 2009), p. 51; and William F. Althoff, *Forgotten Weapon: U.S. Navy Airships and the U-Boat War* (Annapolis, MD: Naval Institute Press, 2009), p. 300.

125   Its protective air service accomplishments are highlighted in Rosendahl, *United States Navy Airships in World War II*, p. 7; Richard G. Van Treuren, *Airships vs. Submarines* (Edgewater, FL: Atlantis Publications, 2009), pp. 24–28, 410; and William F. Althoff, *Forgotten Weapon: U.S. Navy Airships and the U-Boat War* (Annapolis, MD: Naval Institute Press, 2009), pp. 232–233.

125   William F. Althoff, *Forgotten Weapon: U.S. Navy Airships and the U-Boat War* (Annapolis, MD: Naval Institute Press, 2009), pp. 16, 298.

125   Admiral Rosendahl's lament is from Richard G. Van Treuren, *Airships vs. Submarines* (Edgewater, FL: Atlantis Publications, 2009), p. 328.

125-126   The Donitz statement is referenced in Rosendahl, p. 152; and J. Gordon Vaeth, *Blimps & U-Boats: U.S. Navy Airships in the Battle of the Atlantic* (Annapolis, MD: US Naval Institute Press, 1992), p. 172.

126   See Richard G. Van Treuren, *Airships vs. Submarines* (Edgewater, FL: Atlantis Publications, 2009), p. 32. Also, pp. 54–55.

126   See *This Man's Navy*, Metro-Goldwyn-Mayer, January 4, 1945.

127   Joel Mokyr is quoted in Virginia Heffernan, "Vidi Estas Kredi* Seeing Is Believing," *The New York Times Magazine*, November 16, 2014, p. 55.

127   Goodyear's current activities are variously reported. See James R. Schock and David R. Smith, *The Goodyear Airships—A Photographic History* (Bloomington, IL: Airship International Press, 2002); James Ewinger, "Goodyear rolls out newest blimp with help of Zeppelin," *The Plain Dealer*, March 14, 2014; Rich Heldenfels, "A new blimp is christened: Wingfoot One makes its formal debut," *Akron Beacon Journal*, August 23, 2014

127   Doug Grassian is quoted in James Ewinger and Aubrey Cohen, "Goodyear's new 'Wingfoot One' isn't a blimp," *Seattle Post-Intelligencer*, August 25, 2014, p.1.

127   The US Army initiative is discussed in Joshua A. Krisch, "A New Quest Borne Upon a Relic," *The New York Times*, August 26, 2014, p. D6; and Dion Nissenbaum, "Technical Woes Scuttle Army Spy-Blimp Project," *The Wall Street Journal*, February 15, 2013, p. A3.

127   Senator McCain's criticism is reported in Dion Nissenbaum, "Builder to Ask Army for Canceled Blimp," *The Wall Street Journal*, March 19, 2013, p. A3.

128   The recent Maryland collapse is discussed in Tom Vanden Brook, "Military blimp goes AWOL for a joy ride up the East Coast," *USA Today*, October 29, 2015, p. 6A.

128   The Worldwide Aeros initiative is described in "Aeros," *The Noon Balloon*, Summer 2015, p. 33; and Billy Witz, "A Colossal Ambition," *The New York Times*, November 11, 2014, p. B1. Also "Airships in the Artic," *The Economist*, June 11, 2016, p. 36.

128   Professor Sarah Miller is quoted in Joshua A. Krisch, "A New Quest Borne Upon a Relic," *The New York Times*, August 26, 2014, p. D1.

129   Victor Hugo's "tyranny of gravity" is found in Jonathan Rosen, "'Our Place Is In the Sky,'" *The Atlantic*, December 13, 2014, p. 46.

129   The Chinese proverb on the miracle of walk is from Jonathan Rosen, "'Our Place Is In the Sky,'" *The Atlantic*, December 13, 2014, p. 46.

Chapter 9. Meals on Wheels

132   See Mufi Hannemann, "From the Stage to the Kitchen..." *MidWeek*, June 2, 2015, p. 27. Also Betty Shimabukuro, "Sam Choy's Seattle enterprise primed, ready for expansion," *The Honolulu Star-Advertiser*, April 13, 2016, p. C1. More recently, Mr. Kinimaka's passing was reported in "Hawaiian musician made a lasting impact" by John Berger, *Honolulu Star-Advertiser*, August 5, 2016, p. A-22.

133   For more on the history of mobile vendors, see Daniel Engber, "Who Made that Food Truck?" *The New York Times Magazine*, March 22, 2014; Danielle Bowling, "The business of street food," *Hospitality Magazine*, August 23, 2012; Kai Ryssdal, "Food Truck Nation," *American Public Media*, July 30, 2010; and Katie Robbins, "The Food Truck Economy," *The Atlantic*, July 21, 2010.

133   Daniel Engber, "Who Made that Food Truck?" *The New York Times Magazine*, March 22, 2014, p. MM21.

133   Bryan Urstadt, "Intentionally Temporary," *New York Magazine*, September 23, 2009.

133   Joel Stein, "Gourmet On the Go: Good Food Goes Trucking," *TIME*, March 29, 2010, p. 1.

134   Zachary Sniderman's quote is from his "How Social Media Is Fueling The Food Truck Phenomenon," June 16, 2011, Mashable, http://www.mashable.com/2011/06/16/food-trucks-social-media.

134   The Emergent Research study is reported in http://www.emergentresearch.com.

134-135   The IBISWorld study on growth is from Chris Bibey, "Food Trucks, Street Vendors Move Up In Business," *SurePayroll*, May 8, 2015.

135   Tod Schifeling and Daphne Demetry's "new authenticity economy" is from their "Study identifies factors that contribute to food trucks' fast spread," *University of Michigan News*, August 16, 2014.

135-136   The Banán story is reported in Mindy Pennybacker, "A Banan for the man," *The Honolulu Star-Advertiser*, June 15, 2015, p. D2, and Kawehi Haug, "This Frozen Fruit Treat is Just Bananas," *Honolulu Magazine*, February 5, 2015, p. 12.

136-137   Sam Sifton, "Karma Asada," *The New York Times Magazine*, July 12, 2012, p. MM46; Katy McLaughlin, "The King of the Streets Moves Indoors," *The Wall Street Journal*, January 15, 2010, B3; Zachary Sniderman, "How Social Media Is Fueling The Food Truck Phenomenon," June 16, 2011, Mashable, http://www.mashable.com/2011/06/16/food-trucks-social-media; and Joel Stein, "Gourmet On the Go: Good Food Goes Trucking," *TIME*, March 29, 2010, pp. 1–2. Also Nicole Laporte, "How Roy Choi Built an Empire From One Beat-up Taco Truck," *Fast Company*, November 18, 2014, p. 10; Roy Choi's remarkable life is examined in his *L.A. Son: My Life, My City, My Food* (New York: HarperCollins Publishers, 2013).

137   The "Sweet Caroline" quote is from Corina Knoll, "Learning in reverse brought Kogi chef Roy Choi to the top," *The Los Angeles Times*, August 12, 2014, p. 1.

137   Anthony Bourdain, *TIME* 100 Pioneers, "Roy Choi: Culinary trailblazer," *TIME*, May 2–9, 2016, p. 38.

137   Choi's "Broken spirit" is from Roy Choi, *L.A. Son: My Life, My City, My Food* (New York: HarperCollins Publishers, 2013), p. 131.

137   His "fit like a glove" is from Roy Choi, *L.A. Son: My Life, My City, My Food* (New York: HarperCollins Publishers, 2013), p. 205.

138   His feeling "great" is also from Roy Choi, *L.A. Son: My Life, My City, My Food* (New York: HarperCollins Publishers, 2013), p. 217.

138   Choi's quotes on "big kitchens" is from Jonathan Gold, "The Korean Taco Justice League: Kogi Rolls Into L.A.," *LA Weekly*, January 28, 2009, p. 3.

138   His "changed my life" is from Katy McLaughlin, "The King of the Streets Moves Indoors," *The Wall Street Journal*, January 15, 2010, p. 3; and Roy Choi, *L.A. Son: My Life, My City, My Food* (New York: HarperCollins Publishers, 2013), p. 185.

138   The UCLA turning point is discussed in Nicole Laporte, "How Roy Choi Built an Empire From One Beat-up Taco Truck," *Fast Company*, November 18, 2014, p. 4.

139   For more on the industry's explosion, see Jonathan Gold, "How America Became a Food Truck Nation," *Smithsonian Magazine*, March 2012, pp. 1–3. There are even food trucks dedicated to dogs. See Kim Holcomb, "This food truck caters to canines," *USA Today*, May 31, 2016, p. 4A.

139   The Kapoor's experience is from Curry Up Now, www.curryupnow.com.

139   David Schillace's story is told in Janet Morrissey, "Mixing Cuisines, Mexicue Moves Beyond the Food Truck," *The New York Times*, May 14, 2015, p. B1.

139   Mintel's Gallo-Torres is quoted in Janet Morrissey, "Mixing Cuisines, Mexicue Moves Beyond the Food Truck," *The New York Times*, May 14, 2015, p. B4.

140   The Coolhaus story, see www.eatcoolhaus.com/about#aboutstory. Also Bekah Wright, "Summer Scoops," *UCLA Magazine*, July 2015, p. 38.

140   Sonja Rasula is quoted in Katie Robbins, "The Food Truck Economy," *The Atlantic*, July 21, 2010, p. 3.

140   Her "truck model is fantastic" is from Katie Robbins, "The Food Truck Economy," *The Atlantic*, July 21, 2010, p. 3.

141   For Shana Dawson's "tip of the iceberg," see Katie Robbins, "The Food Truck Economy," *The Atlantic*, July 21, 2010, p. 4.

141   Heidi Nagle's excitement and Mr. Coccio's quote is from Shelly Rossetter, "Second Tampa food truck rally draws thousands," *Tampa Bay Times*, October 22, 2011, p. 2.

141-142   For more on the Askews and their Street Grindz operation, see Shannon Tangonan, "Poni Askew," *Honolulu Star-Advertiser*, September 4, 2015, p. F1; Garett Kamemoto, "Elevating the Food Truck Experience," *Honolulu Star-Advertiser*, September 14, 2015, p. C14; Jay Jones, "Cheap (but creative) eats at Honolulu food trucks and tents," *Los Angeles Times*, October 7, 2015, pp. 1–2.

142-143   For Japan's mobile experience and the Neo operation, see Sarah E. Needleman, "Street Fight: Food Trucks vs. Restaurants," *The Wall Street Journal*, August 9, 2012; and Lauren Shannon, "Great eats on the go," *Japan Today*, June 3, 2013, pp. 1–2.

143   The Australian acceptance of street eats and Stephanie Raco's quote are from Danielle Bowling, "The Business of Street Food" *Hospitality Magazine*, August 23, 2012, pp. 1–5. Also Tim Grey, "Meals on wheels: Australia's best food trucks," *The New Daily*, January 21, 2014.

143   For the Parisian experience, see Julia Moskin, "Food Trucks in Paris? U.S. Cuisine Finds Open Minds, and Mouths," *The New York Times*, June 3, 2012, p. B1; and Elena Barton, "Awestruck by food trucks: Trend on a roll in Paris," *USA Today*, August 31, 2015, p. 3A.

143   Ms. Frederick's quote is from Julia Moskin, "Food Trucks in Paris? U.S. Cuisine Finds Open Minds, and Mouths," *The New York Times*, June 3, 2012, p. B1.

144   Mayor Hidalgo's quote is from Elena Barton, "Awestruck by food trucks: Trend on a roll in Paris," *USA Today*, August 31, 2015, p. 3A.

144   The projection is from "Dorothy Cann Hamilton Talks About the World Expo" by Shivani Vora, The *New York Times*, June 17, 2015, p. TR3.

145   Jonathan Salvatore is quoted in Kai Ryssdal, "Food Truck Nation," *American Public Media*, July 30, 2010, p. 3.

145   Ms. Rasula's "shakeout" prediction is from Katie Robbins, "The Food Truck Economy," *The Atlantic*, July 21, 2010, p. 4.

Chapter 10. Ghost Stories

147   The love letter is presented in Jennie Erdal, *Ghosting: A Double Life* (New York: Doubleday, 2004), p. xi.

148   The high-voltage remarks are from Jennie Erdal, "The invisible woman," *The Guardian*, October 23, 3004, p. 2.

148   Erdal's description of her master and subsequent quotes are from *Ghosting: A Double Life* (New York: Doubleday, 2004), pp. 35, 164, 230, 244.

148   Erdal's thoughts on collusion and related comments are from *Ghosting: A Double Life* (New York: Doubleday, 2004), p. xiii.

148	Erasmus' quote is from www.quotationspage.com.
148-149	*The Daily Telegraph* review is by Catherine Taylor, "The Missing Shade of Blue by Jennie Erdal: review," March 27, 2012, p. 1. Also Anne VanderMey, "The Ghost In The Memoir," *Fortune*, December 15, 2015, p. 28.
149	Joel Hochman's remarks are from Alex Mayyasi, "The Ghosting Business," *Princeconomics*, December 3, 2013, p. 12.
149	Sean O'Casey's thoughts on money are found at www.write-out-loud.com.
149	Erdal's likeness of ghosting to prostitution is from her *Ghosting: A Double Life* (New York: Doubleday, 2004), p. xiii.
150	For more of the life of Edward Stratemeyer, see http://www.online-literature.com/stratemeyer/; Jennifer Furlong, "Edward Stratemeyer (1862–1930)," *Immigrant Entrepreneurship* (a monograph), August 28, 2014; Meghan O'Rourke, "Nancy Drew's Father," *The New Yorker*, November 8, 2004, pp. 120–129. Alex Mayyasi, "The Ghosting Business," *Princeeconomics*, December 3, 2013, pp. 109–12; and Deidre Johnson, *Edward Stratemeyer and the Stratemeyer Syndicate* (New York: Twayne Publishers, 1993).
150	The most influential assessment is from "Answer the Question," *Sheboygan Press*, December 3, 1931, p. 8. Also John T. Dizer, "Young People of America, Bright Days and Edward Stratemeyer," *Dime Novel Round-up*, 71.6 (2002), pp. 183–200.
150	Trudi Johanna Abel's thoughts are from her *A Man of Letters, A Man of Business: Edward Stratemeyer and the Adolescent Reader, 1890–1930*, (New Brunswick, NJ: Rutgers University, 1993), p. 205.
151	Stratemeyer's "wide awake lad" is from Jennifer Furlong, "Edward Stratemeyer (1862–1930)," *Immigrant Entrepreneurship* (a monograph), August 28, 2014, p. 16; and Meghan O'Rourke, "Nancy Drew's Father," *The New Yorker*, November 8, 2004, p. 124.
151	Meghan O'Rourke, "Nancy Drew's Father," *The New Yorker*, November 8, 2004, p. 122.
152	For more on Leslie McFarlane, see his *Ghost of the Hardy Boys* (Toronto: Methuen Publishers, 1976); Marilyn S. Greenwald, *The Secret of the Hardy Boys: Leslie McFarlane and the Stratemeyer Syndicate* (Athens, Ohio: Ohio University Press, 2004); and James D. Keeline, "The Writings of Charles Leslie McFarlane (1902–1977)," October 26, 2008.
152	Carl Spadoni's thoughts are from Michael Posner, "A reluctant author of bestsellers," *The Globe and Mail*, May 17, 2008, p. 2. Also Meghan O'Rourke, "Nancy Drew's Father," *The New Yorker*, November 8, 2004, p. 126; and Leslie McFarlane, *Ghost of the Hardy Boys* (Toronto: Methuen Publishers, 1976), p. 62, 188–139.
152	Mrs. Perez's views are offered in Posner, p. 2

152	Brian McFarlane's quotes are from Posner, p. 2.
152-153	Leslie McFarlane's thoughts on fair play are also from Posner, p. 2; and Leslie McFarlane, *Ghost of the Hardy Boys* (Toronto: Methuen Publishers, 1976), p. 205.
153	His "encountering boredom" is from Leslie McFarlane, *Ghost of the Hardy Boys* (Toronto: Methuen Publishers, 1976), p. 202.
153	Brian's comments on his father's legacy are from Posner, p. 2.
153	For more on Mildred Wirt Benson, see http://nancydrewsleuth.com/mildredwirtbenson.html; and Melanie Rehak, *Girl Sleuth: Nancy Drew and the Women Who Created Her* (Fort Washington, PA: Harvest Books, 2006.)
153	The aggressive assessment is discussed in Meghan O'Rourke, "Nancy Drew's Father," *The New Yorker*, November 8, 2004, pp. 120, 127.
153	Benson's prodigious work schedule is highlighted in Jennifer Fisher, "'Who Is Carolyn Keene?'" *The Los Angeles Times*, March 28, 2010, p. 1.
154	Her comments on the popularity of the Nancy Drew series is discussed in "Ohio Reading Road Trip: Carolyn Keene (Mildred Wirt Benson Biography)," Greater Dayton (Ohio) Public Television, 2004.
154	O'Rourke's "two heads" is from Meghan O'Rourke, "Nancy Drew's Father," *The New Yorker*, November 8, 2004, pp. 120–129, p. 127.
155	The *Forbes* wealthiest list, see "The Hightest-Paid Authors," August 23, 2016, p. 24.
155	Joe Queenan, "New Books, Dead Authors," *The Wall Street Journal*, June 27–28, 2015, p. C11.
155-156	See Alex Mayyasi, "The Ghosting Business," *Princeeconomics*, December 3, 2013, p. 8.
156	Hilary Liftin's quotes are from Sheila Marikar, "A Celebrity Ghostwriter Flips the Script," *The New York Times*, July 26, 2015, p. 4.
156	The Phillips quote is also from Marikar, p. 4.
157	William Novak's remarks are found in Jack Hitt, "The Writer Is Dead," *The New York Times*, May 25, 1997, p. 2; and William Novak, "Writing Books Very Few Will Read," *The New York Times*, July 12, 2015, p. 11.
157	Jack Hitt's thoughts on ghosting are discussed in his "The Writer Is Dead," *The New York Times*, May 25, 1997, p. 2. Also Anne VanderMey, "The Ghost In The Memoir," *Fortune*, December 15, 2015, p. 28.
157	See Anonymous (later revealed as Joe Klein), *Primary Colors* (New York: Random House, 1996).

158   Professor Huth's remarks are from his "Authorship from the Reader's Side," *The Annals of Internal Medicine*, 1982, pp. 613–613.

158   James-Enger's quote on work is from Susan Johnston, "Veteran freelancer Kelly James-Enger: 'There is plenty of work to go around,'" *Urban Muse Writer*, May 2013, p. 1.

158   Wendy Walker is quoted in Lynn Andriani, "Ghost Stories," *Publishers Weekly*, May 29, 2006, pp. 1–3.

158   George Orwell's description of writing is from www.whatquote.com.

158   Mark Sullivan is quoted in Paul Farhi, "Who wrote that political memoir? No, who actually wrote it?" *The Washington Post*, June 9, 2014, p. 3.

159   See Madeleine Morel's remarks in Lynn Andriani, "Ghost Stories," *Publishers Weekly*, May 29, 2006, pp. 1–3; and Anne VanderMey, "The Ghost In The Memoir," *Fortune*, December 15, 2015, p. 28.

159   Mr. Novak's quote is from Josh Getlin, "Ghost to the Stars: William Novak Is the Invisible Writer Behind the Memories by Lee Iacocca, Nancy Reagan and—Soon—Magic Johnson," *The Los Angeles Times*, September 17, 1992, p. 1.

159   John Mason Brown's comment is from www.quoteshut.com.

159   Jack Hitt's remarks are from his "The Writer Is Dead," *The New York Times*, May 25, 1997, p. 3.

159   Hockman's assessment of ghosting's size is from Alex Mayyasi, "The Ghosting Business," *Princeeconomics*, December 3, 2013, pp. 7–8.

160   Morel's quote is from Lynn Andriani, "Ghost Stories," *Publishers Weekly*, May 29, 2006, p. 2.

160   Demian Farnsworth's problems are described in his "The Brutally Honest Truth About Ghostwriting," https://raventools.com/blog/truth-about-ghostwriting/, June 7, 2013.

160   Sally Collings' experience is from Alex Mayyasi, "The Ghosting Business," *Princeeconomics*, December 3, 2013, p. 6. Also www.sallycollings.com.

160-161 David Jacoby's remarks on the benefits of ghosting are found at https://www.plus.goole.com/__/o/115630079405940076652/posts/gNDpY;NQAFW.

161   William Novak's positive experiences are discussed in Josh Getlin, "Ghost to the Stars: William Novak Is the Invisible Writer Behind the Memories by Lee Iacocca, Nancy Reagan and—Soon—Magic Johnson," *The Los Angeles Times*, September 17, 1992, p. 1.

161   His comments on voice are also from Josh Getlin, "Ghost to the Stars: William Novak Is the Invisible Writer Behind the Memories by Lee Iacocca, Nancy Reagan and—Soon—Magic Johnson," *The Los Angeles Times*, September 17, 1992, p. 2.

161   See Philip Roth, *The Ghost Writer* (New York: Farrar, Straus & Giroux, 1979), p. 72.

161   The voice quote is from Ilima Loomis, "My Job: Author Lets You Take All the Credit," *Hawaii Business*, February 2016, p. 18.

161   Mr. Osnos' praise for Mr. Novak is found in Josh Getlin, "Ghost to the Stars: William Novak Is the Invisible Writer Behind the Memories by Lee Iacocca, Nancy Reagan and—Soon—Magic Johnson," *The Los Angeles Times*, September 17, 1992, p. 2; and Alex Mayyasi, "The Ghosting Business," *Princeeconomics*, December 3, 2013, p. 7.

161-162   See Jennie Erdal, *Ghosting: A Double Life* (New York: Doubleday, 2004), p. 175.

162   The Oliver Wendell Homes Sr. quote is from www.famousquotesindex.com.

162   Kevin Anderson's views are presented in Farhi, pp. 2–3.

Chapter 11. Into Thin Air

165   T.S. Eliot's "April is the cruelest month" quote is from www.famousquotesindex.com; and Robert Zaretsky, "Why August Is the Cruelest Month," *The Chronicle of Higher Education*, September 5, 2014, p. A50.

165   See Jon Krakauer, *Into Thin Air* (New York: Villard, 1997) and his "Death and Anger on Everest," *The New Yorker*, April 21, 2014. For more on the great mountain, see Nick Heil, *Dark Summit: The True Story of Everest's Most Dangerous Season* (New York: Henry Holt and Co., 2008); Anatoli Boukreev and G. Weston DeWalt, *The Climb: Tragic Ambitions on Everest* (New York: St. Martin's Press, 1997); Beck Weathers, *Left for Dead: My Journey Home From Everest* (New York: Villard, 2000); Kenneth Kamler, *Doctor on Everest* (Guilford, CT: The Lyons Press, 2000); Matt Dickinson, *The Other Side of Everest: Climbing the North Face Through the Killer Storm* (New York: Crown, 1999); Sean Markey, "First Teams Summit as Everest Season Begins," *National Geographic News*, May 2003, pp. 1–2; and Ed Viesturs with David Roberts, *No Shortcuts to the Top: Climbing the World's 14 Highest Peaks* (New York: Broadway Books, 2006). See also Jemima Diki Sherpa, "Everest's deadly demands: a Sherpa's view," *Financial Times*, May 3–4, 2014, p. 9; and Chip Brown, "Sorrow on the Mountain," *National Geographic*, November 2014, pp. 56–73.

165   George Mallory's 1922 ascent is discussed in Freddie Wilkinson, "The Risks of Everest Are Deadlier for Some," *The New York Times*, April 20, 2014, p. 5.

166   Freddie Wilkinson's quote is from his "The Risks of Everest Are Deadlier for Some," *The New York Times*, April 20, 2014, p. 5.

166   The disposable characterization is from Grayson Schaeffer, "The Disposable Man: A Western History of Sherpas on Everest," *Outside Magazine*, July 10, 2013, p. 1.

166   Kaji Sherpa's experience is discussed in Gordon Fairclough, Raymond Zhong and Krishna Pokharel, "For Sherpas of Everest, A Perilous Life on the Edge," *The Wall Street Journal*, May 23, 2014, p. A1. Also Steve Inskeep, "Injured Sherpa Explains Why He'll Never Climb Mount Everest Again," *NPR News*, April 24, 2014.

166   Pemba Chhoti Sherpa's quotes are from Gordon Fairclough, Raymond Zhong and Krishna Pokharel, "For Sherpas of Everest, A Perilous Life on the Edge," *The Wall Street Journal*, May 23, 2014, p. A12.

167   Kaji Sherpa's escape is from Steve Inskeep, "Injured Sherpa Explains Why He'll Never Climb Mount Everest Again," *NPR News*, April 24, 2014; and Gordon Fairclough, Raymond Zhong and Krishna Pokharel, "For Sherpas of Everest, A Perilous Life on the Edge," *The Wall Street Journal*, May 23, 2014, p. A12.

167   Pasang Dorje Sherpa's brush with death is also from Gordon Fairclough, Raymond Zhong and Krishna Pokharel, "For Sherpas of Everest, A Perilous Life on the Edge," *The Wall Street Journal*, May 23, 2014, p. A12; and Chip Brown, "Sorrow on the Mountain," *National Geographic*, November 2014, pp. 64–67.

167   See Chip Brown, "Sorrow on the Mountain," *National Geographic*, November 2014, p. 68.

168   Pemba Tashi's comments are from Nick Heil, *Dark Summit: The True Story of Everest's Most Controversial Season* (New York: Henry Holt and Co., 2008), p. 120.

168   Nimea Namgyal Sherpa's "freaked out" may be found in Gordon Fairclough, Raymond Zhong and Krishna Pokharel, "For Sherpas of Everest, A Perilous Life on the Edge," *The Wall Street Journal*, May 23, 2014, p. A12.

169   Ang Dorje Sherpa is quoted in Binaj Gurubacharya, "Many Sherpa guides leaving Everest with 3 still lost in snow after avalanche," *Honolulu Star-Advertiser*, April 23, 2014, p. A6; and Chip Brown, "Sorrow on the Mountain," *National Geographic*, November 2014, p. 72.

169   The Rippels' support is discussed in Jon Krakauer, "Death and Anger on Everest," *The New Yorker*, April 21, 2014, p. 8; and in Nida Najar and Bhadra Sharma, "Nepal Tries to Save Season as Everest Tourists Depart," *The New York Times*, April 24, 2014, p. A10.

169   For more on Sherpas, see Krishnadev Calamur, "Who Are Nepal's Sherpas?" *NPR Parallels*, April 22, 2014; Lhakpa Norbu Sherpa, *Through a Sherpa Window*, (Kathmandu: Vasra Publications, 2008); and Ngawang Tenzin Zangbu, *Stories and Customs of the Sherpa* (Kathmandu: Mera Publications, 2000).

170   For more on Gary Guller, see my book *Bright Triumphs From Dark Hours: Turning Adversity into Success* (Honolulu: University of Hawaii Press, 2010), pp. 100–101. Also Gary Guller and Phillip Macko, *Make Others Greater: From Mt. Everest to the Boardroom* (San Diego: Second Starters, 2013).

170   For more on Sherpas' remarkable endurance, see Kenneth Kamler, *Surviving the Extremes: What Happens to the Body and Mind at the Limits of Human Endurance* (New York: Penguin, 2005), especially pp. 183–199, 210–220.

170   Jamling Tenzing Norgay is quoted in Fairclough, Raymond Zhong and Krishna Pokharel, "For Sherpas of Everest, A Perilous Life on the Edge," *The Wall Street Journal*, May 23, 2014, p. A12.

171   See Jon Krakauer, "Death and Anger on Everest," *The New Yorker*, April 21, 2014, p. 7.

171   Kaji Sherpa's comments on the need for money are from Steve Inskeep, "Injured Sherpa Explains Why He'll Never Climb Mount Everest Again," *NPR News*, April 24, 2014.

171   The Super Sherpa, Apa, is discussed in Tommy Heinrich, "Apa Sherpa: A Little Man," http://www.everesthistory.com/sherpas/apa.htm; and Anup Kaphle and Brett Prettyman, "Apa Sherpa summits Everest for the 21st time," *The Salt Lake Tribune*, May 11, 2011, p. 1.

171   Apa's comments on education are from Anup Kaphle and Brett Prettyman, "Apa Sherpa summits Everest for the 21st time," *The Salt Lake Tribune*, May 11, 2011, pp. 2–3.

172   Apa's quote is from Anup Kaphle and Brett Prettyman, p. 3. Also Anup Kaphie and Pradeep Bashyal, "The world's most renowned Sherpa talks Mt. Everest," *The Washington Post*, May 5, 2014, p. 1; and Jon Krakauer, "Death and Anger on Everest," *The New Yorker*, April 21, 2014, p. 4.

172   Tenzing Norgay's description of Everest is cited in Gordon Fairclough, Raymond Zhong and Krishna Pokharel, "For Sherpas of Everest, A Perilous Life on the Edge," *The Wall Street Journal*, May 23, 2014, p. A12.

172   Graham Hoyland's quote is from "Fouling Mount Everest," *The Week*, April 3, 2015, p. 9.

172   Nick Heil, *Dark Summit: The True Story of Everest's Most Controversial Season* (New York: Henry Holt and Co., 2008), p. 5.

173	Sir Edmund Hillary's quote is from Graham Hoyland, "Fouling Mount Everest," *The Week*, p. 9.
173	Peter Hillary's quote is from Kaori Shoji, "Facing death at the Earth's highest reaches," *The Japan Times*, June 27, 2014, p. 16.
174	Apa Sherpa's comments are from Anup Kaphie and Pradeep Bashyal, "The world's most renowned Sherpa talks Mt. Everest," *The Washington Post*, May 5, 2014, p. 3.
174	See Jon Krakauer, "Death and Anger on Everest," *The New Yorker*, April 21, 2014, pp. 6–7.
174	Susmita Maskey's "circus" quote is from Steve Inskeep, "Injured Sherpa Explains Why He'll Never Climb Mount Everest Again," *NPR News*, April 24, 2014; and Gordon Fairclough, Raymond Zhong and Krishna Pokharel, "For Sherpas of Everest, A Perilous Life on the Edge," *The Wall Street Journal*, May 23, 2014, p. A12.
174	Grayson Schaffer's quote is from Steve Inskeep, "Injured Sherpa Explains Why He'll Never Climb Mount Everest Again," *NPR News*, April 24, 2014.
174	Super Sherpa Apa's "leave Everest alone" is from Anup Kaphle and Brett Prettyman, "Apa Sherpa summits Everest for the 21st time," *The Salt Lake Tribune*, May 11, 2011, p. 1.
175	Kami Noru Sherpa's "need to earn" remarks are from Gordon Fairclough, Raymond Zhong and Krishna Pokharel, "For Sherpas of Everest, A Perilous Life on the Edge," *The Wall Street Journal*, May 23, 2014, p. A12; and Bikash Sangraula, "Sherpa Guides return to Everest," *The Christian Science Monitor Weekly*, March 16, 2015, p. 12.
175	Pasang Tenzing Sherpa's comments are from Bikash Sangraula, "Sherpa Guides return to Everest," *The Christian Science Monitor Weekly*, March 16, 2015, p. 12. See, too, Gary Guller and Phillip Macko, *Make Others Greater: From Mt. Everest to the Boardroom* (San Diego: Second Starters, 2013), pp. 90–91.
175	His "act of nature" quote is from Bikash Sangraula, "Sherpa Guides return to Everest," *The Christian Science Monitor Weekly*, March 16, 2015, p. 12.
175	For more on the Nepalese earthquakes, see Jon Krakauer, "Death and Anger on Everest," *The New Yorker*, April 21, 2014; "Into thin air," *The Economist*, May 3, 2014, p. 36; Raymond Zhong and Suryatapa Bhattacharya, "Nepal Hit by New Earthquakes," *The Wall Street Journal*, May 13, 2015, p. A7; and Ellen Barry, "Major Quake Ravages Nepal," *The New York Times*, April 26, 2013, p. A1.
175-176	Katy Daigle and Binaj Gurubacharya, "Death Toll Hinges On Remote Villages," Associated Press reported in *The Honolulu Star-Advertiser*, April 27, 2015, p. A7.

176   Ang Tenzing Sherpa's "state of shock" quote is from Raymond Zhong and Suryatapa Bhattacharya, "Nepal Hit by New Earthquakes," *The Wall Street Journal*, May 13, 2015, p. A7.

177   Kenichi Yokoyama's quote is from Raymond Zhong, "Donors to Meet on Nepal's Painful Recovery," *The Wall Street Journal*, June 24, 2015, p. A8.

177   Min Bahadur Shrestha of the Central Banks is from Raymond Zhong, "Donors to Meet on Nepal's Painful Recovery," *The Wall Street Journal*, June 24, 2015, p. A8. Also Gardiner Harris, "Nation's dysfunction exacerbated by earthquake," *The Honolulu Star-Advertiser*, April 27, 2015, p. A7.

177   Mr. Bonatti's "bleeding its best people" is from Gardiner Harris, "In Nepal, a Better Life with a Steep Price," *The New York Times*, August 15, 2014, p. A4. Also Donatella Lorch, "Voices: Post-quake Nepal a country rattled to the core," *USA Today*, May 1, 2015, p. 2A.

177-178   Tashi Sherpa, "Hundreds return to scale Everest despite disasters," *Honolulu Star-Advertiser*, April 24, 2016, p. A6.

178   Bonatti is quoted from www.amccomb.blogspot.com.

178   The Helen Keller quote is from www.brainyquote.com.

178   See Jon Krakauer, "Death and Anger on Everest," *The New Yorker*, April 21, 2014, p. 12.

179   Erick Shipton is from Freddie Wilkinson, "The Risks of Everest Are Deadlier for Some," *The New York Times*, April 20, 2014, p. 15.

179   Nima Dorma Sherpa's "No tourists mean no jobs" is from "Fouling Mount Everest," *The Week*, April 3, 2015, p. 9; and Gordon Fairclough, Raymond Zhong and Krishna Pokharel, "For Sherpas of Everest, A Perilous Life on the Edge," *The Wall Street Journal*, May 23, 2014, p. A12.

179   Sumit Joshi's thoughts are from Freddie Wilkinson, "The Risks of Everest Are Deadlier for Some," *The New York Times*, April 20, 2014, p. 5.

179   The Chinese proverb is from Lesson 32, p. 84; and www.brainyquote.com.

Chapter 12. Top Billings For Underdogs

181   Robert Browning's quote is from his "Andrea del Sarto." Also Luke Johnson, "Entrepreneurs who curb their ambition to be happy instead," *Financial Times*, January 21, 2015, p. 12.

181   Erma Bombeck's quote is from www.brainyquote.com.

181-182   The Disraeli and Galileo quotes is from www.famousquotesindex.com.

182   Lisa Fischer is quoted in Mandalit Del Barco, "Spotlighting Background Singers In 'Twenty Feet From Stardom,'" *NPR Morning Edition*, June 11, 2013, p. 3.

182   Joseph Campbell's "follow your bliss" is discussed in John M. Maher and Dennie Briggs (eds.), *A Open Life: Joseph Campbell in conversation with Michael Toms* (New York: Harper Perennial, 1990).

183   Super Sherpa Apa is quoted in Anup Kaphle and Brett Prettyman, "Apa Sherpa summits Everest for the 21st time," *The Salt Lake Tribune*, May 11, 2011, p. 3. Also Anup Kaphie and Pradeep Bashyal, "The world's most renowned Sherpa talks Mt. Everest," *The Washington Post*, May 5, 2014, p. 3.

183   Tom Cook's quotes are from his 2015 commencement address at George Washington University. See Motoko Rich, "Now Make the Folks Proud, Oh, and Fix Global Warming," *The New York Times*, June 14, 2015, p. 22.

184   For James Russell Lowell's quotes, see www.brainyquote.com.

184   Langston Hughes' lines "What happens..." are from his "Harlem," cited in Harold S. Kushner, *Overcoming Life's Disappointments* (New York: Knopf, 2006), p.6.

184   Vice President Biden's advice is cited in See Motoko Rich, "Now Make the Folks Proud, Oh, and Fix Global Warming," *The New York Times*, June 14, 2015, p. 22.

184   The famous Keynes quote is from "John Maynard Keynes," *The Economist*, January 5, 2008.

184   Rabbi Kushner's comments on balance are from his "How to Overcome Life's Disappointments," *Bottom Line*, February 1, 2008, pp. 9–10.

185   See Warren Bennis and Patricia Ward Biederman, *Organizing Genius: The Secrets of Creative Collaboration* (Reading, MA: Addison-Wesley, 1997), p. 203.

185   William Faulkner's advice is found in "Wisdom to Live By," *Investor's Business Daily*, June 19, 2008, p. A4.

185   The Webster quote was offered at the signing of the Declaration of Independence, Philadelphia, July 4, 1776.

185-186 See "Stephen Covey on Recharging Creativity," *USA Weekend*, November 17–19, 2000, p. 10.

186   The Wooden quote is from Alexander Wolff, "Remembering the Wizard," *Sports Illustrated*, June 14, 2010, p. 32.

186   Carole Kai is quoted in Kaysen Jones, "True Grit," *Generations Hawaii*, February/March 2007, p. 4.

187   Colin Powell's remarks on optimism is from www.famousquotesindex.com.

187   Professor Stretcher's thoughts are cited in Julie Halpert, "The Importance of Having a 'Transcendent' Mission," *The Wall Street Journal*, March 20, 2014, p. R4.

187   The Katie Couric charge is from Motoko Rich, "Now Make the Folks Proud, Oh, and Fix Global Warming," *The New York Times*, June 14, 2015, p. 22. Also Kerry Hannon, "Lost midlifers have a Sherpa," *USA Today*, February 5, 2013, p. 8A.

187   Phil Silvers' "banana" thoughts are found in Robert E. Kelley, *The Power of Followership* (New York: Doubleday Currency 1992), p. 53.

188   See David Zweig, "Managing the 'Invisibles,'" Harvard Business Review, May 2014, p. 100. Also David Zweig, *Invisibles: The Power of Anonymous Work in an Age of Restless Self-Promotion* (New York: Portfolio, 2014); and "Hidden Talents." October 2015, p. 57. Also Amy Showalter, *The Underdog Edge* (New York: Morgan James Publishing, 2011).

188   Warren Bennis and Patricia Ward Biederman, *Organizing Genius: The Secrets of Creative Collaboration* (Reading, MA: Addison-Wesley, 1997), p. 213.

188   Admiral James Stockdale is cited in his *A Vietnam Experience: Ten Years of Reflection* (Stanford, CA: Hoover Institution, Stanford University, 1984).

189   Victor Prince's remarks are from Sonja Carberry, "Play To Team's Strengths," *Investor's Business Daily*, September 28, 2015, p. A4. Also Ed Frauenheim, "What Business Can Learn From the Golden State Warriors," *Fortune*, December 22, 2015, p. 16.

189   Alexis de Tocqueville's "longing to rise" is from www.famousquotes.com. See also Amy Chua and Jed Rubenfeld, "What Drives Success?" *The New York Times Magazine*, January 26, 2014, pp. 1, 6.

189   The Catherine the Great quote is from "Wisdom To Live By," www.investors.com, November 2, 2015. See, too, Herminia Ibarra, "When your mentor does more harm than good," *Financial Times*, January 5, 2016, p. 10.

189   Lily Tomlin's quip is from www.brainyquote.com.

189   David Zweig, "Managing the 'Invisibles,'" Harvard Business Review, May 2014, p. 103.

189-190   See Tony Schwartz's "Tips for elevating jobs from drudgery," *The International New York Times*, June 10, 2014, p. 15; Barbara Bradley Hagerty, "Quit Your Job," *The Atlantic*, April 2016, p. 22; and Sharmila Devi, "Quirky employee benefits no match for peer recognition," *Financial Times*, February 26, 2016, p. 8.

191 Margaret Mead's observation is from Richard L. Leider and David A. Shapiro, *Something to Live For: Finding Your Way in the Second Half of Life*, (San Francisco: Berrett-Kohler Publishers, 2008), p.115. Also Bill George, *7 Lessons for Leading In Crisis* (San Francisco: Jossey-Bass, 2009), p. 127.

191 Mitch Albom, *Tuesdays with Morrie: An Old Man, a Young Man, and Life's Greatest Lesson* (New York: Doubleday, 1997), p. 43.

INDEX

Abel, Trudi Johanna 150
Adams, Henry Brooks 77
Adams, William T. 150
Agrella, Robert 111
Albom, Mitch 191
Ales, Omar 70
Alger, Horatio 150
Allen, George 39
Allen, Gracie 54
Althoff, William F. 117, 122, 124–125
Amazing Dunninger, The 49
Anderson, Kevin 162
Anderson, L.V. 78
Andrée, Salomon August 119
Andrews, V.C. 155
Anzivino, Joe 24
Apa 171, 174, 178, 183
Aristotle 9
Armstrong, Lance 6, 149
Askew, Brandon 141–142
Askew, Poni 141–142
Astaire, Fred 21, 69, 71
Atkinson, Ant 27
Avalon, Frankie 47

Bach, Johann Sebastian 58
Barnes, Brook 58
Barnum, P.T. 28
Barry, Zak 135
Báthory-Kitsz, Dennis 87
Beamish, Mike 34, 38, 40
Bednarik, Chuck 32
Beery, Wallace 126
Benedict, Alan 69–70
Bennett, Tony 54
Bennis, Warren 185, 188
Benson, Mildred Wirt 153–154
Bernstein, Leonard 47
Bernstein, Mark 54, 60
Beyoncé 7, 58, 60
Biden, Joseph 184
Biederman, Patricia Ward 185, 188
Bishop, Joey 47–48
Blackstone 49
Blackwood, Grant 155
Blake, Lauretta 69
Blanchard, Sophie 118–119
Bloom, Harold 149

Boggs, George 110
Bombeck, Erma 181
Bonatti, Walter 178
Bourdain, Anthony 137
Boyle, Patrick 38
Branch, John 21
Branson, Richard 1
Brawer, Florence B. 104, 110, 112
Brawner, Tammy "T-Time" 27
Bridges, Jeff 51
Brooks, David 3, 9
Brower, K.B. 93
Brown, Chip 167
Brown, John Mason 159
Browning, Robert 181
Bruni, Frank 100
Bryant, Paul "Bear" 42
Bryant, Peter S. 106
Buckley, Thomas 132
Burns, George 54
Burrell, Marques 41
Busatti, Maurizio 177

Cage, Nicolas 51
Cai, Ed 38
Calhoun, M. Grace 37
Campbell, Joseph viii, 182
Carlin, George 57
Carlyle, Thomas 1
Carroll, Constance M. 110
Carson, Johnny 48
Carter, Jimmy 34
Case, Natasha 140
Case, Steve 135
Cash, Johnny 1
Catherine the Great 189
Cerasoli, Mary-Faith 81–82
Chaka Khan 58
Chamberlain, Wilt 19
Chaney, Kate 64
Chaney, Robert A. 112–113
Chaney, Rose 64
Charles, Alexander 118
Chhoti, Pemba 167
Chiri, Babu 170
Choi, Roy 136–139, 145
Chong, Reuben 97–99, 104, 113
Chopra, Deepak 90

Cicero 6
Clancy, Tom 155
Clark, Robin 59
Clifton, Nat "Sweetwater" 18
Clinton, Bill 159
Clinton, Hillary 159
Clooney, George 51
Clooney, Rosemary 56
Coccia, Roberto 141
Cohen, Arthur M. 104, 110, 112
Collings, Sally 146, 160–161
Confucius 87
Cook, Tim 183
Cooper, Chuck 18
Copperfield, David 49
Cosby, Bill 6
Couric, Katie 187
Covey, Stephen 186
Crow, Michael 94
Cullen, Terry 32, 36, 42, 45
Cyrus, Miley 156

Dale, Brendon 38
Dana, Bill 55
Dawson, Shawna 140–141
de La Rochefoucauld, François 147
De Sieyes, Jacques 115
de Tocqueville, Alexis 189
Del Cueto, Mario 39
Demetry, Daphne 135
Deming, David 103
Diamond, Neil 137
Disraeli, Benjamin 68, 181
Dixon, Franklin W. 152
Doma, Nima 177
Donitz, Karl 125
Dorje, Ang 169
Dorje, Pasang 167
Drew, Peter 70
Dylan, Bob 59

Eckhouse, Mort 125
Einsenhower, Dwight D. "Ike" 20
Einstein, Albert 12
Eliot, T.S. 165
Elliott, John 22
Engber, Daniel 133
Epstein, Jack 38

Erasmus 148
Erdal, Jennie 147–149, 157, 161, 187
Estreller, Freya 140
Euripides 11

Fahey, Joseph J. 93
Farnworth, Demian 160
Farrell, John 71
Faulkner, William 185
Fell, Sara Sutton 84
Ferrari, John 27, 29
Fischer, Lisa 7, 10, 58–60, 182
Fitzgerald, F. Scott 32
Flanders, Sascha 86
Foo, Ching Ling 49
Ford, Henry 4, 90–91
Franklin, Aretha 59
Franklin, Ben 31
Frederick, Kristin 143
Frost, Robert 94
Fruscione, Joseph 85, 87, 93
Fudge, Kevin 108

Galileo 182
Gallo-Torres, Julia 139
Gandhi 95
Garner, Jennifer 51
Gates, Bill 1, 12
Gates, Thomas Sovereign 33
Ginsberg, Nate 83
Glaisher, James 119
Gold, Jonathan 139
Goodale, Tom 73
Goodnight, Charles 132
Grand Baton 60
Grant, Cary 65
Grant, Ulysses S. 149
Grassian, Doug 127
Green, Ben 18–19
Greene, Shecky 56
Greer, Judy 8, 51–54
Griffin, Chad 12
Griffith, Andy 55
Grossman, Dan 121
Guller, Gary 170

Hall, Rob 171–172
Hamilton, Dorothy Cann 144

Hanks, Tom	10, 102, 104
Hannemann, Mufi	132
Hartle, Terry	84, 89
Haslam, William E.	109
Hastert, Dennis	6
Hatanaka, Robert	76
Hayes, Jamie	73
Haynes, Marques	18–19
Heil, Nick	174
Heisman, John	32
Helgeson, Stu	38, 44
Hess, John	78
Hiaasen, Carl	42
Hiam, C. Michael	122
Hickey, Ken	71
Hidalgo, Anne	144
Hill, Judith	60
Hillary, Edmund	166, 171–173
Hillary, Peter	171, 173
Hirsch, Rosemary	74
Hirten, Tim	22
Hite, Matthew	39
Hitler, Adolf	121
Hitt, Jack	157, 159
Hochman, Joel	149, 159
Hollande, François	2
Holmes, Oliver Wendell Sr.	162
Hong, Matt	135
Hoodie Allen	34
Houdini, Harry	49, 149
Howe, Samuel Gridley	181
Hoyland, Graham	172
Hudgins, Gene	22
Hughes, Langston	184
Hughey, vanLee	73
Hugo, Victor	129
Hulbert, Ann	106
Huth, John Edward	158
Iacocca, Lee	157
Ibárruri, Dolores	63
Icarus	116, 121
Infeld, Ronne	71
Izenberg, Jerry	32, 41, 45
Jackson, Mannie	25
Jackson, Phil	21
Jacoby, David	160

Jagger, Mick	58–59
James-Enger, Kelly	158
James, Henry	81
Jenkins, Rob	104
Jenner, Caitlyn	157
Jessel, George	47
Jobs, Steve	8
Johnson, Bobby	42
Johnson, Magic	157
Jones, Del	6
Jones, Doug	68
Joshi, Sumit	179
Kahlenberg, Richard	109
Kai, Carole	56–58, 186
Kaji	166–167, 171, 175
Kapoor, Akash	139
Kapoor, Rana	139
Kardashians, The	11
Katsinas, Stephan G.	109
Keene, Carolyn	153–154
Keller, Helen	98, 178, 181
Kelly, Tim	21, 27
Kennedy, John F.	3
Kerr, Deborah	65
Kezar, Adriana	82, 92, 94
Khrushchev, Nikita	15–16
King, Tony	59
Kinimaka, Iva	8, 130–132
Klein, Joe	157–158
Klotz, Red	9, 16, 19–25, 27–29, 184
Klum, Heidi	53
Kottner, Ann	93
Kovalik, Daniel	80
Kraft, Robert	34
Krakauer, Jon	165, 171, 174, 178
Kupper-Herr, Beth	98
Kushner, Harold S.	184
Kutcher, Ashton	51
Lacro, Erika	96, 111–112
Ladd, John	107
Lagasse, Emeril	137
Lake, Kavan	33
Lang, Leslie	161
Lemmon, Jack	62, 70
Lemon, Meadowlark	24, 28
Leno, Jay	56

Lewis, C.S. 11
Liftin, Hilary 156–157, 159
Lloyd, Earl 18
Lombardi, Vince 15
Lopez, Jennifer "J. Lo" 51, 53
Lopresti, Mike 42
Louis-Dreyfus, Julia 158
Love, Darlene 60
Lovecraft, H.P. 149
Lowell, James Russell 75, 184
Ludlum, Robert 155

Mabler, Jonathan 21
Maddox, Antoine 29
Madonna 181
Maisto, Maria C. 94
Mallory, George 165–166
Manby, Joel 25
Manguera, Mark 138
Maskey, Susmita 174
Mason, Henry 38
Matthau, Walter 62, 70
Maurer, Carol-Ann 46, 49–50
Maurer, Harry 10, 46–51
Maynard, John 184
Mayyasi, Alex 155
McCain, John 127
McCleary, Galen 135
McCullough, David 149
McCurdy, Mike 37, 39–40
McFarlane Perez, Norah 152
McFarlane, Brian 152–153
McFarlane, Leslie 152–153
McGill, Stuart 143
McGuire, Al 28
McGuire, Patricia A. 104
Mead, Margaret 191
Melville, Chuck 17
Merman, Ethel 58
Messing, Debra 53
Mettler, Suzanne 99, 101
Meyer, Henry Cord 121
Migoya, Carlos 83
Miller, George 93–94
Miller, Sarah 128
Moffett, William A. 120, 188
Mokyr, Joel 127
Monaco, A.G. 88

Morel, Madeleine 159–162
Morris, Bob 69–70
Morrison, Herbert 122
Morrison, Van 54
Morton, John 109–110, 189
Moser, Richard 91
Moskin, Julia 143
Moya, Jack 71
Mozart, Wolfgang Amadeus 149
Murdoch, Rupert 11
Murphy Paul, Annie 6
Murray, Arthur 71–72
Musk, Elon 1
Muslimah, Maha 89

Nabors, Jim 54–56, 187
Nagle, Heidi 141
Namgyal, Nima 168
Napoleon 118
Neal, Fred "Curly" 27
Neiderman, Andrew 155
Nel, Philip 81, 88
Neville, Morgan 60
Nietzsche 187
Norgay, Jamling Tenzing 170
Norgay, Tenzing 164, 166, 170, 172–173
North, Oliver 157, 161
Norton, Harry 71–73
Noru, Kami 175
Nostrand, Rob 71
Novak, William 157, 159, 161

O'Banion, Terry 113
O'Casey, Sean 149
O'Donnell, Rosie 47
O'Neal, Tatum 156
O'Neill, Tip 161
O'Rourke, Meghan 151, 154
Obama, Barack 2, 16, 92, 106–109, 113, 135
Orwell, George 158
Osnos, Peter 161
Outland, John 32
Owens, Jesse 19

Pannapacker, William 89–90
Parton, Dolly 7, 58
Pasternak, Igor 128
Pate, SooJin 90, 105

Patrick, Danica	90, 183
Patterson, James	155, 190
Pavarotti, Luciano	54, 189
Phillips, MacKenzie	156–157
Plato	99
Platt, Fran	74
Poitier, Sidney	19
Pope Francis	11
Porath, Christine	189–190
Potter, Claire	88
Powell, Colin	187
Prince, Victor	189
Pyle, Christian	84, 86, 89
Queenan, Joe	155
Quiggin, John	100
Raco, Stephanie	143
Rashid, Rafael	143
Rasula, Sonja	140, 145
Reagan, Nancy	157
Redstone, Sumner	11
The Reagans	161
Regan, Marilou	60
Rhoades, Gary	92
Rickles, Don	57
Rippel, Becky	169
Rippel, Tim	169
Rivers, Joan	56
Robinson, Douglas H.	116
Robinson, Jackie	18
Robison, Tracy	68, 73
Rockefeller	150
Rockne, Knute	43
Rodich, David	92
Rogers, Ginger	21
Rogers, Will	2
Rolfing, Bill	70
Rolling Stones	7, 58–59
Roosevelt, Franklin D.	122
Rosenblatt, Roger	54
Rosendahl, Charles E.	123, 125, 188
Ross, Jack	71
Roth, Philip	161
Rowling, J.K.	149, 157
Rumsfeld, Donald	34
Russert, Tim	157

Saban, Nick	43
Salvatore, Jonathan	145
Santos-Dumont, Albert	119
Saperstein, Abe	16–20, 23–24
Sasso, Richard	65
Schaffer, Grayson	174
Schifeling, Todd	135
Schiller, David	139
Schneider, Kurt	25, 27
Schultz, Howard	11
Schuman, Rebecca	85
Schwartz, Morrie	191
Schwartz, Tony	189
Scott, Debra Leigh	93
Scott, Walter	132
Selingo, Jeffrey	111
Shimer, Barbara	86
Shimer, William	86
Shin-Manguera, Caroline	138
Shipton, Eric	179
Shrestha, Min Bahadur	177
Shulock, Nancy	108
Silvers, Phil	187
Smith, Alex	40
Smith, Betsy	86
Sniderman, Zachary	134
Snyder, Bill	43
Solman, Paul	89
Sowards, Robin J.	78, 91
Spadoni, Carl	152
Spelling, Tori	156
Spivey, Bill	20
Staples, Andy	42
Starr, Kay	56
Steffensen, Ingrid	90–91, 183
Stein, Joel	133
Stephanopoulos, George	157
Stevenson, Adlai	20
Stewart, Doug	22
Stewart, Jimmy	52
Sting	58, 60
Stockdale, James B.	188
Stone, Spencer	2–3, 191
Stratemeyer Adams, Harriet	154
Stratemeyer, Edward L.	150–155, 190
Strecher, Victor	187
Streisand, Barbra	54
Stutz, Todd	141

Sullivan, Mark	158
Supremes	47
Sussman, Carol	68
Tashi, Pemba	168
Tatum, Goose	18–20
Tenzing, Ang	177
Tenzing, Pasang	175
Thompson, Adam	44
Tomlin, Lily	51, 189
Trachtenberg, Stephen	90
Trump, Donald	11
Tunis, John R.	15
Turner, Tina	7, 58
Tuthill, Matthew	104, 111
Twain, Mark	97, 149
Untermann, Luke	135
Vaeth, J. Gordon	121
Van Lustbader, Eric	155
Van Treuren, Richard G.	123, 126
VanderZwaag, George	41
Vandross, Luther	7, 58–59
Vernon, Jack	48
Vojtko, Margaret Mary	77–82, 91, 95, 188
von Zeppelin, Ferdinand	119
Wachtstetter, Leona Davis "Mama Lee"	63–64, 67, 75
Wagner, Bill "Wags"	30, 36–40, 42, 45
Walker, Wendy	158
Wallenbrock, Nicole Beth	11, 85, 91
Warhol, Andy	113
Waters, Alice	133
Weaver, Sigourney	51
Webster, Daniel	50, 185
Wellman, William A.	126
Wellmon, Eric	39
West, Mark	41–42, 45
Wie, Michelle	135
Wilder, David	88
Wilkinson, Freddie	166
Williams, Jeffrey	84
Winfrey, Oprah	12
Wise, John	119
Wolfe, J. Watthew	38
Wooden, John	186
Woods, Ross	125
Yangjin	171
Yokoyama, Kenichi	177
Zammel, Diane	70
Zedong, Mao	104
Zeitlin, Dave	38
Zeno, Phyllis	69
Zweig, David	188–189

About the Author

DAVID HEENAN is a trustee of the Estate of James Campbell, one of the nation's largest landowners, as well as a visiting professor at Georgetown University. Formerly he served as chairman and CEO of Theo. H. Davies & Co., the North American holding company for the Hong Kong-based multinational Jardine Matheson. He has been vice president for academic affairs at the University of Hawaii and, before that, dean of its business school.

Educated at the College of William and Mary, Columbia and the University of Pennsylvania, Heenan has served on the faculties of the Wharton School, the Columbia Graduate School of Business and the University of Hawaii. His articles have appeared in such leading publications as the *Harvard Business Review*, the *Sloan Management Review*, *The Wall Street Journal*, *The New York Times* and *The Christian Science Monitor*. He is author or co-author of nine other books, including *Leaving On Top*, *Bright Triumphs from Dark Hours*, *Flight Capital*, *Double Lives* and *Co-Leaders*.

Heenan lives in Honolulu, Hawaii. He can be reached at davehee@aol.com.